THE DIGITAL BORDER

CRITICAL CULTURAL COMMUNICATION

General Editors: Jonathan Gray, Aswin Punathambekar, Adrienne Shaw
Founding Editors: Sarah Banet-Weiser and Kent A. Ono

Dangerous Curves: Latina Bodies in the Media
Isabel Molina-Guzmán

The Net Effect: Romanticism, Capitalism, and the Internet
Thomas Streeter

Our Biometric Future: Facial Recognition Technology and the Culture of Surveillance
Kelly A. Gates

Critical Rhetorics of Race
Edited by Michael G. Lacy and Kent A. Ono

Circuits of Visibility: Gender and Transnational Media Cultures
Edited by Radha S. Hegde

Commodity Activism: Cultural Resistance in Neoliberal Times
Edited by Roopali Mukherjee and Sarah Banet-Weiser

Arabs and Muslims in the Media: Race and Representation after 9/11
Evelyn Alsultany

Visualizing Atrocity: Arendt, Evil, and the Optics of Thoughtlessness
Valerie Hartouni

The Makeover: Reality Television and Reflexive Audiences
Katherine Sender

Authentic™: The Politics of Ambivalence in a Brand Culture
Sarah Banet-Weiser

Technomobility in China: Young Migrant Women and Mobile Phones
Cara Wallis

Love and Money: Queers, Class, and Cultural Production
Lisa Henderson

Cached: Decoding the Internet in Global Popular Culture
Stephanie Ricker Schulte

Black Television Travels: African American Media around the Globe
Timothy Havens

Citizenship Excess: Latino/as, Media, and the Nation
Hector Amaya

Feeling Mediated: A History of Media Technology and Emotion in America
Brenton J. Malin

The Post-Racial Mystique: Media and Race in the Twenty-First Century
Catherine R. Squires

Making Media Work: Cultures of Management in the Entertainment Industries
Edited by Derek Johnson, Derek Kompare, and Avi Santo

Sounds of Belonging: U.S. Spanish-language Radio and Public Advocacy
Dolores Inés Casillas

Orienting Hollywood: A Century of Film Culture between Los Angeles and Bombay
Nitin Govil

Asian American Media Activism: Fighting for Cultural Citizenship
Lori Kido Lopez

Struggling for Ordinary: Media and Transgender Belonging in Everyday Life
Andre Cavalcante

Wife, Inc.: The Business of Marriage in the Twenty-First Century
Suzanne Leonard

Homegrown: Identity and Difference in the American War on Terror
Piotr Szpunar

Dot-Com Design: The Rise of a Useable, Social, Commercial Web
Megan Sapnar Ankerson

Postracial Resistance: Black Women, Media, and the Uses of Strategic Ambiguity
Ralina L. Joseph

Netflix Nations: The Geography of Digital Distribution
Ramon Lobato

The Identity Trade: Selling Privacy and Reputation Online
Nora A. Draper

Celebrity: A History of Fame
Susan J. Douglas and Andrea McDonnell

Fake Geek Girls: Fandom, Gender, and the Convergence Culture Industry
Suzanne Scott

Locked Out: Regional Restrictions in Digital Entertainment Culture
Evan Elkins

The Digital City: Media and the Social Production of Place
Germaine R. Halegoua

Distributed Blackness: African American Cybercultures
André Brock, Jr.

Beyond Hashtags: Racial Politics and Black Digital Networks
Sarah Florini

Race and Media: Critical Approaches
Edited by Lori Kido Lopez

Dislike-Minded: Media, Audiences, and the Dynamics of Distaste
Jonathan Gray

Media Distribution in the Digital Age
Edited by Paul McDonald, Courtney Brannon Donoghue, and Tim Havens

Digital Black Feminism
Catherine Knight Steele

The Digital Border: Migration, Technology, Power
Lilie Chouliaraki and Myria Georgiou

The Digital Border

Migration, Technology, Power

Lilie Chouliaraki *and* Myria Georgiou

NEW YORK UNIVERSITY PRESS
New York

NEW YORK UNIVERSITY PRESS
New York
www.nyupress.org

© 2022 by New York University
All rights reserved

References to Internet websites (URLs) were accurate at the time of writing. Neither the author nor New York University Press is responsible for URLs that may have expired or changed since the manuscript was prepared.

Library of Congress Cataloging-in-Publication Data
Names: Chouliaraki, Lilie, author. | Georgiou, Myria, 1971– author.
Title: The digital border : migration, technology, power / Lilie Chouliaraki, Myria Georgiou.
Description: New York : New York University Press, [2022] | Series: Critical cultural communication | Includes bibliographical references and index.
Identifiers: LCCN 2021037353 | ISBN 9781479844319 (hardback ; alk. paper) | ISBN 9781479873401 (paperback ; alk. paper) | ISBN 9781479850969 (ebook) | ISBN 9781479830503 (ebook other)
Subjects: LCSH: Emigration and immigration—Social aspects. | Internet and immigrants. | Boundaries—Social aspects. | Borderlands—Social aspects.
Classification: LCC JV6225 .C46 2022 | DDC 304.8—dc23
LC record available at https://lccn.loc.gov/2021037353

New York University Press books are printed on acid-free paper, and their binding materials are chosen for strength and durability. We strive to use environmentally responsible suppliers and materials to the greatest extent possible in publishing our books.

Manufactured in the United States of America

10 9 8 7 6 5 4 3 2 1

Also available as an ebook

CONTENTS

Introduction: The Digital Border: The Techno-Symbolic
Assemblages of Power   1

SECTION I: THE TERRITORIAL BORDER

1. The Outer Border: Assemblages of Humanitarian
   Securitization   31
2. The Inner Border: Assemblages of Entrepreneurial
   Securitization   58
3. The Inner Border as Networked Commons   81

SECTION II: THE SYMBOLIC BORDER

4. Narrative and Voice in News Stories   105
5. Visibility and Responsibility in News Imagery   128
6. Subaltern Voice and Digital Resistance   148

   Conclusion: The Crisis Imaginary: The Digital Border
   and Its Crises   171

   Acknowledgments   191
   Notes   195
   Bibliography   203
   Index   233
   About the Authors   245

Introduction

The Digital Border: The Techno-Symbolic Assemblages of Power

What Is the Digital Border?

Who are the rightful inhabitants of this earth? Achille Mbembe asks, and What do we do with those who do not have a claim to earth? (2020). These are the questions that we, too, pose in this book. In asking about rightful ownership of the earth, Mbembe's questions are not new. They are part of a long struggle over mobility, land, property, and borders that has historically been underlying colonial conquest and imperial expansion since early modernity. Even though today human mobility is less a matter of imperial conquest and more of a broader "planetary entanglement" of people, technologies, and environments, struggles over movement and relocation are nonetheless still met, for many, with attempts at deterrence, encampment, and incarceration. At a moment when international migrants number almost 272 million globally, or 3.5% of the world population (IOM 2020), and when refugee numbers are at 26 million, the highest since WWII (UNHCR 2018), Mbembe's questions remain more pressing than ever. What they throw into relief is perhaps the most difficult conundrum of international geopolitics: namely, how to understand and manage human mobility in a world where migration is not an option but a necessity, especially, but not only, for the millions who leave their countries on the grounds of war and persecution and at the risk of death.

This is not an abstract challenge. While migration has been a fundamental constituent of all human societies throughout history, in recent decades—what de Haas et al. (2003/2019) define as "the age of migration"—it has been elevated into a key parameter of global order, shaping governmental policies and public imaginaries on who has the right to cross borders. Migration as a constant but shifting force of human mobility has become increasingly diversified in its causes (existential, economic, environmental) and its flows (regional and global). From the historical predominance of unidirectional flows from global South to global North driven by colonial and postcolonial change as well as industrialization (Haas et al. 2003/2019), contemporary migration has become much more multi-dimensional and multi-directional, reflecting the asymmetrical but interconnected geographies of transnational mobility. Far from being an issue concerning the US or Europe alone, as western media often claim, migration is differentially but persistently global. In fact, currently, many migrants stay within their own region (31% in Asia, 10% in Africa, 26% in the Americas, 30% in Europe, IOM 2020), and this includes the vast majority of displaced people, with 73% of those seeking refuge remaining in neighboring countries within the global South (UNHCR 2020).

While diversified, migration nonetheless still remains primarily driven by systemic inequalities and violence, grounded in the legacies of a colonial and neocolonial past, and on the contemporary realities of continuing and growing poverty, oppression, and conflict in the global South. These asymmetrical geographies of migration suggest that migrants, as Purkayastha observes, cannot be thought of as a universal category but "are relatively privileged or marginalized because of their social location relative to the *intersecting structures* of nationality/gender/class/race/ethnicity/caste/religion/sexuality/age and, consequently, their ability to move and access substantive rights after internal or international migration" (2018: 171). These asymmetries also suggest not only that people cannot be conceived as a universal category—"the migrant"—but neither can migration be understood from a singular vantage point (Marino 2020). In this book, we show how specificities of context—of Europe and of a "crisis"—reveal facets of migration and the digital border that are both spatially and temporally distinct and, at the same time, interconnected with other migrations and their patterns of border control. Not long after the peak of Europe's migration "crisis," in 2015, the Rohingya refugee crisis exploded in Southeast Asia, with those seeking safety in both regions confronted not with sanctuary but with closed borders (Ellis-Petersen 2019) and denial of their communication rights (Hussain et al. 2020; Molnar 2019). Indeed, we now know that practices of migration control are strikingly transnational. Australia's system of indefinite detention of asylum seekers in the islands of Nauru and Manus, which has been internationally condemned (Doherty 2016), is now reproduced in the camps where most of the new arrivals to Greek islands are also infinitely detained; at the same time, the inhumane conditions of the Greek camps are not dissimilar to those observed at the US southern border (Sky News 2019), and the digital systems that monitor people and territories are multiplied across borders, often contracted to the same big-tech industries all the way from the US borders to Greece (Howden, Fotiadis, Stavinoha, and Holst 2021; Naranjo and Molnar 2020).

This global control of migration takes place within the hegemony of a western epistemology of the earth, which, in Mbembe's (2020) words, views the planet as a site of domination over land and sea circumscribed by borders between nations and people. Migration also takes place, we add, within a technological rationality, which expands transnationally through data, AI, and drones to mediate and monitor mobility within and across territories and through media narratives and images that legitimize its techniques of control and surveillance. The aim of *The Digital Border* is to interrogate this dominant rationality, unpack and explore its networks of mediation and discourse, as well as critically reflect on the implications that these have both for migrants and the societies where migrants arrive. This means that, while Mbembe's postcolonial critique of migration informs our own normative concerns, as developed in the concluding chapter of this volume, our conceptual language, in the analytical chapters, is fertilized by vocabularies from many other fields of study, including media and migration studies, international relations, and security and border theories—all of which help us highlight the constitution of borders as technological and symbolic constructs dividing people, territories, and access to rights.

Our conception of the digital border is similarly expansive, encompassing the outer and the inner spaces of Europe in the context of the so-called 2015 "migration crisis" and its aftermath—the complex geography and timeline of migration's techno-symbolic governmentality. At Europe's outer border, for example, not unlike the technologization of borders across the world, a recently developed AI project of border security, called iBorderCtrl, has been hailed by the European Union (EU) as a "unique approach to deception detection" (iBorderCtrl 2021). Receiving more than 4.5 million euros of European research funding, iBorderCtrl combines digital identification (face or finger-based such as Eurodac) with emotional recognition technologies (lie detectors) to make decisions on who can or cannot cross into Europe (iBorderCtrl No! 2020; Sánchez-Monedero and Dencik 2020). Far from exceptional, iBorderCtrl represents a European trial of new technologies within the increasingly crowded field of "experimental" border governance. From the US to Europe and Asia, such "predictive intelligence" (Accenture 2017), combined with "smart" technologies including drones, cameras, and sensors (Mattern 2018), draws heavy investment from government–tech-industry collaborations in border control. The advantages of such "smart" regulation of transnational mobility for nation-states is perhaps best described by one of the key players in the tech field: as Accenture (2017) promises in its promotional material, the goal is "the transformation of the border" into "an asset . . . that can drive a lot of value for a nation."

What Accenture's reference to "value" hints at is the idea that "smart" tech corporations can deliver border control services in ways that are perceived to be beneficial to nation-states in terms of both economy and security—Accenture being not only a key corporate partner in the EU's human mobility management but also a core player in the border-industrial complex globally (Lemberg-Pedersen et al. 2020). As part of such service delivery, biometric data are indeed today spearheading the sorting of migrants into categories of "legitimate" or "illegitimate," while populating transnational databases that mediate migrant mobilities and monitor their behaviors as they cross and when they settle. Through the thorough digitization of the outer border, such data thus represent an established parameter of territorial governance and its increasing orientation towards a comprehensive biopolitical management of human mobility—what Madianou aptly names the "biometric assemblage" (2019). This ever-converging synergy of media technology and human mobility subsequently turns the territorial border into a configuration of intersecting logics of identification, classification, and control that not only profoundly shapes how we should today understand the politics of migration and security (Andersson 2017) but also how we should understand the constitution of western states' own political projects of belonging (Yuval-Davis et al. 2019).

Alongside the territorial border, narratives of migration in online news, social media, and institutional web platforms engage in parallel practices of power. Embedded within their own networks of mediation, such narratives also form part of the border's logics of identification and control in that they publicly legitimize certain discourses of migration over others and, in so doing, contribute to the biopolitical power relations of human mobility—what we refer to as the symbolic border. Visual and linguistic mediations of the migrant in western networks of news storytelling, for instance, situate those who, fleeing poverty or war, arrive in the global North to claim a new life, and who Pallister-Wilkins calls precisely "life seekers" (2020: 1005), within the linguistic binary of "victim"/"terrorist." This binary has long been mobilized to divide newcomers between those deserving care and those requiring containment or expulsion, yet it is now increasingly complemented by another one: the binary of the "entrepreneurial"/"parasitical" migrant who is either capable of "making it" in western urban markets or is unworthy of joining the national community. In their variations, these systems of identification consistently detach migration from the global trajectories and histories of human mobility, reproducing the myths of migration as "crisis" (de Genova 2017), a sudden emergency that requires extraordinary measures, and of the migrant as an unknowable stranger who is fundamentally different from "us." Such networks of discursive mediation do little to speak of migrants as human beings with diverse capabilities and talents and oversimplify the story of migration, often turning migrants into "illegals" who seek a "back door," in Trilling's words in *The Guardian* (Trilling 2019).

Decontextualized narratives circulate in news media but also become caught up in social media struggles, turning networked public spheres into discursive battlefields, sites where voices of solidarity and welcome, such as those of #refugeeswelcome and #migrantlivesmatter, are systematically countered and attacked by anti-migrant rhetoric, as seen in #refugeesnotwelcome across Europe or #buildthewall in the US. In this way, social media platforms such as Twitter and Facebook sustain antagonistic but insulated conversations which may partly enable diversity in migrant representations, yet also, in ways that are different to mainstream journalism, perpetuate stereotypes, and "reinforc[e] nationalism and an ethnocentric understanding of citizenship" (Bozdağ 2020: 712).

The symbolic border relies, then, on narrations of migration that largely mobilize reductive formulas of "us" and "them," consolidating stereotypical positions of "otherness," yet also enable alternative voices, which challenge the mainstream, to be heard and seen in public.

The consequences of these two intersecting dimensions of mediation—the techno-symbolic infrastructures of the territorial border and the platformed narratives of the symbolic border—drive the analysis of this book. Throughout its chapters, we define those dimensions not simply as novel add-ons to pre-existing systems of border control but as constitutive parameters of what the border has become and how it works on migrant bodies and identities today. In adopting this conceptual starting point on the digital border, we draw on two sources. The first is Christophe Sohn's Deleuze-inspired understanding of assemblages as "heterogeneous and open-ended groupings of material and semiotic elements that do not form a coherent whole but that allow us to explain how different meanings derived from various actors (and thus not only the state) may interact and endure in a contingent and provisional way" (2016: 183). In line with this understanding, our own theorization of the border as material and symbolic assemblages that operate across space and time aspires to show how such assemblages position migrants on an elastic, adaptable, yet persistent boundary of inside/outside and how, in so doing, they provisionally stabilize the power relations of migration on the ground as much as in language. While we acknowledge that the territorial and the symbolic entail different empirical realities and are studied through different methodological lenses, our distinction emphasizes that the two are not opposites but always exist in mutual reference to one another within shifting space-times and relations of power (Paasi 2012; Mattelart 2019).

In order to disentangle their intersecting dynamics, we further situate these assemblages of the territorial and the symbolic within what Roger Silverstone (1994) calls the "double articulation" of mediation—the second theoretical source we draw upon in our thinking about the digital border. The concept of "double articulation," which was originally proposed to describe how "information and communication technologies, their hardware and their software, are the focus of meaning construction at the same time as they enable it" (Silverstone and Mansell 1996: 213), is useful insofar as it enables us to grasp the processes by which such assemblages work precisely as a border, that is, how they produce relations of inclusion/exclusion by operationalizing their own constitutive duality: as digital technologies located in particular geopolitical settings, whether crossing points or city centers, and as textual/visual communication located within broader orders of socio-cultural relations of power, whether on paper or online. A full and proper integration of the two—the territorial and the symbolic—is actually impossible, yet our aim in this book is to offer illuminating snapshots of their intersections *both* in the form of digital networks of surveillance and control in the territorial border *and* in the form of the media narratives that stereotype and "other" migrants in the textualities/visualities of the symbolic border. Our argument is that, if we wish to grasp the struggles over exclusion, classification, and voice that are played out at the border under conditions of digitization, it is not enough to attend solely to the automated controls of its geographical crossing points, nor to focus exclusively on the different forms of storytelling in western mediascapes. We need instead to bring the two, surveilled territories and social categorizations, together in an integrated conceptual account that acknowledges the centrality of both in the power struggles over migration flows around the world (Wodak 2020) and citizenship rights within and across states (Anthias 2021); as Didier Fassin has put it, "borders as external territorial frontiers and boundaries as internal social categorizations are tightly related in a process in which immigrants are racialized and ethnic minorities are reminded of their foreign origin" (2011: 214).

Our inquiry into the digital border, then, is an inquiry into how, both on location and on screen, the technological and symbolic resources of the border—its double articulation—work through specific networks of mediation to situate migrant bodies and identities on the boundary of inside/outside, but, importantly, also how they offer spaces of resistance and struggle against the exclusions of the border. In developing this account, we proceed in three moves. First, we elaborate on the digital border as a boundary-drawing process by contextualizing its workings within different relations of power, each configuring different assemblages of mediation with their distinct norms of inclusion/exclusion—what, after Foucault, we call "regimes" of border power; and we situate these regimes of power within existing theoretical accounts that, while thinking about the border as deterritorialized and processual, do not adequately attend to the interconnections between its territorial and symbolic dimensions. Second, we propose a conceptual language to describe the digital border as assemblages by focusing on three of its key operations: its networks of mediation, that is how the techno-symbolic resources of the border are organized across space (on-location and online); its dialectics of resistance, highlighting the spaces that these assemblages open up for migrants to challenge the effects of border power; and its trajectories of historicity, describing how the border's regimes of power emerge and change in time (in the context of "crisis" and post-"crisis"). Finally, we present the chapter outline of our book as a series of theoretically informed case studies based on diverse data sources (fieldwork notes, interviews, online news, and social media text analysis) that were collected through extensive emperial research at crossing points as well as within Europe's urban centers. Together, these case studies offer illuminating, albeit inevitably partial, glimpses of the digital border and its exclusionary but contested taxonomies of mobility.

The Digital Border and Its Regimes of Power

At the heart of the digital border, we have suggested, lies a theory of power as techno-symbolic assemblages of mediation that produce boundaries of inside/outside across space and time (de Genova 2013; Dijstelbloem and Broeders 2014; van Houtum et al. 2005). Given the dispersed nature of these assemblages, we refer to their power relations as regimes of power/knowledge; in doing so, we follow Foucault's conception of power not as a top-down system of authoritarian imposition but as localized and malleable formations of "procedures, practices, objects of inquiry, institutional sites, and, above all, forms of social and political constraint" that are particular to their contexts of emergence (Fraser 1989: 274).

Indeed, technologies such as iBorderCtrl, among others, suggest that the digital border emerges within a regime of power—what Foucault (Foucault, Marchetti, and Burchell 2003) calls biopolitics—that, by targeting individual bodies, identities, and affects (finger or face recognition, lie detection) operates no longer by force of punishment, whether corporeal or emotional, but by force of micro-interventions that "identify, treat, manage or administer those individuals, groups or localities where risk is seen to be high" (Rose 2007: 70). These are combined with a range of genres and narratives that operate through those biopolitical techniques: for instance, the debriefing interviews with arriving migrants in the Greek islands (Chapter 1), or the job center interviews with asylum seekers precariously settling in London (Chapter 2), both of which feed into national and transnational databases, recording migrant whereabouts and behaviors. The datafication of migrant profiles also co-exists with and informs other meaning-making practices of the border, such as news storytelling, photojournalism, or social media posts, insofar as all of these often draw on official border discourses of security and surveillance to construct their narratives.

This biopolitical regime of the border is responsible not so much for identifying risky individuals as it is for producing knowledge about who is potentially risky—knowledge "about the becoming-dangerous of some risky subjects" (Vaughan-Williams 2015b: 40). Border biopolitics, in other words, performs the security work of sorting migrants in terms of who is granted or denied legitimacy for entry or settlement in western nation-states on the basis of individual data profiling (Sánchez-Monedero and Dencik 2020) as much as narratives of victimhood, criminality, or entrepreneurship that may be cast in new, platformed genres yet reproduce an age-old suspicion "of whatever is produced as non-European" (De Genova 2018: 1779). What indeed connects these diverse interventions into an assemblage of mediation is that, through their technologies and platforms, they mobilize normative criteria of valorization that are inherently racialized—whether in machine code or language semantics—yet appear as natural and necessary practices of protection for western citizens, territories, markets, and cultures (Ibrahim 2005). Here, who is allowed entry and who remains outside not only depends on the biopolitical practices of racialized classification and valorization that each techno-symbolic assemblage mobilizes but comes also to reproduce and legitimize these same hierarchies of human life that lead to migration in the first place.

And while much current research on the biopolitics of the border focuses on datafication, and rightly so—for instance, in the form of the residual colonialism inherent in the racialized profiles of border data policing (Leurs and Shepherd 2017) or the dehumanizing mathematization of data-driven decision-making on border crossing (Dijstelbloem and Broeders 2014)—it is clear by now that we understand the border in more expansive ways. Namely, we see the digital border as: i) involving *a hybrid configuration of space-time* that encompasses both the liminal contexts of cross-points and the urban contexts of migrants' everyday life; ii) relying upon *various double articulations of technology with meaning*: datafication with embodied encounters, for instance, when border officers at crossing points apply their own cultural judgements on arriving migrants, or organizational bureaucracies with mainstream narratives, when job centers' data profiling is coupled with online news storytelling about "migrant invasions"; finally, iii) entailing *both regulation and resistance*, in that the border's regimes of power offer, at the same time, opportunities for alternative expressions of voice and acts of subversion that destabilize, at least temporarily, the border's hierarchies of life.

Even though the regimes of power embedded in such assemblages are always constitutive of the border, nonetheless each regime differs from others depending on the context in which it emerges and the techno-symbolic resources of mediation available. This means that, in each assemblage, the technologies, bodies, and meanings of the border are mediated somehow differently, and so each produces its own historically-situated rules of inclusion and exclusion. How and to which extent specific assemblages of mediation produce and reproduce specific regimes of power at any point in time is consequently not a matter of conceptual definition but, we argue in line with a Foucauldian sensibility, an empirical question that forces us to engage in detail with the specificities of the border in its concrete contexts of emergence (Flyvbjerg 2002). It is in this spirit that our analysis of the digital border is centered specifically on Europe's migration "crisis," which peaked in 2015 but which still frames the lives of the continent's migrants, while, at the same time, points to the global interconnectedness of the politics, technologies, and narratives of migration—powerfully outlined in Amitav Ghosh's (2019) *Gun Island*, for instance, where the fates of earth and people are tied together through climate breakdown and migration.

Zooming into the European context, when in 2015 more than a million people crossed the continent's southern borders, migration took the world by storm—not so much because such large-scale, forced mobility was unprecedent but because humanitarian disasters of large scale had so far been largely contained within the Asian and African continents (Awumbila 2017). As a result, western media headlines and social media quickly started to speak of a "crisis." Naming those events as a "crisis," and even more so as a "European migration crisis," has in itself been a discursive process of boundary-making—one that we problematize in-depth in the concluding chapter. Decontextualizing its time and space from global developments such as conflicts in Syria and the Middle East or unrest and poverty in South Asia and North Africa, as well as from broader trends of migration and the rising numbers of forcibly displaced people worldwide (79.5 million at the end of 2019, 26 million of whom are refugees; IOM 2020), public discourse in the global North construed the arrival of these people as a spectacular media event, an unexpected European "emergency" that had to stop. "Crisis" appears in inverted commas throughout the book, as we recognize this term precisely as performative discourse, or, as we rename it later, a "social imaginary": a discursive order that encompasses the totality of public representations within which we are collectively invited to imagine what migration means for "us" as western publics. Within this understanding, we historicize the "crisis" not only as a specific moment, 2015, but also as a temporal continuum, where the meaning of "crisis" spills over subsequent years and still infuses the meanings of the digital border today; empirically, this means that we examine the trajectory of the "crisis" through the period of 2015 to 2020—what could be referred to as its performative peak and performative aftermath.

The "crisis" peak, we argue, is defined by the mobilization of *humanitarian securitization*, a regime of border power that combines concerns of national security—protection against risky migrants—with care for those same migrants as precarious, vulnerable populations (Chandler 2014; Marino 2020). Expressed as a regime of both openness and enclosure, "where the actual borders of states and gateways to the territory become themselves zones of humanitarian government" (Walters 2011: 139), the humanitarian security of the territorial border operated through and depended upon networks of mediation that attended both to risk management and compassionate engagement—and where migrants were largely cast as either "risks" or even "terrorists," in need of encampment, and as "victims" in need of care (Walters 2011; Marino 2020). These networks consisted of datafied systems of biometric assessment, drone, and satellite surveillance of the Mediterranean Sea—such as Eurodac and Eurosur—alongside other digital technologies, such as smartphones and social media by NGOs, activists, and migrants, that constructed European crossing points as both "digital passages and borders" (Latonero and Kift 2018); but they also involved mass and social media narrative patterns that framed much of the reporting on the "crisis" throughout its duration and across the continent. Such practices of power notwithstanding, this border regime also allowed for alternative performances of migrant voice and identity that in persistent, albeit minor ways, challenged the contours of humanitarian securitization.

Following the settlement of more than a million newcomers inside Europe's territories, a different regime of biopolitical power emerged across the urban centers of the continent, what we call a regime of *entrepreneurial securitization*. Rather than crossing points, the main locus of this new biopolitics is now the host city. Within it, the construction of the migrant no longer takes place within the binary of victim or threat, as before, but now shifts into the binary of the entrepreneurial migrant versus the parasitical and aggressive (and hence still threatening) "other" of the city; that is, those who manage to become financially self-sustained through employment and those who are not and are seen as relying on benefits or crime to survive (Gürsel 2017).

We argue that, while this regime produces racialized and exclusionary hierarchies of migrant identity similar to those of humanitarian security, it nonetheless reflects a different and more persistent articulation of territorial and symbolic resources, where new systems of classification and valorization, specific to the market-driven rationalities of western metropoles, now construe the migrant as a self-governing, self-optimizing neoliberal subject (Georgiou 2019; Georgiou et al. 2020). As before, this regime operates as much through institutional technologies of migrant surveillance—datafied profiles at health and educational institutions, job centers, and airlines (Vukov and Sheller 2013; Yuval-Davis et al. 2019)—as it does through storytelling that ties western norms of "good citizenship" onto market securitization (Musarò 2017; Tyyskä et al. 2018). By the same token, this entrepreneurial assemblage also cuts across territorial and symbolic borders in ways that not only consolidate the power relations of security but also allow for possibilities of voice and connectivity among migrants entangled in its urban networks.

What these two assemblages of mediation and their regimes of power throw into relief, then, is not only the difficulties inherent in defining where and how the border works as a site of performative classifications and migrant agency. Importantly, they also highlight the challenges of analyzing the multiple and shifting ways in which the border performs its work at different places and moments in time—challenges that, as we shall see, the social sciences have already grappled with. While our study is inspired by such research, we nonetheless identify two limitations to it. First, existing scholarship gives its attention either to the material/discursive constitution of the territorial border as a biopolitical affair of control *at* the outer border (at crossing points), or to the linguistic constitution of the symbolic border through narratives of migration *inside* the border (the territory of the nation). Second, and consequently, this division of scholarly attention prevents a full grasp of the border as an assemblage of mediations that may indeed be grounded in concrete contexts and moments in time, yet variously performs its power operations of boundary-drawing across and beyond specific times and locations (Mattelart 2019).

Territorial Border

Influenced by International Relations (IR) and Critical Border Studies (CBS), one side of this scholarly divide centers around debates on what the border is and how it works (Vaughan-Williams 2015a). Approaches to the border in the twentieth century, for instance, focused on the sovereignty of the nation-state as a territorial and judicial entity that is ontologically connected to the integrity of its land and has the enduring power to decide who has legitimate access to this land and who does not (Coleman and Grove 2009). Tightly linked to the historical project of European empires, this view of sovereignty already reflects a colonial imagination that seeks to separate the inhabitants of the "center" from those of the "periphery" within an epistemology of the earth as divided in spheres of power and subordination; and, even today, as Walters (2004) aptly notes, the EU's borders still reflect Europe's imperial trajectories and their contradictions, including the ambivalent coexistence of cultural openness with anxiety, assimilation with exclusion. This centrality of territory and its focus on military violence as a form of border control has, however, since been problematized in favor of what we earlier encountered as the biopolitical conception of the border. With its emphasis no longer on military might but on the micro-monitoring of human bodies (de Genova 2015; Mezzadra 2019), biopolitics entails a radical rethinking of the border itself no longer as a fixed line between adjacent states but rather as an open-ended process of ongoing boundary-drawing that occurs wherever and whenever the distinction between inside/outside is drawn. As Parker and Vaughan-Williams put it, the border has today become "increasingly ephemeral and/or impalpable: electronic, non-visible, and located in zones that defy a straightforwardly territorial logic" (Parker and Vaughan-Williams 2009: 583; see also Amoore, Marmura, and Salter 2008; Dijstelbloem 2009).

Instead of thinking of sovereignty and biopolitics as separate moments in the historical dynamics of modern power, however, our own account of the territorial border fully acknowledges the continuities and complicities between them and so approaches the two as operating in tandem—performing, as Nick Vaughan-Williams puts it, various kinds of "borderwork" (2015a). This means that, in our analysis, we understand biopower to be manifested as an imperative of sovereign power and its various forms of racialized and neocolonial control in the everyday techniques of migration management. The subtle forms of border regulation over migrant bodies, for instance, exercised in the spaces of humanitarian care at crossing points (ID bracelet or hand stamps) are themselves implicated in the geopolitical rationality of nation-states and its racialized hierarchies insofar as they take place side-by-side with military operations and hence complement and facilitate the enforcement of national security rather than challenge it (Vaughan-Williams 2015a). Similar biopolitical micro-techniques of security are also applied within the territory of the nation, as when migrants' medical information in western cities is cross-checked against biometric databases collected at entry points so as to determine their right to receive care, or its denial (Nedelcu and Soysüren 2020). The "smart" border here operates, in the words of Bigo, "via a multitude of points that are linked together through networks of computerized databases constantly exchanging information about the traces left by the individuals when they travel, and constantly updating them in order to be able to anticipate what may happen" (2014: 217).

These different kinds of "borderwork" suggest not only that processual borders always entail biopolitical practices that serve the territorial interests of national sovereignty, namely to safeguard its borders by way of exclusion, but, as we noted, that they do so in ways that are shifting and mutating in time; as Andreas put it, "states have always been in the business of territorial exclusion"; what changes is simply "the focus and form of their exclusionary practices [. . .] over time" (2003: 109). The emphasis on a processual conception of the border, then, matters here in that this fluidity alerts us both to the synergies between sovereignty and biopolitics as these work through techno-symbolic assemblages of the border to selectively inscribe the inside/outside distinction; *and* to the blurring of the territorial and the symbolic border as such assemblages operate both on the ground and in discourse to legitimize this inside/outside as natural. Yet, even though this processual reconfiguration the border has become increasingly prominent in the literature of IR and CBS, this body of work still largely ignores the symbolic dimension of the digital border (but see Bleiker 2019; Hansen 2011) and the ways in which the two articulate with and complicate each other.

Symbolic Border

On the other side of the divide, digital media and migration research has identified the symbolic border both in the stories and voices of migration produced and circulated by means of digital technologies (Georgiou 2018; Leurs and Smets 2018; Marino 2020) and in the journalistic narratives about migration that continue to shape public conversations about human mobility in Europe (Berry et al. 2016; Musarò 2017; Tyyskä et al. 2018). Literature on digital technologies, to begin with, focuses on the use of smartphones and social media platforms in "crisis" contexts so as to explore the potential of such personalized technologies to negotiate the power relations of the border. Indeed, even though, as Madianou et al. have put it, the global spread of mobile technologies has been hailed for its "capacity to give voice to affected people," including migrants, the extent to which such voice is heard, by whom, and to what effect, is a matter of contention (2016: 960).

The key problematic here is one of digital harms, which emerges in research on smartphones across migrant routes, highlighting, on the one hand, their indispensability in helping migrants to communicate with others and navigate their journeys (Dekker et al. 2018; Zijlstra and van Liempt 2017), and, on the other, their potential to render migrants vulnerable vis-à-vis malevolent actors and state surveillance (Pötzsch 2015). While such vulnerabilities stem from digital regimes of surveillance that collect digital footprints (Madianou 2019), they are also related to disinformation, that is, migrants' engagement with incorrect or misleading online content—for example navigation tips—that can put their lives at risk; as Bokert et al. point out, "the outcomes of receiving poor or false information can cause bodily harm or death, loss of family, or financial ruin" (2018: 1). Reflecting on the ambivalence of the mobile phone, Gillespie et al. thus strongly recommend a rethinking of current definitions of migrant security to include not only their privacy set-ups but also their "content (e.g. these resources should provide warnings regarding the dangers of financial exploitation by certain groups such as taxi/private drivers and smuggling networks)" (2016: 98).

If, in digital media and migration research, the symbolic border manifests itself in harmful sources of knowledge that may impact migrants' destinies, the strand of journalism studies and migration media studies identify the symbolic border in practices of storytelling—especially, though not exclusively, news storytelling of migration in western mediascapes. Literature on the migration and refugee "crisis," despite its internal diversity, converges on the fact that such storytelling systematically misrepresents migrants as either victims or villains (Crawley et al. 2016; Berry et al. 2016; Musarò, 2017; Georgiou and Zaborowski 2017; Zaborowski and Georgiou 2019). Caught largely between the positions of helpless sufferer or evil threat, as we have already noted, migrants rarely appear on their own terms and often exist within orientalist narratives that silence and objectify them (Malkki 1996).[1] The digital border is here performed through linguistic strategies that mostly portray migrants in terms of numbers, or, again, as one-dimensional figures existing outside biographical contexts and geopolitical histories (Georgiou et al. 2017). In parallel to these studies, research on post-"crisis" storytelling shows how the figure of the migrant-entrepreneur is positioned within a hierarchy that validates this figure as a "successful businessman" while vilifying and excluding those who are unable (or refuse) to engage with the economic rationalities of western capitalism (Georgiou 2019; Munkejord 2017).

Even though journalism is indeed instrumental in drawing boundaries of inside/outside within western mediascapes, literature on news storytelling, we argue, tends to overemphasize the linguistic binaries of victim and threat (and, increasingly, entrepreneur and criminal) and so downplays a more versatile spectrum of meanings that emerge as news stories themselves reflect and renegotiate the changing relations of power at the territorial border. While this trend has been complexified, for instance, in Benson and Wood's (2015) text analysis of three national press cultures in 2011–12, where migrant stories are mostly informative (or "frameless") rather than evaluative, we argue that, in moments of "crisis," this persistent emphasis on the migrant as victim or threat is problematic. This is because such binary naming operates as itself an evaluative frame that tends to fix the meaning of the term migrant within a narrow spectrum of static categories, perpetuating stereotypes of "otherness." To use a key example from the 2015 "crisis," the death of Syrian toddler Alan Kurdi in September 2015 triggered a temporary media shift towards humanitarian care for migrant children and families as victims—a shift that was, however, abruptly reversed after the Paris attacks in November of the same year, taking up a denunciatory vocabulary against migrants as terrorists. What this example highlights is not only that migrants are "trapped" in the polarity of innocence and malevolence, but also that it is important to focus on the semantic politics of substitutability around the signifier "migrant"—particularly on the ways in which such politics is deeply embedded in the power regimes of the border and performs the ideological work of "othering" migrants in various ways, across of the regimes of humanitarian and entrepreneurial securitization. The vocabulary of the migrant, it follows, should not be seen as a binary but as consisting of differential and relatively diverse "floating signifiers" (Russo 2017) that attach different meanings to those arriving from elsewhere (or those perceived as not belonging here), in line with the power context within which each signifier occurs.

In summary, journalism studies and migration media studies have insightfully illustrated how the symbolic border is reproduced through two separate but interrelated processes: digital disinformation, where unreliable or malevolent online sources of knowledge may perpetuate the precarity of migrants' lives; and linguistic misrepresentation, where dominant news vocabularies "other" and dehumanize migrants in western mediascapes. However, because this research tends to analyze the border in partial terms, either as a terrain of content surveillance or as a site of harmful representation, it has overlooked the interpenetration of the territorial and the symbolic in defining the border. Consequently, it has also downplayed the border's dimensions of mediation—how, that is, the border is constituted simultaneously through the biopolitics of migrant phone use and the harms these create for them on the ground, as much as through those textual practices that narrate migrants on screen and the distinct but real harms these also create for them. This by no means suggests that there is a conscious synergy between territorial and symbolic borders; it implies, nonetheless, that, as our experience of the border emerges through assemblages of digital platforms and their meaning-making practices, we can only grasp the diverse ways in which the border regulates (and potentially harms) migrant populations, if we attend to the entanglements of power at the heart of these assemblages within their specific historical contexts.

The Digital Border as a Field of Study

Informed by this view, our methodological approach similarly aspires to put forward a theoretically informed account of the digital border that is grounded upon concrete case studies of its territorial and symbolic dimensions—one that aims to interrogate how its networks of mediation engage migrants in power struggles around mobility control. In producing this account, we are fully aware of our positionality in the field we have delved into—being privileged researchers working at the core of western academia with its inherent biases (Shome and Hedge 2002), but also being ourselves migrants who moved from the southern "periphery" of Europe to its "core" and so having experienced, over the years, Europe's own racialized migration and competing nationalisms (Lambrianidis 2013). Aware of our own contradictory subjectivities, intensified even more in the context of the migration "crisis" that accentuated divides of responsibility between European North and South, we have, throughout this project, questioned the limits of both our knowledge and privilege. In doing so, we committed to expanding our engagement with literature from across regions and to employing participatory methods that destabilize the hierarchies of the western "knowing subject" and the silenced "other" (Maalki 1996; Signona 2014).

In practice, and when conducting fieldwork at the outer border of the Greek island of Chios during the 2015 moment of "transit" migration, when people would pass through the island onto mainland Greece within 24 or 48 hours, we decided not to integrate migrants into our data collection; we felt that it would be ethically inappropriate to approach them for quick, "soundbite" interviews as they stood in line for hours, tired and anxious, waiting for their debriefing interviews or as they tried to rest in the UN camp before continuing their trip. Instead, we committed to engaging with local islanders receiving newcomers, as their voices have been silenced as much as those of migrants in (his-)stories of migration often told on their behalf. When conducting fieldwork in the inner border, which now engaged with migrants' voices, we similarly built sustained relationships with a range of actors of migration—not only newcomers but also civic actors—and employed co-creative and participatory methods that enabled those voices and experiences to be heard in the narrative of our encounters.

Throughout these moments of encounter and in writing up the chapters of this volume, our aim has always been to illustrate the workings of the digital border from the perspective of those who are close to it and shape it but also to do so in ways that further conceptualize and clarify how the power relations of the border work, "with what consequences to whom" (Flyvbjerg 2004: 283). Within this approach, our distinction between the territorial and the symbolic is, then, not simply an empirical one, as we have argued so far, but also an analytical one in that it opens up the space for us to examine the inner workings of each dimension of the border and to develop the conceptual language required for us to understand how these workings may impact the lives of migrants and other border actors. Three key questions are relevant to this analytical task, namely: how the techno-symbolic assemblages of the border work (*mediation*); how they restrict or enable struggle and resistance (*agency*); how they change in time (*historicity*). It is to the meanings of these terms and concepts that we now turn.

The Digital Border: Mediation, Agency, and Change

The digital border, we have established, can be understood as shifting assemblages of technologies and meanings organized around historically embedded power relations that regulate the inside/outside boundaries of migrant mobility across space and time. While this description opens up a new perspective for a broader account of the relationship between digital mediation, mobility, and power, nonetheless it poses three further analytical/conceptual questions. The first one concerns the *constitutive elements of the digital border*: what do its techno-symbolic assemblages consist of, and how are they organized? The second question refers to the *position of migrants in the power relations of the border*: are these relations of total domination, or does the border allow spaces of subaltern agency? And the third question relates to the *historicity of the border*: what does the shift from humanitarian to entrepreneurial securitization entail, and what does it mean for the lives of migrants and those of other border actors? By addressing these questions recursively throughout this volume, we present our account of the digital border, both territorial and symbolic, in terms of its dynamics of mediation, its dialectics of resistance, and its trajectories of historicity.

The dynamics of mediation refers to the specific configuration of techno-symbolic resources particular to the border at specific points in time: how these resources map onto one another and so connect (or disconnect) migrants with (or from) each other and other border actors and to what effects. While each epoch's border technology has always been enabled by particular border infrastructures (from barbed wires to watch towers), each with its own arrangements and hierarchies of power, digitization, we argue, has reorganized this architecture of the border through three specific infrastructural networks (Chouliaraki and Georgiou 2017): the network of *remediations*, which refers to the role of mass and social media in the public representation of the border; the network of *intermediations*, where various digital networks, from Eurodac to Instagram, link up migrants with security forces, humanitarian groups, local populations, and with one another; and the network of *transmediations*, where online connections enable offline relationships between those arriving and those receiving them (NGOs, activists, volunteers) at various border locations.

Rather than belonging exclusively to one dimension of the border, each of these networks cuts across territorial and symbolic borders, blurring the distinctions between them and shaping the identities and relations for those involved. The territorial border as a site of reception,[2] for instance, is remediated in news journalism through narratives of illegal migrants or the human cost of risky sea crossings, thereby intersecting with the symbolic border and its imaginaries of security, humanitarianism, and migration; but it is also intermediated through migrant "arrival" selfies on the island's coast as they spread horizontally, on WhatsApp or Facebook, to their families and friends in narratives of survival and celebration—as well as remediated on western news, again, as objects of curiosity or suspicion (see Chouliaraki 2017 on migrant selfies as newsworthy stories). Across its networks, the digital border integrates digital, pre-digital and embodied technologies that together work to draw boundaries of inside/outside not only as geographical markers of separation but also as narrative tropes of "othering" and embodied ways of being. We focus on the dynamics of mediation at the territorial border in Chapter 1 in particular, when we explore how the border's three networks, from remediation to transmediation, organized the regimes of humanitarian securitization at a key EU crossing point during the "crisis" moment of 2015; and we focus on how the dynamics of (re)mediation in the symbolic border in Chapters 4 and 5, as we detail how news in eight European countries employs its own techno-narrative affordances to amplify portrayals of migrants as racialized "others."

Addressing the second analytical question about the *agency of migrants* in the power relations of the border, we argue that, in contrast to certain claims in Critical Border Studies, the digital border is not to be understood as a totalizing space of sovereign or biopolitical subjection, but rather as a contradictory space where military security, humanitarian care, and activist solidarity co-exist. It is the nature of the border precisely as an assemblage of intersecting networks of mediation, enabling multiple connectivities and interactivities among relatively powerless actors, that renders it a site of struggle for alternative forms of inclusion and belonging; in this, we echo Squire's powerful argument that "borderzones may be marked by struggles around abjectification, but do not necessarily produce abject subjects" (2011: 14).

Grounded in migrant experiences of profound precarity, the border's potential for resistance depends specifically on the tactical mobilization of what we call intermediation and transmediation processes that connect border actors across online and offline networks and potentially turn migrants' claims to rights and voice into a "new form of commons through mobility" (Trimikliniotis et al. 2015: 1). Such mobilizations open up the possibility for migrants, activists, and volunteers to challenge the criminalization practices at work both in humanitarian securitization, fighting, for instance, against laws that turn migrant rescue at sea into a punishable deed (Tazzioli and Walters 2019); and in entrepreneurial securitization, hosting and educating non-entrepreneurial migrants who are marginalized and excluded in big cities (Mekdijian 2018). In Chapters 3 and 6, we explicitly engage with the question of resistance by theorizing the digital border (both territorial and symbolic) from the perspective of migrants, as they speak out online and offline within the urban environments of Athens, Berlin, and London.

Our discussion on resistance is, in turn, intrinsically linked to our final analytical category of the digital border: its spatiotemporal trajectories. This concern with *the historicity of the border* is here relevant because resistance does not occur in a vacuum but is always embedded in the border's shifting assemblages of mediation that, by configuring different regimes of power, also offer different possibilities for claiming agency. Humanitarian and entrepreneurial regimes of power, from this perspective, entail their own techno-symbolic resources of surveillance—interviews and biometric technologies, in the case of humanitarianism; or online employment registration forms and start-up training programs, in the entrepreneurial regimes of power—so that each inevitably requires its own distinct performances of migrant identity. At the same time, while humanitarian securitization in 2015 was met with calculated performances of "abject victimhood" as migrants sought to model and mimic the normative identities of the border in order to successfully cross it, so the marketized securitization of urban living in 2020 mobilized migrant acts of "everyday resistance" in the networked commons of the city to undermine the norm of neoliberal citizenship (Georgiou 2019). And it is precisely this spatiotemporal grounding of its regimes of power that, for us, enables a reading of the border's security (humanitarian and entrepreneurial) not as totalizing practices of subjection but also as spaces of creative self-expression (Hall 2015) and political activism, where migrants do not simply claim citizenship but already act as citizens themselves (Mezzadra 2011).

In the following chapters, we incorporate this historical sensibility into our argument by viewing the digital border through a diachronic lens. Three of our empirical cases, in Chapters 1, 4, and 5, are taken from the period of migrant arrivals between June 2015 and March 2016, the period between Europe's intermittent border openings and their eventual closing; and the remaining ones, in Chapters 2, 3, and 6, engage with the subsequent period, what we refer to as post-"crisis" period, from 2016 to 2020, when arriving populations settled in European cities and sought to make a new life for themselves.

Chapter Outline

Based on six case studies and organized in two sections, each of our chapters captures a particular snapshot of the border's assemblages of mediation and the struggles over exclusion and voice that they made possible. Section I focuses on the territorial border: the initial arrival points at the island of Chios, as much as the urban arrival settings in Athens, Berlin, and London; and Section II on the symbolic one: the online news of the migration "crisis" or the social media and institutional online accounts of migrants seeking self-expression and recognition. Both sections offer new theoretical insights into the mutations of the border's regimes of power, their networks of mediation, and their struggles over migrant agency, and each section is organized around a deliberate balance between narratives of control and narratives of resistance: the first two chapters of each section highlight processes of subjection (Chapters 1 and 2, and 4 and 5), whereas the final chapter of each section illustrates how struggles of resistance emerge within and against such contexts (Chapters 3 and 6).

Chapter 1 introduces the territorial border with a description of Chios island as one of the two main reception sites for migrants in 2015. Drawing on on-location observations and interviews, collected during our visit to the island in December of that year, the chapter details the regime of humanitarian securitization—a regime organized around a robust but invisible assemblage of remediations, intermediations, and transmediations that organized the bureaucratic monitoring, professionalized care, and activist hospitality for arriving migrants across three domains of reception: military securitization (at the reception center); securitized care (at the UN camp), and compassionate solidarity (in the spaces of volunteer activists). Moving from the continent's outer border on Chios to its urban centers, Athens, Berlin, and London, Chapter 2 explores how Europe's "inner borderlands" activate their own hierarchical networks of digital intermediation and transmediation via social media and web projects to give rise to entrepreneurial securitization—a regime premised upon the obligation for migrants to comply with a neoliberal logic of work in order to obtain not only economic benefit, but also legal status, a sense of self-worth, and community belonging. While being employed represents the predominant pathway for migrants to potentially achieve citizen status, we show how this potential is both facilitated and skewed by the cities' border assemblage across three domains of migrant employment: securitized self-responsibility (via digital job training programs); securitized precarity (via job center databases and their profiles of migrant employment skills); and conditional conviviality (in informal contexts that mix online with face-to-face community work). Chapter 3, the last in this section, highlights the ways in which urban networks of digital intermediation and transmediation, organized horizontally on smartphones and social media and enacted in fringe spaces on the ground, generate their own networked commons: fragile but lively collectivities of communication, collaboration, and self-expression between urban citizens and noncitizens that challenge the normative contours of the border: the commons of grassroots pedagogy (in language learning cafés as spaces of spontaneous sociality); of cultural encounters (in mobile libraries and workshops, where people meet, talk, and play together) and political activism (in squat networks and solidarity centers that take care of the most vulnerable migrants).

Section II of the volume turns its attention to the dynamics by which securitization, humanitarian and entrepreneurial, is intrinsically connected to the digital mediations of the symbolic border. Online journalism and social media, we here argue, are crucial sites where these regimes of power and their possibilities for resistance are legitimized or challenged: "discourses and social realities are mutually constitutive," as Wodak puts it, "and discursive practices may have major ideological effects helping [. . .] to legitimize inclusion and exclusion, particularly in regard to ethnic and religious minorities, refugees, immigrants and asylum seekers" (2020: 160). The centrality of the symbolic border in our study stems precisely from the role that the digital infrastructures of institutional news and social media play in remediating and amplifying narratives of the "migrant" that are "othering" and exclusionary, but also from the role of NGO websites and social media accounts that challenge these imaginations and enable migrant self-representations and voices to be heard.

Chapter 4 focuses on the remediation of migration in online news storytelling from the standpoint of voice—who speaks (subjects of voice), in which capacity (status of voice), and within which context (context of voice). Our analysis of 1,200 news articles shows that the systematic silencing of migrants in European news during the "crisis" relied not so much on an either/or binary of "victim" and "terrorist" as on the shifting articulation of the two within the fluid regime of humanitarian securitization, which fluctuated between moments of tolerance, empathy, and fear for them. Silencing in this erratic discursive context, we demonstrate, is accomplished through persistent representations of migrants as abstract and ahistorical figures that lack voice and agency. Chapter 5 interrogates the visual remediation of migrants in the photojournalism of migration during the same period of time. This chapter takes its point of departure not from migrant voice but from the question of western responsibility vis-à-vis the migrants' arrival. Approaching photojournalism as a moralizing project that invites its publics to offer a response to the spectacle of migration, the chapter reflects upon five key patterns of migrant visibility across 51 front-page online images from five EU national news websites: the patterns of monitorial, charitable, securitizing, activist, and post-humanitarian responsibility. Despite this broad range of proposals, we conclude, the news' economy of visibility systematically employs strategies of dehumanization that, throughout these images, represent the migrant as a deeply ambivalent figure, whether this is a body-in-need, a powerless child, a racial "other," a celebrity token, or a sentimental drawing. By reflecting on those visual patterns, our analysis invites us to fundamentally rethink how we understand the media's own responsibility towards migrants and how "we" see ourselves as responsible publics of "our" news. Chapter 6 moves away from remediation and into networks of intermediation and transmediation through which migrants emerge as speaking subjects addressing their own communities and western publics. Through an analysis of four Europe-wide institutional and grassroots online initiatives in the course of the past five years, we illustrate the potential of the migrant as a "subaltern" actor to unsettle, at least briefly, the symbolic border and its binaries of inside/outside and to appear as a sovereign speaker in control of their discourse. As these network diversify over time, we show how subalternity is mobilized in different and sometimes competing projects of voice: subordinating this voice to official discourse (in governmental sites) and so denying recognition to migrants or enabling it to speak in its own terms (in grassroots ones) and so claiming an autonomous identity.

Our Conclusion wraps up our argument by returning to the two key questions of this volume. On the one hand, the conceptual question of what the digital border is and how we can describe it, and, on the other, the normative question, posed by Achille Mbembe, of what we do with those who do not have a claim to earth. In response to the first question, we conceptualize the digital border as a hybrid terrain of techno-symbolic contestations where security, care, solidarity, and activism co-exist in different combinations across space and time; and where, consequently, the boundary-drawing capacity of the border also shifts and mutates at different scales, in ways that bring its primary function of security together with other political imperatives of the (neo)liberal west—namely the imperative to care and the imperative to profit. The digital border, it follows, can only be grasped in glimpses and studied through various methodologies in its multiple granular details rather than as a total institution. Our response to the second, normative question begins by revisiting the very idea of "crisis," so far cast as a linguistic act that construed the 2015 migration event as an unexpected mega-challenge, and now problematizes it as a "social imaginary." More than a linguistic act, the imaginary refers here to a whole order of discourse that delimits our sphere of the perceptible, and regulates what we see and understand as migration while also regulating what is hidden from view and thus falls below the radar of critical faculties. Given that the "crisis" imaginary has been at the heart of the techno-symbolic assemblage of the digital border since 2015, spreading fear of the "other" and fueling demands for more borders in the global North, we argue that we now urgently need a new social imaginary—one that values dignity, inclusion, and recognition for migrants as for everyone else.

SECTION I

The Territorial Border

1

The Outer Border

Assemblages of Humanitarian Securitization

In this chapter, we set out an account of the digital border as it emerged at a busy crossing point in Europe's outer frontiers, the island of Chios, in December 2015. Chios, a small island of 52,000 inhabitants located in the Eastern Mediterranean (the Aegean Sea), is only eight kilometers away from the coast of Turkey. Because of this proximity, Chios had always been a point of reception for migrants crossing the short distance from the Asia Minor coast to the edges of Europe, yet, in the summer of 2015, this flow of arrivals reached an unprecedented peak.[1]

By December of that year, Chios, together with the adjacent islands of Lesbos and Kos, became the crossing point for 818,654 migrants, most of whom wished to eventually settle in Northern European countries such as Germany, Sweden, France, and the United Kingdom (ECFR 2015; IOM Report 2020). It was at that point that the island turned from a relatively low-key entry point to Greece into a major site of infrastructures and actors that both controlled mobility flows and provided assistance to new arrivals. Bringing together the Registration Center, run by Greek and European police forces (Frontex), the UNHCR-run reception migrant camp, and the activist spots of located action and migrant support, this new assemblage of technologies, actors, and narratives comprised the networks of mediation that in turn constituted humanitarian security as the dominant regime of power on the island (ECFR 2015).

But what exactly did it mean for the island of Chios to participate in the border regime of humanitarian securitization? And what were the complications of this regime as it sought to care for those it regards as a risk? It is these questions that we address in detail in this chapter. In our response, we partly concur with existing accounts of the border in Critical Border and Critical Data Studies, which view the border as a site of collusion between geopolitical and biopolitical rationalities that dehumanize migrants by assigning to them the "paradigmatic status [of] the outsider par excellence" (Darling 2009: 649). Our analysis nonetheless allows for a more open-ended understanding of the border assemblage on Chios, which shows how, in co-articulating two distinct imperatives, military monitoring and humanitarian assistance, this assemblage entails tensions within its own constitutive rationalities—between policing and caring or challenging and reproducing the power relations of the regime—thereby giving rise to practices of reflexive critique and solidarity.

Specifically, we begin with problematizing the accounts of humanity and dehumanization that dominate literatures on Border Studies and develop a conception of migrant humanity as a matter of the ongoing struggles over classification and voice inherent in the mediations of the border assemblage: its networks of remediation, intermediation, and transmediation. We subsequently offer our own reconstruction of Chios Island as a site of reception traversed by these intersecting networks across three domains of border practice: military securitization, securitized care, and compassionate solidarity, where local actors contribute to caring for and supporting migrants at arrival points. What this detailed cartography of one of Europe's busiest entry points shows, we conclude, is how the humanization of migrants is intricately linked to the techno-symbolic networks of the island and their own situated tensions around migrant bodies, their voice and their agency.

Theorizing the Outer Border

The Datafication of the Outer Border

The starting point of our critical engagement with Critical Border Studies and Critical Data Studies is the dehumanization thesis: a thesis claiming that humanity does not preexist the body as a fixed quality that belongs to all but, rather, that it is an attribute selectively attached to certain bodies over others in the process of giving meaning to these bodies within certain contexts of power. In this account, migrants are selectively construed as "human" in the context of the datafied border as the latter employs its own technologies and narratives to classify their bodies as legitimate or not (Ticktin 2006; Millner 2011). Practices as diverse as face-to-face interview protocols and face recognition employed by the digital border work, in the Critical Border Studies narrative, to deprive migrants of their human quality as unique individuals with biographical and psychological depth and situate them in another order of existence, that of "bare life." They become, in Agamben's (1998) argument, ambivalent subjectivities whose life may be worthy of protection yet whose death is not a cause for prosecution and may go unpunished or ungrieved.

This impunity that border violence can enjoy, continues Agamben, does not only inform the security mandate of the border to safeguard the sovereignty of the nation at all costs. Rather, sovereignty also penetrates the domain of care by subordinating the biopolitical mandate of humanitarianism to its own violent ends—for instance, through charitable micro-interventions upon migrant bodies, whether it is the UNHCR identification bracelet of the camp or the minimal provision of survival goods (a nutrition bar and a blanket per person) distributed among migrants upon arrival. Through such interventions, as Jenny Edkins writes, "victims appear only as a form of life that can be saved (as bare life), not as people whose communities and livelihoods have been destroyed but who still have political views" (2000: 14).

Biopolitics should not here be seen simply as the micro-management of migrants' biological lives in ways that deprive them of the status of the citizen and turn them into bare life, or "bios," instead of engaging them in "zoe," or civic life. More than this, biopolitics physically restricts those lives within spaces that entail forms of lethal violence—what Edkins, after Agamben, calls "exceptional places: zones such as the Nazi concentration camps" (2000). Agamben's point here is not that humanitarian camps are in any way comparable to Nazi extermination camps—certainly not the transitional camp of Chios in 2015, though, as we discuss in the Conclusion, modern camps have since morphed into "exceptional places" of extreme suffering where, as he puts it, "whether or not atrocities are committed depends not on law but on the civility and ethical sense of the police who temporarily act as sovereign" (1998: 174). For our purposes, Agamben's point is that the life form of the camp, which is central to the biopolitical administration of all bodies-in-need, is always entangled with the strictly constrained life forms of sovereign violence: in grasping "human life in the figure of bare life," he says, "humanitarian organisations [. . .], despite themselves, maintain a secret solidarity with the very powers they ought to fight" (1998: 133).

The dehumanization of migrants, in this account, is then not a consequence of a failed process of border management but an inherent feature of how the regime of humanitarian securitization works. Integral to this regime of border violence are the data-driven infrastructures that today underpin the techno-symbolic assemblages of the border. In the narrative of Critical Data Studies, this is the case with biometric identification and AI-driven technologies, which have introduced face or dialect recognition, name transliteration, and mobile phone data analysis into the digital border (Sánchez-Monedero and Dencik 2020). Even though, as Ana Beduschi argues, these are adopted to benign ends, namely to accelerate migrant selection and asylum determination that, for example, "would otherwise require lengthy human expert linguists' assessment" (2020: 4), they nonetheless dehumanize migrants by reproducing the racial biases that are already coded into the human-made algorithms of their automated classification systems.

This dehumanization of the border's identification practices operates on the basis of what Cheney-Lippold calls an "algorithmic fit" between coding categories and Black or Brown populations, which assigns "categorical membership" to migrants so that "if one's data is spoken for 'as if' it was produced by a 'terrorist,' for example, one is seen to be a terrorist" (2017: 47). It is in this sense of systematically subjecting "almost exclusively non-European/non-white migrant and refugees" to what de Genova calls forms of "structural violence and generalized suffering" that the European migration "crisis" can effectively be seen as a "racial crisis" (2018: 1768). A key consequence of this mathematical reduction of individual profiles to abstract codes of race, ethnicity, and religion is that such datafied systems of border control condense the migrant as a person into one category or the "other" of a rigid binary of "risky" or "safe," while rendering their origins, biographical narratives, and personal trajectories irrelevant to decision-making. As a consequence, Leurs and Shepherd claim, "individual people, faces, stories and motives are not of interest to 'smart' border processes" (2017: 216).

It is this erasure of the migrant in the dehumanization accounts of Critical Border Studies and Critical Data Studies that we complexify in our reconstruction of the Chios site. We do so by shifting focus from an epistemological gaze privileging the power effects of the datafied border to a grounded approach that grasps the inner workings of the border as a dialectical space of struggle over who controls the networks of mediation and who speaks in the narratives of its assemblages. By engaging with the overlapping and competing networks, actors and narratives of reception across the border's three domains of action, this approach challenges the key assumption of the datafied border, which constructs the newly arrived as a disembodied matrix of computerized data patterns (Raley and Amoore 2017), and opens up the possibility to read the outer border also as a space for tactical self-expression, political agency, and resistance.

Dehumanization consequently emerges as a more complex process that, on the one hand, encompasses the situated micro-practices in which border power classifies migrant bodies but, on the other, also highlights the diverse ways in which such bodies, and those of other actors, may subtly interrupt power, attempt to speak out, and tactically exercise their agency within the regime of humanitarian security. As we proceed with our reconstruction of Chios's digital border, our aim is to offer a more nuanced narrative of border power than established accounts currently do—one that specifically highlights three crucial tensions of the border: how *bodies* challenge the disembodied abstractions of the migrant in the datafied border; how migrant *voices* remain a key stake in the power struggles of the border; and how migrant *agency* in the form of self-expressive and performative identity always persists as a possibility of resistance for the actors of the border.

The Outer Border and Humanitarian Securitization

Our criticism of much Agamben-informed Critical Border and Critical Data Studies literature relies on a slippage that conflates a *theoretical* account of power as datafied biopolitics with the *empirical* account of how historical practices of the border, in Chios and elsewhere, actually engage with and manage migrant populations; how, in other words, power works in context. Criticizing Agamben for his ahistorical "Europeanization" of the contemporary migrant in the model of the persecuted Holocaust victim, Ahmed problematizes "Agamben's methodological tendency to subsume historical and theoretical work under a reductivist conceptualization of homo sacer [. . .] outside its own historico-material context" (2019: 157). Autonomy-of-migration scholars, such as Papadopoulos and Tsianos, similarly critique his "frenetic fixation with security" (2013: 178), which ignores the infrastructures of connectivity, affective cooperation, and mutual support that counter the repressive regime of the border.

In line with these arguments, our own analysis aims at producing an account of the border that places the empirical micro-realities of migration in reflexive tension with macro-theories of border power. It is in this in-between space that the most productive questions arise: How exactly does the digital border operationalize this regime of power? What techno-symbolic assemblages does it require and how do these unfold and intersect? What networks of mediation traverse it and how do these connect and disconnect the actors of the border?

Our point of departure in addressing these questions is that, even though the Chios assemblage of the outer border produces and reproduces humanitarian securitization as the dominant regime of power on the island, its mobilization of technologies, actors, and narratives is not always fully aligned within this regime. Further, this non-alignment opens up the possibility for other modes of care and subjectivity to emerge—ones that overlap, complement, or conflict with the dominant regime of the border.[2]

The Chios assemblage, in this sense, is best thought of as a configuration of intersecting networks of mediation and narrative that respond to an emergent situation of uncertainty—a "crisis"—by fusing the mandates of security and care in the course of situational and often contingent engagements. Such engagements, in turn, enable different actors of security and care, state and EU staff and NGOs and activists, to communicate with one another so as to facilitate the swift management of migrant arrivals; an example here is the Registration Center, a meeting point for army and police staff de-briefing migrants, Doctors of the World professionals offering medical support, and local activists distributing hot soup to those waiting.

Following this open-ended understanding of the nature of the Chios border as a techno-symbolic assemblage, our analysis is organized around this assemblage's networks of mediation and networks of discourse. The island's *networks of mediation* refer to the distribution of technological platforms and information flows across our familiar media routes: *remediation*, which is either about traditional news reporting from or about the island or it is about the vertical mobility of social media content as it shifts upwards onto mass media platforms (for instance, from local Facebook posts to the local or national press); *intermediation*, which is about horizontal mobility across social media contexts and contents (for instance, when an activist Facebook message becomes a Twitter hashtag or when an activist Twitter message appears in local or national websites); and *transmediation*, which is about movement from online to offline contexts (for instance, from online Facebook contact to offline cooking sessions and food distribution by a group called the Collective Kitchen). It is, we propose, the contextual articulations of these networks and their meanings that define the extent to which the digital border may challenge (or not) the hierarchies of migrant voice and their potential for agency in the context of the island.

The island's networks of discourse refer to the distribution of discourses of international law (rights), geopolitical interests (policy mandates), activism (solidarity), or management (information, coordination, etc.) that circulate within and across domains of reception and their media platforms. While each domain is constituted by its own distinct discourses—for instance, security by geopolitical and military ones or humanitarianism by those of human rights and diplomacy—networks of mediation enable the permeation of each domain by discourses of the other—as when the Greek army referred to small gestures of care to migrants or when they showed appreciation for the humanitarian work accomplished by NGOs—as well as the diffusion and amplification of these discourses within broader public spheres. Our analytical task next is to map out how these various routes of mediation work—which intersect with what others, and which discourses they disseminate across the spheres of the digital border: military securitization at registration, humanitarian securitization at the camp, and compassionate solidarity in the volunteers' kitchen, among others.

Reconstructing the Outer Border

Our empirical discussion emerges out of ten days of intensive fieldwork on Chios in December 2015; this included interviews and participant and nonparticipant observations conducted by the two of us across locations of reception. While the study came with inevitable limitations, its conduct and relevance have to be understood in the context of the spatial and cultural geography of the island, especially at that moment of intense transitional movement. It is in that context that we, as researchers, decided it would be morally more appropriate to refrain from engaging with populations-on-the-move—migrants who had just landed, anxious, exhausted, and desperate for boat tickets—and pursued instead encounters with the actors of reception.

Given our own identities as Greek women and having the great privilege of pre-existing local connections, as we have also noted in Chapter 1, access to a range of actors was much easier and numerous interviews and meetings were organized before our arrival. We gratefully benefited from one of our key informant's strategic position between local government and networks of solidarity, as well as of many actors' warm welcome to us as individuals; and, naturally, from our native, intuitive understanding of the local culture and people (and we are fully aware of the nationality, professional, gender, and age dynamics that put us in a favorable position vis-à-vis other researchers or activists, and migrant newcomers).

Benefiting from this positionality and local support, our relatively brief period of fieldwork on the island was filled with unending interviews and observations from dawn till late at night. From the moment of our arrival, we visited repeatedly different locations of reception, including the Registration Center (the sphere of military securitization), formal and informal meetings of the humanitarian professionals on the island (the sphere of securitized care), and the fishing village of Ayia Ermioni (the sphere of compassionate solidarity), where migrants were arriving in dinghies. The actors of reception in both these locations were surprisingly (or perhaps unsurprisingly, considering our own positionality) willing to talk to us at length. Relations of trust developed fast, partly as a result of initial local introductions, and partly because of our identities as women happy to participate in practices of care. Contacts with the humanitarian sector were established equally swiftly on our first day of arrival; key actors in the sphere of securitized care agreed to be interviewed and provided access to spaces of care and to NGOs' organizing meetings. In addition, we strategically divided our work between the different sites, maximizing the potential of our research time. In the course of this intensive fieldwork, between us we visited the Registration Center three times and spent hours of participant and nonparticipant observations on site; twice visited and spent time with volunteers at the fishing village of Ayia Ermioni; twice visited the UNHCR-run refugee camp and once the informal camp of Dipethe, the local theater turned into shelter for newcomers; three times participated in the Collective Kitchen's activities; and, finally, we conducted 14 interviews with actors within all three domains of reception. In many cases, the interviews took the form of informal conversations and, occasionally, took place in-between hectic activity; for this reason, we chose to prioritize informality and mutual trust and kept notes instead of using tape-recorders. These interviews were complemented by multi-sited participant observation and encounters with approximately 40 actors across the three domains. Where appropriate, participation extended to online spaces through our inclusion in local Facebook groups, which we continued to interact with throughout the course of this study.

The main strength of our fieldwork lies in the multi-sited observations and lengthy encounters with key actors of reception, which surpassed our expectations. It is these dense encounters that enabled us to break with the theoretical tradition of Critical Border and Critical Data Studies and develop instead a richer, albeit "more modest understanding," as Barnett puts it, "of what state and non-state actors are capable of doing, for good or ill" (2015: 21), and how they do it on the ground through the networks of mediation and discourse available to them. While we have already explained why migrant voices are absent from this chapter, we here also wish to make a more emphatic point about the significance of listening to and engaging with the voices of the local actors—the islanders on the police force, the pensioners living by the coast where migrant boats arrive, and the (mostly but not exclusively) young people organizing to help people-on-the-move, whose voice often goes unheard and whose contribution to the workings of the border assemblage remains largely under-researched. Using observations and interviews with these different groups of citizens, we next map out Chios's assemblage at work across the spheres of security, military and humanitarian, as well as the volunteering work of solidarity.

Military Securitization: Classifying "Others"

Military securitization's networks of mediation and discourse render the border a site of identification and classification for mobile populations. During the peak of arrivals, military securitization took place exclusively at the Registration Center of Chios. There was a conspicuous absence of the state (army, police) at various other locations, such as arrival bays, by the port, en route to the Registration Center, or any other transit spots, and this absence was filled by NGOs and local volunteers.

The Registration Center was the space where migrants were subjected to the compulsory process of passport control, de-briefing (short interviews), and digital identification—a process that determined whether they could continue their journey towards Northern Europe (if they were Syrian, Iraqis, or Afghanis) or go to Greek detention camps (if they belonged to any other nationality). Military staff consisted of 14 Greek army and police officers as well as seven Frontex (European Border and Coast Guard Agency) officers. The Registration Center was hosted gratis in a derelict factory and our initial visit to it was organized through local government contacts consequent visits were organized independently. The factory was a large, sheltered area with broken glass in a number of the windows and without proper heating, lighting, or flooring—the latter just uneven and partially destroyed cement. Power was provided by a temporary electrical generator and the space divided into two: a medical area at the back; the queuing corridor and the interview and identification areas at the front, consisting of six passport control desks as well as four Eurodac PCs (the digital system of fingerprint identification); next to this, there was the translation desk, where the certified NGO Metadrasi offered translation services in Arabic and Farsi.

Despite this inadequate working infrastructure, assembled piecemeal through the personal initiative of local officers, the pace and efficiency of the process rendered Chios an example of what the news called "best practice in refugee management." Given the combination of low resources/high arrival numbers (up to 1,800 people a day), this achievement was largely due to the work ethos of its team, with its relentless processing rates (shifts 24/7) and coordination abilities. The Chief of the registration process (a 30-year-old Special Forces officer) justified this performance on multiple grounds, speaking of the team's sense of patriotic duty and professional commitment, but also their compassionate spirit: "We can't let those poor people and their small children wait for days, as they do in Mytilene [Lesbos]." One of the officers further mentioned that they did it because of their team spirit and professional devotion to their Chief: "We would never let our Chief or each other down."

This exceptional performance needs to be contextualized within the wider frame of the Greek economic crisis (Knight 2018) that was, at least partly, responsible for the inability of the state to support local securitization infrastructure and to pay staff adequately. While, therefore, the infrastructure was scrambled together by the entrepreneurial initiative of the military Chief and his staff, local salaries remained deplorably inadequate, especially in comparison to those of the European Frontex team. Income discrepancies consequently became the focus of self-mocking jokes that the Greek staff shared with us, despite the disproportionate burden of work that fell on them. What, then, were the networks of mediation and discourse that organized these processes of securitization?

Even though the Registration Center was a critical node in the migrants' route of travel, it was absent from the process of *remediation*—hardly ever republished or broadcast in mass or social media. This is for obvious reasons. Regarded as matters of national security and classified as top secret, de-briefing and identification processes were kept resolutely outside the spotlight of publicity. We, as researchers, were allowed to take only a very limited number of photographs. Media reports, as we shall see, in general, relied on elite sources, such as politicians or EU officials, and NGO reports with statistics on entry numbers, security updates, or dramatic stories of migrant rescue and survival. Consequently, the networks of discourse available in mainstream media throughout the 2015 period involved the remediation of both securitization claims (such as the appeal made by the Greek Minister of Humanitarian Aid, requesting "European partners to send more officials to help register and process refugees") and human rights claims (when the same minister pleaded for Europe to stop using racist criteria for reception: "statements such as 'we want ten Christians,' or 'seventy-five Muslims' . . . are insulting to the personality and freedom of refugees" [Tagaris 2015]).

The efficiency of registration, in those early days, rested on the fingerprint identification system of Eurodac (European Commission 2016a).

A digital technology that works across space in near real-time, Eurodac offered confidential information on the biometrical make-up of each migrant, enabling the insertion of their data into global data banks and their subsequent classification in categories of legality and illegality. *Intermediation* operated thus as a digital practice of border biopolitics, separating "authentic" from "non-authentic" claims to entry on the basis of bodily parts here used as "instruments in the politics of mobility" (Ticktin 2011b: 319).

Rather than a stand-alone technique of power, however, this digital biopolitics of intermediation was used in conjunction with the face-to-face cross-examination of suspect cases of entry—and hence intersected with transmediation practices. The most prominent example of these hybrid practices of securitization was the arrest of two Chechen criminals posing as Afghan migrants, who, as was described to us, having come under suspicion due to their accents, were held in a provisional detention area and eventually exposed as illegal entries when the Chios officers brought into their detention cell a couple of Russian women (see Katrine Côté-Boucher 2020 for sexist dynamics in border regulation). As one of the officers told us, after 24 hours of waiting and chatting together, one of the suspects accidentally used the original name of his co-traveler in a clear Chechen accent—a detail that the women passed on to the border officers.

A discourse of humanitarian care also informed the Center's practices of intermediation, in that the speed and efficiency of Eurodac[3] were highly appreciated by registration officers for reducing the waiting time of families with small children or the sick who "should not stand in queue for too long." Yet, the predominant understanding of the process was one of security. Eurodac helped protect Europe from what the Chief officer termed an "invasion" of foreigners and potential terrorists—particularly in light of allegations that one of the November 2015 Paris attack terrorists had entered Europe through Leros, an island in Chios's vicinity.

Moving from online to offline contexts, *transmediation* was about corporeal encounters, for instance, in passport control and de-briefing (though these are inextricably linked to intermediation, as the Chechen example demonstrated). The process inevitably also foregrounded the role of migrants' bodies, physical demeanor, and voice as distinct biopolitical sites that yielded information about where individuals came from (attire, accent), and how safe or potentially risky they might be (body movement, gaze, and overall composure). Indeed, according to the officers, the newcomers' readiness for eye contact, their posture, tone of voice, and dress code predisposed them to be perceived in particular ways—with the middle-class habitus of Syrian families seen as respectable and dignified and thus regarded as "like ours," while the habitus of others (for instance, Pakistanis and Africans or Chechens) seen as indicative of outsiders and potential "cheaters." As the officers observed, migrants were, in turn, acutely aware of the role of their bodies in border control and attempted their own performances of "the refugee": claiming to have lost their passports (Pakistani and Algerian passports were reportedly accumulating by the main road outside the town of Chios) and pretending to be Syrians in the hope of being granted asylum.

Discourses of transmediation, similar to those of intermediation, thus subordinated humanization and care of migrants to security and the protection of the border. These discourses, however, simultaneously offered resources for migrants to negotiate their identities in the hope of claiming entry and continuing their trip. Military securitization, in summary, relied on a network of mediations that combined (i) official practices of censored mainstream publicity, such as political leaders visiting camps (remediation), with (ii) digital practices of biometrical governance that guarantee the security prerogative (intermediation) and (iii.) local engagements, juridical and cultural, through the mediation of bodies (transmediation). This network, in turn, articulated the dominant discourses of threat, where migrants figure as potential terrorists, with ambiguous discourses of humanization, reflected in the evocation of international law as well as in the selective recognition by security forces of some migrants as "people like us" and in the denial of such recognition to others.

Military securitization emerges here as a relatively heterogenous regime of power that is subject to the pressures of its specific historical and geopolitical context. On the one hand, security, rather than purely a matter of digital surveillance, seemed also to be a matter of co-presence and cultural sensibility; as we observed and heard, gazes and bodies appeared as important to the biopolitical management of mobile populations as the long-distance operations of digital media. On the other hand, security discourses incorporated not only elements of professional duty and nationalist rhetoric but also self-mockery, hints of compassion, and an implicit but intense distrust of state authority; similarly, migrants did not simply figure as passive "bare life" but also as active and creative agents who sought to direct their own fates. Far from a monolithic structure of biopolitical power, securitization operated as an impure regime of meanings, which revealed its actors' heterogenous range of reflections, desires, and commitments and which, at least momentarily, managed to humanize the dehumanizing practices of those who enact it.

Securitized Care: Ambivalent Humanitarianism

Unlike security, which is about protecting European borders, the mandate of care is about protecting migrant lives through the provision of humanitarian assistance and human rights advocacy by international and national agencies. Assistance and advocacy on Chios were geared towards emergency care, addressing the urgent needs of the continuous migrant flow and enabling agencies to collaborate with one other, as well as with the local authorities. The largest agencies present were the UNHCR (accommodation and nutrition, rights), the Red Cross (ICRD; missing persons, psychological care), Doctors of the World (DoW; medical care) and the Norwegian Refugee Council (NRC; information) but there were also smaller ones, such as WAHA and Drop in the Ocean (group offering assistance at sea).

The priorities of emergency care, to offer immediate aid and information on asylum applications and traveling options, were shaped by two considerations: first, the temporary character of the migrants' sojourn, since, unlike the long-term camps of Turkey or Lebanon, the duration of their stay on Chios in 2015 was seldom longer than two days; second, the outcome of the migrants' border experience, which, brief as it may have been, was also the moment of decision, whether asylum or deportation. These twin considerations shaped care provision on the island in terms of what NGOs called "proactive humanitarianism": care oriented towards "transit," rather than "resident" needs, that is, temporary shelter, emergency food, and health provisions, as well as towards the provision of information for the continuation of migrants' journeys (from advice about registration to ferry itineraries and maps). In the process, the areas and practices of care were closely articulated with security ones, as for instance, Doctors of the World shared the securitized space of the Registration Center and had a say in the registration protocol—that is, who of the sick migrants should take priority over others in the registration queue. Similarly, in the rare cases of unrest at the camp, NGO staff would help ensure that order was re-established, as one of our NGO interviewees explained, noting that sometimes they just need to "calm down conflict and diffuse heated arguments."

The transit character of securitized care rendered speed an important challenge to proactive humanitarianism (how to take equally good care of everyone in 48 hours?) and so had a further impact on the emotional dynamics of the site. We often encountered migrants who, though anxious and tired, were also euphoric for having survived the sea crossing and who were hopeful about next steps (their first question upon arrival to the UN camp was often "where is the port?"). As a number of NGO staff told us, however, such a fast pace deprived them of deeper bonds with individuals. Even though for some staff this meant minimizing interaction with migrants and simply handing out leaflets to them, others nonetheless made a point of speaking to and connecting with them; some defended as "legitimate options" the brevity and automation of care in the form of the distribution of emergency food (nutrition bars instead of warm food), or the color-coded ID bracelets identifying the status of new arrivals. Whereas for some staff, this minimal contact with newcomers was necessary to manage the mass needs of the camp, others sought to nurture more personalized relations of care: "At nights, I cannot sleep for long. I need to visit the camp again and again to make sure they sleep well and have a good rest. They are in the middle of a long journey," confessed NRC's head. Within this complex, multi-organizational set-up, what then were the networks of mediation and discourse that communicated the practices and affects of securitized care?

There were two ways in which securitized care was *remediated* in mainstream media: first, through news reports of what NGOs did on the ground and how they reacted online and offline to political developments that affected their practice; and second, through news reports on other actors' (e.g., politicians', celebrities', etc.) evaluations of the NGOs through social media and public statements. This coverage was dominant across key mass media outlets and observed on a daily basis by us as well as commented on by our informants during the fieldwork. Even though we did not do a detailed content analysis of all press/television media during our stay, we incorporated a regular practice of media monitoring across selected newspapers and television channels into our fieldwork observations (and see Chapter 4 for a content analysis of European media during the summer–winter 2015 migration "crisis").

Remediation primarily relied on journalists' own reports from the island, registering the invaluable work of securitized care in the absence of state infrastructures, but also expressing concern for the implications of the minimal regulation of their operations. Journalistic criticism focused on a number of minor NGOs plus volunteer groups and individuals, some of whom did not even register with local authorities and acted without coordination with others, potentially creating "more chaos on their small islands rather than a coordinated response" (Nianias 2016). As we observed in a number of news stories during our study, journalists often depended on social media to find out more about these NGOs' actions. Remediation also consisted of quoting the humanitarian sector's statements about various political actors—for instance, the UN's demand for "stronger leadership" from Greece in the face of massive incoming flows (Tagaris 2015). By the same token, what was also remediated was the Greeks' mixed reactions to the UN (and other global actors) for such criticism, as local politicians both thanked the UNHCR for their assistance and accused them of having unrealistic expectations of a country in economic crisis.

Remediation, consequently, established a contradictory network of discourses around securitized care. On the one hand, there was a positive discourse of gratitude towards the humanitarian sector, where media acknowledged its crucial role in the management of migration flows, often by drawing evidence from NGOs' own social media messages; yet, on the other, there was a negative discourse of suspicion and critique towards them—either for voicing their own criticisms against Greece for its inadequate border response (in the case of global players) or for their dubious intentions and their potential for damaging rather than assisting caring practices (in the case of minor aid groups).

If remediation enhances the global visibility of securitized care, *intermediation* represents the backbone of their horizontal communication on the ground. As it was shown to us by key NGO communication actors on the ground, two intermediation networks coordinated NGO activism in Chios: between NGOs themselves and between NGOS and external parties—notably migrants. The former relied on WhatsApp's instantaneous and multi-participant communication affordances that enabled major NGOs to be on a 24/7 alert and keep constantly updated on both NGO and migrant activity, rendering their mobile phones their most important work instrument.

Even though it was geared towards collaborating with local authorities and minor agencies, this closed circuit nonetheless established an internal hierarchy in the field, relegating minor humanitarian players to satellite status. The hierarchical communication arrangement—more of a pyramid rather than a network—of the humanitarian sector on the island was the subject of exchanges we had with the communication officer of a leading NGO on the island and one of the key actors of another international NGO. We also observed how smaller NGOs were involved in the circuit only through hashtag groups or Twitter accounts (e.g., @wahaint) rather than WhatsApp and heard how local organizations felt unhappy with this hierarchy; as a local member put it, "they [international NGOs] are friendly with us, but they just want us to follow."

Nonetheless, it is in the second intermediation network where the most significant hierarchy was established, that between NGOs and migrants. While intermediation was multi-platform, utilizing a range of media to reach out, we observed no social media links between NGOs and migrants—despite an estimated 80% of the latter owning smartphones.[4] As we were told by a key actor in the humanitarian sector, online communication for migrants was restricted to "Nethope," a minimum-function WhatsApp circuit that simply enabled them to forward pre-formulated messages, such as "I'm ok," to a narrow number of contacts (migrants' families or friends). Despite therefore the celebration of mobile phones as giving rise to, what Diminescu calls, the "connected migrant" (2008), a subjectivity constituted through their ability to connect and communicate online, humanitarian security insisted on perceiving the migrant as a speechless recipient of care situated in a pre-digital realm of communication (for this critique, see Awad and Tossell 2019).

Indeed, as we observed, the bulk of intermediation occurred through pre-electronic and hence non-connective technologies: pamphlets, maps, diagrams, posters, or announcement boards or screens. Printed UN pamphlets, for instance, offered information on rights and asylum appeals at Registration while announcement boards were used for information on further travel. Pre-electronic forms of intermediation further encompassed rumor or word-by-mouth, which NGOs regarded as an effective way to spread news; "the ripple effect" of these modes of communication was instrumental in "raising awareness" and "inspiring trust" among local populations, as we were told, but also reaching those on the Turkish coast waiting to cross. While maximizing communication efficiency was a priority among care structures, NGOs were nonetheless reluctant to contemplate using social media more inclusively, with the exception of NRC. This was a topic we repeatedly discussed with leading figures on the ground, yet received little response on NGOs' plans to expand their social media connections with newcomers. While more recently concerns of mobile surveillance and migrant safety at the border have been raised (Latonero et al. 2019), such concerns, we need to emphasize, were not on the agenda of any Chios-based NGO in winter 2015 and the lack of horizontal communication with migrants was, at that point, simply regarded as a "necessary evil" in the context of emergency care (and see Madianou et al. 2016 for a similar argument to ours on asymmetries and exclusions of populations-in-need regarding the use of mobile phones in disaster emergencies). Consequently, and despite their smartphone ownership and literacy (UNHCR 2015), migrants were kept outside the digital mediation and discourse networks of securitized care.

The *transmediations* of securitized care similarly took a dual form. The first was through the use of online platforms, notably WhatsApp, which updated and coordinated NGOs' offline action; for instance, the nocturnal arrival of boats (anytime between 3:00 and 5:00 a.m.) would be signaled on mobile phones and get everyone on their feet and on their way to their posts. The second transmediation was through pre-electronic technologies, used to coordinate the mobility of migrants on the island, for instance, through speaking trumpets upon arrival at Registration. Even though these transmediations did succeed in guiding large groups through the often-chaotic process of queuing, their effects were restricted to contexts of physical proximity, inevitably having no impact across extended and multiple space-times; nor did they offer options for interactivity, feedback, and fine-tuning with the receivers. As we observed and heard from our interviewees, migrants' smartphones remained, as before, largely unexploited as a local communications resource inevitably perpetuating the hierarchical order that excluded them from the networks of care and deprived them of having their voices heard.

The communicative structure of securitized care sustained, in turn, a polyphonic but stratified discourse network. This consisted of two major discourses: an operational discourse of emergency care that intermediated and transmediated connections among major NGOs; and a mixed discourse of practical guidance (where to buy boat tickets or eat) and advocacy (UN's asylum application advice or the human rights of refugees) that included migrant groups, as well as local populations. These networks were organized around a differential distribution of media use: inter- and transmediations among bigger NGOs occurred through digital media, only selectively including satellite ("secondary") NGOs, but those between NGOs and mobile populations occurred through pre-digital technologies; finally, inter-migrant digital communication was further restricted to minimal, formulaic phrases.

Even though then this mediation network allowed for a range of relevant voices to be heard, its structure was ultimately strictly stratified. The major actors of securitized care not only perpetuated uni-directional, top-down channels of communications with all actors other than themselves but, by being reluctant to explore interactive technologies, they fully silenced the migrants.

Compassionate Solidarity: Networks of Care

Driven by a progressive politics of solidarity and operationalized through informal and emotionally charged acts of support towards newcomers, the network of compassionate solidarity was distinctly different to securitized care. Despite its informality, this network was impressively effective: for example, the Collective Kitchen used to cook up to 1,600 portions of food a day; the volunteers of the fishing village Ayia Ermioni provided, on a daily basis, dry clothes to dozens and sometimes hundreds of migrants landing soaked at their shores; and the lawyer group "Lathra?" prided itself on exposing a case of torture by the port authorities on the island, a case that migrants won. We had the chance not only to interview members of these different groups, but also to observe and participate in their activities on the ground. Different in their constitution and values to the security forces and NGOs, these non-institutional local structures of care represented an organic element of the bordering architecture, as they themselves were a product of their unplanned but inescapable encounter with the arriving migrants.

Despite their intense local presence, mainstream media only occasionally focused on the work of the compassionate solidarity groups. "Chios does not attract much attention [in the media]. That can only be a good thing," said a volunteer who explained that the media were always looking to *remediate* negative stories, and the story of Chios was not one of those. The mass media had little interest in the acts of these groups, as we could hardly ever find stories about the solidarity networks in such outlets. At the same time, activists did not seek mass media attention; on the contrary, they were wary of them. In fact, their engagement with digital platforms was itself a contestation of mainstream media authority. The only case when these groups were systematically remediated, therefore, was in the course of a social media-driven campaign for the "Nobel Prize to Greek islanders" (December 2015–January 2016), which eventually became a mass media-led one—a nationalist campaign that depoliticized their solidarity, turning it into a manifestation of the "Greek spirit" of benevolence and hospitality.

The effectiveness and accountability of activist groups on the ground relied on two digital sub-networks of *intermediation*: their inter-group platforms of coordination and action (SMS, Facebook, WhatsApp, Viber); and the public platforms that communicated narratives of solidarity to the local population. Intermediation was about engaging civic voices beyond those of institutional militarization and securitized care, as key informants emphasized. To this end, members of the volunteer and activist networks used the online newspaper *Aplotaria*—popular among Chios locals. Alongside their Facebook network, *Aplotaria* allowed activists to be vocal about their own experience of reception, by producing their own alternative media news stories that condemned both Europe's security policy and major NGOs' bureaucratic care provision. Thus, as a popular portal to the local society, *Aplotaria* became an interface between the wider population of Chios and the activists' alternative voices of resistance.

Most encounters among activists and between activists and migrants were face-to-face and *transmediated* as collective action, including meal distribution and provision of dry clothes at the shore. We observed those acts at Ayia Ermioni, at the informal camp of Dipethe, and at the Registration Center, where meals were distributed among those waiting their turn to register. Yet, these embodied forms of care were both managed and regulated through a feedback loop that linked the digital to the territorial, in three ways.

First, it was through social media that calls for help were circulated beyond the core group of activists, appealing for collaborations, for instance, through invitations to bring donated goods to particular locations or participate in low-key fundraising activities. Second, transmediation through Facebook groups or WhatsApp facilitated social get-togethers among groups of volunteers and activists, which functioned as support mechanisms of "decompression" after the intense emotional and physical strain of reception (we heard volunteers reporting depression and inability to sleep, while one activist reported recently developed heart problems). Third, transmediation enabled semi-public systems of accountability or feedback, as in the case of the volunteers at Ayia Ermioni; every time a dinghy arrived at the village port, locals hectically mobilized to support the new arrivals and, at the end of their exhausting shifts, lasting up to 12 or even 18 hours, one of them would regularly return to Facebook to report on the day. In this way, local groups managed to keep a record of their activities in a transparent and interactive way.

The networks of mediation in the sphere of compassionate solidarity articulated a complex discourse of care that worked both as activist resistance to the security of the border and as a gesture of recognition to vulnerable humanity—both of which contested the securitization of the island. This discourse was founded on an ethics of unconditional commitment to help those in a predicament of precarity without asking for something in return, and, indeed, the Chios activists and volunteers not only dedicated all their efforts to assist newcomers without asking back, but even disliked any manifestation of public acknowledgment by third parties. This reluctance emanated from their politicized understanding of compassion as part of a power struggle against established border structures rather than as charity inviting praise by the establishment—such as, for instance, media proposals for them to be nominated for the Nobel Prize. Thus, compassionate solidarity combined empathy with a discourse of socio-political critique and, from this perspective, its actors criticized humanitarian NGOs as a space of simply "administering needs" rather than also challenging the exclusionary policies of the European order. As one of the interviewees said to us, "We are a movement, not a bureaucratic organization . . . we need to be prepared to defend the refugees against the fascists."

The treatment of migrants as "people like us" highlights the notion of humanity as the second dominant discourse of compassionate solidarity. The key feature of this discourse is its explicit references to the activists' affective identification with migrants: "It is obvious why we help them. They could have been us," a member of the Collective Kitchen explained. "The difference between those in-solidarity movements and others is that the former are emotionally attached," another added. Such claims are important because they entail an explicit recognition of the humanity of migrants, that is, "a concern for the existential fate of other human beings, a concern that extends into the affective" (Honneth 2007: 123), which has not quite been there in the proactive humanitarianism of NGOs. Through this act of affective recognition, the volunteers and activists on Chios differentiated the sphere of compassionate solidarity both from military securitization, with its emphasis on policing, and from securitized care, with its reliance on professionalized service provision, while also offering a glimpse of the invisible contestations that take place at the border—thus also challenging the dehumanization thesis of much of Critical Border Studies.

Having said this, we need to emphasize that the actors of compassionate solidarity are neither pure nor unaffected by securitization. Despite stark opposition to it, they still functioned within the wider regime of the digital border, and their discourses contributed to the classification of newcomers from an uneven position of privilege and recognition (as citizens of Europe "inside" the border). For example, some volunteers criticized some migrants' eating habits, manners, or gender roles, mobilizing mechanisms of "othering" that reproduced racialized conceptions of humanity in line with "our" own conceptions of civility.

Such familiar narratives represented local people's attempts to make sense of these "new strangers" from within pre-existing cultural frameworks and discourses, in a context where the brevity of their encounters, combined with pressures for timely care and severe linguistic constraints, resulted in significant ruptures in communication and an inevitable depersonalization of solidarity relations—a fact that activists and volunteers were themselves painfully aware of. As an activist told us, "We . . . used to know them [in earlier stages of the 2015 arrivals]; now we don't anymore. They have all become one. The voice of the people has been lost. And the political work to this direction is also lost, as we are just trying to meet needs."

The Outer Border and the Tensions of Humanitarian Security

What we have sought to achieve, in this chapter, is to reconstruct the outer border of Europe at the peak of the 2015 "crisis" as a techno-symbolic assemblage of mobility control and to reflect on the implications of this assemblage for those who are subjected to its power. To this end, we developed a conceptual vocabulary for the digital border in terms of its networks of mediation and discourse, which problematizes existing accounts of the border as a totalizing regime of dehumanization in favor of a view of the border as a site of tensions and resistance within Europe's regime of humanitarian security.

Our reconstruction of these networks identified the means by which the border sustained and connected the three spheres of security and care traversing the 2015 "crisis" at large: military securitization, humanitarian securitization, and compassionate activism. Through these interwoven networks, the border's two imperatives, to national sovereignty and to the biopolitical management of human needs, mix and fuse in ways that do not simply safeguard the continent's integrity at the expense of migrants but also carve out contingent spaces of care, compassion, and solidarity.

Our discussion of *military securitization* highlighted the significance of *embodied encounters* vis-à-vis the centrality of the digital at the border. This is evident in our observations from the registration process, which, as we know, used the Eurodac platform to digitally access transnational data and establish migrant identities as genuine and safe; simultaneously, however, we showed that it also relied on corporeal and cultural clues to "read off" authenticity and trust from migrants' posture, face, and language.

This focus complicates accounts of the datafied border, where migrants appear as algorithmic subjects—disembodied aggregations constituted through data patterns stored and archived in the border's big data banks (Parks 2014). Our observation highlights instead how such data-driven processes work side-by-side with face-to-face contacts that allow border officers to make their own racialized judgments, and so throws into relief the intimate complicity of technology with bodies in reinforcing the control mechanisms of the border. Digital technology may have produced new biometrical epistemologies of exclusion, yet it appears that these epistemologies continue to be undercut by the older epistemologies of co-presence—faces, gazes, spoken words. Similarly, unlike accounts of biopolitical security as all-encompassing surveillance, we showed how the border allows for practices of *performative refugeeness*, where migrants reportedly throw their passports away and turn to face-to-face connectivities and the sharing of "insider" information on the migration system (Trimikliniotis et al. 2015) in the hope of being granted asylum.

At the same time, we see further how bodies matter in the discourses of security agents. While they spoke proudly about their commitments, both national ("protecting of 'our' borders") and professional ("need to process them"), to the sovereignty of the nation-state and the continent, they were also emotionally impacted by their personal meetings with migrants and employed a range of self-reflexive discourses to process this experience—from empathy ("can't let them wait"), to light-hearted but scathing commentary on state failures to support them, to camaraderie with colleagues for sharing the burden of border control (doing it "for each other"). While fully cognizant of the border's dehumanizing effects, we also saw that military securitization did not simply operate as an impersonal technology of power, devoid of humanity. It is instead infused with tenuous judgments and emotions, where the "perpetrator/benefactor/victim" nexus can be fluid, rendering biopolitical monitoring a more complex and self-reflexive process than we have seen in relevant literature.

Our discussion on *securitized care* underscored the significance of migrant voice as a key stake in the power relations of the border assemblage. We specifically pointed to the fact that the very media connections that offer valuable transitional support for migrants simultaneously marginalize their voices. For all their celebrated horizontal connections, social media platforms were ultimately embedded within pre-existing hierarchical orders of humanitarian care that they reproduced and consolidated. Who got to speak and who was listened to, in other words, is a matter of the institutional structures of power through which the platforms' enabling practices emerged in the first place (Madianou et al. 2016). Nonetheless, while this position does point towards migrants as subjects of biopolitical power, as "lives to be saved" (Edkins 2003: 80), we can see that humanitarian securitization is a more ambivalent site of reception than this. Its actors, for instance, were caught in a struggle of competing discourses between keeping a professional distance and just doing their job, and feeling sad for not being able to sustain more meaningful bonds with migrants. Even though the failure to acknowledge the individuality of those cared for has always been intrinsic to the professionalization of compassion (Krause 2014), ultimately, it was now the size and transitory character of mobile populations that marginalized the question of voice and connection in favor of pragmatic concerns of "getting the job done." Therefore, just as in the case of military securitization, securitized care also emerges as a contradictory regime of reception: it inevitably dehumanized migrants by rendering them voiceless, yet it was also informed by unspoken desires and minor acts of emotional attachment and personalized contact, while subjecting itself to an introspective critique of the limitations that emergency care brings to its ethos and effects.

Finally, our discussion of *compassionate activism* offers the clearest manifestation of the border assemblage as a site of resistance that, by attending to the needs of migrants, sought to establish the border as a space of provisional hospitality. Going beyond the professionalized charity of securitized care, this sphere opened up a real possibility of meaningful connection and emotional identification with migrants—a possibility for their humanization. In so doing, it came closest to any other sphere of reception to highlighting the agency of border actors: volunteers and activists as much as the migrants themselves. Its use of social media platforms, from Facebook and WhatsApp to blogging and online journalism, brought together a considerable number of people to maximum effect, online and offline.

Simultaneously, however, contact with the arriving migrants remained limited and fragmentary and the latter were given little voice in the process. Local activists, in this sense, formed part of the privileged European population that military securitization seeks to protect, and so excluded the very subjects of their solidarity in the process of supporting them. As Millner puts it, "how can activists protest against the racial and economic biases of contemporary border controls, without appealing to their own condition of citizenship as a basis for political speech?" (2011: 323). The same ambivalence was further evident in the discourses of compassionate solidarity, which often reiterated racist stereotypes and moral judgments towards Europe's "others," combining a socio-political critique of the west with orientalist sensibilities. This contradiction constituted a major existential challenge for those involved in practices of compassionate solidarity, compelling them to engage in a constant negotiation of often opposing affective orientations: compassion and guilt, dedication and powerlessness, sadness and indignation, hope and despair.

In conclusion, Chios's border assemblage was both digital and pre-digital; datafied and embodied; automated and self-reflexive; undercut by competing emotions, desires, and judgments; and traversed by fluid and fragile social relationships. Even though this assemblage did not challenge the border's raison d'être, namely the protection of national sovereignty, nonetheless understanding its techno-symbolic workings in detail does enable us to read the border as a dialectical site of intersecting forces of control and resistance; to challenge the one-sided normativity of biopolitical accounts of datafied security and, alongside the autonomy-of-migration scholars, to recognize migrants' own contribution to shaping the meanings of transnational mobility, to adopt a "a different *gaze*" (Mezzadra 2011: 121, emphasis in original) and to register the subjective practices of all actors involved in the reception process. It is, we argue, by keeping this dialectic in sight that we can deepen our understanding of the structures of power that operate at Europe's border. And it is this dialectic that can help us better understand both how such structures of power dehumanize others in the name of humanity but also how minor acts of resistance are still possible in the midst of such dehumanization. In the next chapter, we move to the inner border of western metropolises, where the border is secured through the surveillance and self-responsibilization of migrant lives, but also reconfigured through infrastructures of digital connectivity that make possible their acts of creativity and resistance.

2

The Inner Border

Assemblages of Entrepreneurial Securitization

In the previous chapter, the outer territorial border of the migration "crisis" emerged as a hybrid space, tangible and locatable yet also immaterial and virtual, that monitors bodies and identities at the edges of Europe through a combination of security and care. Useful as this conception of the border may be, however, the singular focus on the space-time of "crisis" alone does not fully grasp how the territorial border works as part of a more expansive and long-lasting techno-symbolic assemblage of transnational governance, one that transcends both the checkpoints at the edges of Europe and the peak moment of migrant arrivals in 2015. In line with our processual conception of the border, we here illustrate how the border reveals itself throughout a five-year timeline as an ongoing, elastic, and versatile regime of power whose technologies and discourses of control follow migrants as they move and settle inside the nation that receives them.

It is the cities where migrants eventually settle, we propose, that now work as an exemplary inner border, not least in that, in their new communities, migrants remain subjected to data and physical controls similar to those at the outer border, as well as to media stories that cast them as part of a problem, of a perpetual "crisis." And it is this ever-expanding and ever-morphing techno-symbolic assemblage that renders the digital border an incomplete process of border*ing*: a process of systematic exclusions of racialized bodies not only *at* crossing points but also *inside* western nation-states (Yuval-Davis et al. 2019). In the course of this deterritorializing process, humanitarian securitization is substituted by a more strategic and resilient regime of power, that of entrepreneurial securitization—a regime that situates the surveillance of migrant lives no longer within technologies of humanitarian care but within the market rationalities and narratives of entrepreneurial competition.

This urban regime, we argue, is both about routine practices of ordering and "othering" settled migrants and, at the same time, about the promise of opportunities for migrants to find safety, work, and recognition. As we interrogate these dual processes of the inner border, our aim, in this chapter, is to understand how three major European cities, Athens, Berlin, and London, mobilize digital infrastructures to regulate migrants' pursuit of a new life within their local communities, but also how migrants themselves use these infrastructures to navigate the circumstances they find themselves in. We begin by developing a theoretical account of migrants' urban participation as the digital enactment of claims to recognition that occur outside, beyond, and towards formal citizenship. And, driven by observations and interviews with migrants and activists across the three cities, we subsequently contend that these cities' horizontal networks of intermediation cut across and reorganize the domain of migrant life through three spheres of entrepreneurial security: securitized self-responsibility, securitized precarity, and conditional conviviality. The city as an inner border, we conclude, emerges here as a site of contestation, where diverse struggles over participation and recognition take place: those of the datafied city and its dominant discourses of entrepreneurial success but also those of informal intermediation among grassroots organizations and migrants with their claims to rightful inclusion.

Theorizing the Inner Border

Our account of the city as inner border draws on literature in Critical Migration Studies, Digital Urban Studies, and the philosophy of recognition to help us conceptualize, on the one hand, the ways in which the everyday life of migrants is caught up in the power relations of the city, particularly the dominant discourse of neoliberal citizenship, and, on the other, the ways in which migrant agency is shaped through self-expressive and creative work, yet always within the neoliberal norms and practices of entrepreneurial securitization.

Migration and Recognition

Cities have historically been sites of opportunity and self-realization, and for this reason, they remain, to this day, primary migrant destinations. Indeed, cities are primary destinations for migrants for their openness but also for their diverse employment prospects and, at the same time, the life of cities, both cultural and economic, is created through migration. According to the 2020 IOM report, migrants "tend to have higher entrepreneurial activity compared to natives," or, as Hall puts it, they possess "entrepreneurial agility" (2018)—a result of the need to creatively respond to exclusionary formal markets, as well as to seek new economic opportunities for trading across diasporic and transnational networks (Yamamura and Lassalle 2020).

This entrepreneurial overperformance of migrants across western national and urban markets has been widely recorded in relevant literatures as evidence of migrants' creative agency and their will to prosper (see Baycan-Levent and Nijkamp 2009; Ward and Jenkins 1984; van Delf et al. 2003). Yet, as observed within Critical Migration Studies (see, for example, de Genova 2015; Hall et al. 2016; Hall 2018), migrant agency ends up benefiting not only individuals but also cities. Rath and Schutjens, for instance, speak about how "migrant entrepreneurs" are crucial to economies of urban regeneration, transforming derelict neighborhoods or streets into vibrant local markets (2019). No matter how dynamic these economies are, however, they remain subjected to various market hierarchies, including racially discriminatory structures, so that, as Ram et al. say, "the obstacles faced by racialised entrepreneurs are of a different order to those confronting their 'mainstream' peers" (2017: 7).

In this context, migrant's entrepreneurial success should not be seen to be driven by economic benefit only, but appears instead to be a more complex matter informed by ontological, socio-cultural, and, crucially, legal rewards for migrants. This means that being employed is not just about generating income, though this is obviously paramount, but is also increasingly regarded as the predominant pathway for migrants to reach safety—that is, to be able to claim recognition as respected residents of western cities, and thus move closer to the possibility of (eventually) achieving the legal status of the citizen. In between full precarity and the promise of recognition, for many, lies the status of asylum seeker, that is, the waiting period during which nation-states process asylum applications, leaving migrants suspended in a legal limbo of no (or informal) work until they receive—if indeed they do—a temporary residence permit (which can, in time, eventually lead to citizen status). For those who never make it into the asylum registries, the precarity remains unending, with little prospect of any kind of formal recognition by the state. That space of suspension is one that many migrants occupy, given that, in 2015 alone, 1.3 million asylum seeker applications were launched in Europe (Bansak et al. 2017). Capturing this fluidity of status over the course of a migrant' s lifetime, Wyss explains that legal precarity indeed shifts "between different statuses—including asylum seeker, rejected asylum seeker, undocumented migrant, and holder of temporary residence permit (cf. Goldring & Landolt 2013; Schuster 2005)" (2019: 79).

Across these categories, for some of which legal recognition may only be a distant possibility, different options for participation are available as migrants involve themselves, online and offline, in the life of their urban communities—through, for instance, job or language training, artistic creation, or neighborhood initiatives—and so acquire social status in the form of tightly knit bonds of appreciation and solidarity. Whether these are forms of socio-cultural recognition, what Honneth calls the social "worth" of individuals as useful community members, "measured by the degree to which they appear to be in a position to contribute to the realization of societal goals" (1995: 123), or ontological recognition, which he defines as "the mutually dependent relations of care and respect between its [a community's] members" (van den Brink & Owen 2007: 26), they are both crucial to migrants' sense of self-worth and belonging. More than this, they can act as first steps towards further claims, for, as Isin points out, recognition "involve[s] multiple and overlapping scales of rights and obligations" that may, in time, lead all the way to citizenship (2002: 370). As such, struggles over recognition, as we show, constitute crucial stakes in migrants' efforts to overcome the challenges of entrepreneurial securitization and succeed in the new urban markets they find themselves in.

Entrepreneurialism and Networks of Mediation

While our earlier reference to migrant entrepreneurialism signaled migrants' desire to engage in creative and profitable labor within western markets—after all, as the IOM report puts it, "74 per cent of all international migrants were of working age (20–64 years)" (2020: 3)—in fact, this same term simultaneously situates migrant agency within the framework of neoliberal economics. Entrepreneurialism, in this framework, goes beyond narrow definitions of labor-related agency and has, in the past two decades, come to mean a specifically business-oriented agency, where individuals navigate globally competitive markets in ways that "embrace risks, capably manage difficulties and hide injuries" (Scharff 2016: 108). Embedded within a larger, late twentieth-century restructuring of western markets that rolls back state support and encourages individual competitiveness as the model of financial success the world over (Davies 2014), migrant entrepreneurship has been defined along similar lines as "a system of self-reliance, where new immigrants are held more responsible for their own economic well-being" and where they are regarded "as mature citizens who are able and encouraged to look after themselves with a fine-tuned but limited support of the public sector" (van Delf et al. 2003: 2).

Absent from this idea of labor as business are the racialized structures of western markets and the systemic obstacles of unequal access that such structures place on disadvantaged or subaltern social groups entering urban markets. As a result, entrepreneurialism glosses over the scarcity of resources and opportunities for migrants in those markets, especially under conditions of austerity, while, at the same time, by classifying them as worthy or unworthy on the basis of their financial progress, making them feel personally responsible for the failures of not being "entrepreneurial enough." Even though, then, creative work is instrumental to socio-cultural recognition, entrepreneurial labor reserves recognition for those who succeed only within its own terms. Given that such recognition is instrumental to mechanisms of social inclusion and exclusion that occur in the context of migration (Cox 2012), those who, for whatever reason, are unable to access national labor markets are regarded as losers and scroungers rather than as in need of support (Davies 2014). As Scharff claims, the neoliberal subjectivities of entrepreneurialism "disavow vulnerability and instead manifest an intensified individualism" (2016: 109).

The neoliberalization of labor markets, however, is not a stand-alone development. It goes hand in hand with the expansion of digitization and, specifically, with the penetration of digital networks of migrant connectivity—what we call intermediation networks—within the domains of work and everyday life, opening up spaces for migrant inclusion, participation, interaction, and recognition online. As hundreds of thousands[1] of new migrants, in other words, are now hosted across European cities, it is social media platforms and website initiatives for digital training, self-representation, and self-expression as well as community conviviality that promise to connect migrants, "regularized" or not, within their local environment (Hintz et al. 2018).

Even though such activities can lead to non-competitive forms of recognition, which do not always overlap with entrepreneurial notions of self-worth, they are nonetheless far from innocent. For, just as they invite people to participate and connect, at the same time, such networks of intermediation also require migrants to voluntarily share work-related information online, thereby monitoring their profiles and consolidating their surveillance—what Tazzioli calls "lateral data extraction processes," which "require refugees' active participation in data production and, ultimately, to their own governmentality" (2020). How exactly migrants navigate the ambivalence of such extractive infrastructures as sites of both neoliberal opportunity and datafied surveillance is the overarching question we seek to answer in our analysis.

The Inner Border and Entrepreneurial Securitization

This ambivalence of the city has already been scrutinized within Digital Urban Studies and datafication research. In the former literature, the idea of the "smart city" as the principal host of digital infrastructures of urban connectivity appears as a techno-utopian promise of participation, offering "an imagined democratic space of digital governance" (Datta 2015: 53), where citizens are given "more opportunities to participate in the functioning, design, and governance of the city" (Bibri 2019: 19). Yet, at the same time, it is also criticized as a neoliberal construct that, in the guise of "non-ideological, commonsensical and pragmatic" interventions

(Kitchin 2015: 131), promotes a neoliberal urban vision of progress that benefits corporations and further marginalizes the already marginalized (Georgiou 2013). In the datafication literature, the smart city emerges as a mode of governmentality driven by market interests and big data, which may promise participation to "make urban governance more efficient" (Datta 2017: 406) but, in the process, embeds such participation in data surveillance and citizen profiling practices that undermine individual freedoms (Bigo et al. 2019). Heeks and Shekhar, for instance, speak of these "disbenefits" of surveillance for all citizens, and particularly for the powerless, including, among others, "growing surveillance and loss of privacy, capture of development gains by private corporations, and growing inequalities: especially a relative loss of power for individual citizens and civil society" (2019: 993).

Our own account incorporates elements of these narratives of the city, yet it also problematizes them for their own unexamined positionality. For these narratives, as Critical Race and Class scholarship highlights, ultimately speak from the position of privileged, white, and/or middle-class citizenship (Benjamin 2019; Eubanks 2018). This means that, regardless of whether they celebrate digital participation or are suspicious of the datafication of civic life, both interpretations underestimate the fact that online citizenship presupposes an entrepreneurial order of governance from which non-white, migrant actors are often excluded in the first place. What is more, such precarious actors can be—and, in fact, often are—victimized by this order, as in such initiatives of sousveillance as Neighbourhood Watch in the UK, where citizens are encouraged to monitor their streets for potentially criminal activity and end up predominantly reporting non-white people as suspects (Yuval-Davis et al. 2019). From this perspective, concerns about, for instance, the normalization of surveillance culture (Hintz et al. 2018; Lyon 2017), or data-driven decision-making on people's right to work or consume (Kitchin 2015) already presuppose a taken-for-granted citizenship status, with its own rights regime, that the urban or migrant subalterns do not have access to.

What we are seeing here is the enveloping of the city not only within what Jessop and Sum (2000) call "narratives of enterprise" but also within a securitizing logic that, before it monitors everyone else, has already subjected migrant populations to a long series of restrictions and surveillance measures. Indeed, as we shall see, whether it is databases generated through job center interviews with migrants; data profiles of individuals aggregated and configured through CCTV and facial recognition footage collected on the street and workplaces; or authorities now legally surveilling migrants' social media (Privacy International 2019), ultimately, migrant life in the city is traversed by an assemblage of micro-practices of bordering. In the European metropoles, as Yuval-Davis et al. put it, the border is enacted anytime, "by anyone, anywhere" (2019: 230).

Taking our starting point in this ubiquitous ambivalence of the connected urban market, what we call the regime of *entrepreneurial securitization*, we identify its networks of intermediation and transmediation and situate the everyday practices of its migrant inhabitants within their three spheres of action: *securitized self-responsibility*, which invites migrants to take control of their financial success in line with the normative subjectivity of neoliberal self-reliance; *securitized precarity*, which ignores those who are already too vulnerable to participate in the market and so marginalizes them even further; and *conditional conviviality*, which employs securitized structures and narratives of integration to assert new bonds of conditional belonging and selective solidarity within migrant communities. Across these spheres and in line with our dialectics of resistance, we seek to grasp how the city's intermediation networks reproduce or challenge pre-existing divides in the city. We therefore ask: In which ways do urban networks of mediation, particularly intermediation, enable migrant participation to the city? Which forms does such participation take, and what forms of recognition might this participation lead to? What are the costs of such intermediations for migrants and other local actors and how, if at all, can these intermediations challenge the regime of entrepreneurial securitization in which they occur? In other words, under what conditions do cities emerge as cities of refuge and inclusion or of bordering and exclusion for the migrants who inhabit them?

Reconstructing the Inner Border

Athens, Berlin, and London are very different cities, with distinct histories and experiences of migration. London, the center of financial services in the UK and Europe, is a major global metropole in terms of wealth, prestige, and population size. Berlin is a renowned northern European capital with robust welfare legacy and histories of grassroot activism. And Athens, a historic southern European capital hard-hit by Greece's 2010 bankruptcy during the Euro-crisis, combines persistent economic struggles for its people with vibrant grassroot networks of solidarity. In addition, these cities were differently affected by the 2015–16 migrant arrivals. The UK and Germany have been two of the most popular destination countries for newcomers, yet the former accepted approximately 10,000 Syrian refugees between 2015 and 2018 (with most relocated to the north of England and to Scotland rather than London), while Germany accepted approximately 890,000 people in 2015–16 alone—with some 56,800 asylum seekers ending up in Berlin during the same period of time.[2] Athens originally intended (in migrants' minds) to be a transit city for those heading north, but ended up with approximately 18,500 newcomers out of the more than 77,000 who found themselves trapped in the country after the March 2016 border closures by the EU (OECD 2018a, Greek Refugee Council 2019).[3] Among them, these three cities hosted migrants arriving in Europe from war-torn countries such as Syria, Iran, Afghanistan, and Eritrea, and others torn by poverty and violence such as Pakistan and Bangladesh. These diverse migrant groups possessed differential legal statuses within the restrictive migration and asylum regime imposed by the EU (Yuval-Davis et al. 2019): some were recognized refugees, others were asylum seekers in the process of receiving or being denied recognition as refugees, and others remained fully undocumented (Asylum Information Database 2019).

The intermediation networks we here explore come, specifically, from three multicultural neighborhoods, one from each of our three cities. We selected these locales because of their position in the social geography of the city, especially their constitution through long histories of being settled by newcomers, and because they have been significant points of arrival for newcomers post-2015. Haringey in London was one of the first boroughs in London to receive refugee families post-2015 (Hill 2016) and represents one of the most diverse places in the UK; Neukölln in Berlin has been an impoverished migrant destination since the Cold War, recently transformed through new waves of migration but also through gentrification (Misra 2018); and downtown Athens has become a perilous but inescapable destination for many migrants who, unable to move to Northern Europe, remain trapped in the city (Clarke 2013; Clarke et al. 2016).

Experiencing the three cities through the life of the neighborhood where citizens and noncitizens converge, even at times of rising racism, meant entering spaces of hope and perseverance—spaces that deliberately sought to challenge the divisions between the city's various constituencies and groups on the basis of national hierarchies of citizenship and belonging. Even though these communities inevitably continue to work within such hierarchies, what makes them different from others is that their communicative encounters with migrants purposefully mobilized grassroots participation and collaborative action to create communities of conviviality and solidarity—what Papadopoulos and Tsianos call "the exercising of agency from below" (2013: 11; see also Back and Sinha 2018; Roy and Ong 2011).

Drawing on a multi-method qualitative study, *Resilient Communities, Resilient Cities? Digital Makings of the City of Refuge*,[4] our focus on those neighborhoods' infrastructures of intermediation in the post-"crisis" period of 2016–20 helped us reconstruct three key spheres of horizontal connectivity within which migrants find pathways to urban participation. Through these, we show how digital work-training and employment options, techno-creative expression or mutual care initiatives encourage forms of recognition that are important both to migrants' sense of self-worth and to their access to formal rights, but also how these engagements bear costs as they occur within the regime of entrepreneurial securitization. These are, let us repeat, the spheres of *securitized self-responsibility*, where normative constructions of migrants as self-responsible and business-minded actors dominate; *precarious security*, where the most vulnerable amongst them are marginalized into invisibility; and *conditional conviviality*, where, under the constraints of entrepreneurial security and digital monitoring, migrants and locals strive together to establish spaces of self-expression and mutual care.

Securitized Self-Responsibility

The domain of labor, understood as online and offline spaces that engage migrants with market-related initiatives such as job center interviews and digital skills-training, occupies a central role in migrants' lives. As a strategic pathway to recognition, work contributes both to their sense of personal worth within their new communities and to their economic sustainability, potentially breaking the cycle of deprivation that many newly arrived migrants find themselves in. In Berlin, for instance, there is a "strong correspondence between deprived areas in the center of the city and the percentage of foreign born/native population, in particular [. . .] in the North of Neukölln" (OECD 2018b: 23), and it is this correlation that the networks of intermediation we focus on seek to address.

Job centers in the city are, in this context, crucial spaces of labor in that they are core providers of information on employment vacancies, training opportunities and financial benefits for migrants. Yet, their datafied services, where information on migrants' activities are collected, are not simply a "technical operation" that helps them with job-searching but, rather, what Tazzioli calls (2020: 4) "extractive practices" of routine surveillance. As these services' databases are regularly updated, in other words, migrants' data profiles cumulatively form part of broader evaluative matrices of their employment performance, and can, in turn, decide their status and mark their fate—either as permanent residents or deportees. In their capacity as data extractors, job centers are thus spaces of migrant biopolitics in that they force migrants to participate in the creation of their own surveillance by requiring them to report on their employment and volunteering efforts.

In so doing, however, they also invite minor acts of resistance, where migrants tactically seek to ensure that their data profiles remain "clean"—that is, they avoid registering activity that may classify them as idle or even criminal, and possibly result in imprisonment or deportation. As Hadi in London explained to us, for example, there is an acute awareness among newly arrived migrants that they need to work towards an entrepreneurial data profile, showing initiative and the motivation to work (for free, as asylum seekers are not permitted to work in the UK, even for not-for-profit companies and shops). Hadi described how he volunteered at Poundland, a British thrift shop selling £1 items, as recommended by the job center, to demonstrate his determination to make the best out of a life of forced uprooting and resettlement in the UK. In the absence of formal support, and in order to avoid isolation and appear as a self-responsible actor, Hadi had to depend on data-extracting technologies such as Google Maps to navigate the city on his own and on Facebook to find coding classes offered in a start-up hub that promises digital integration. As he went out of his way to boost his data profile as an active digital trainee and job seeker, Hadi had little choice but to participate in this sphere of securitized self-responsibility. His performance is thus exemplary of a dominant pathway to sociocultural recognition that works as a precondition, though not a guarantee, of legal recognition in the regime of entrepreneurial security.

Caught between, on the one hand, the datafied monitoring of their everyday self in the city and, on the other, stereotypical narratives of the migrant in the media (more in Chapter 4), migrants' experience of work is largely shaped within the narrow roles assigned to them by the border's business-oriented rationality: adventurous entrepreneurs or cheating parasites. While many find this experience particularly stressful, they also know that this is the only safe thing to do if they are to be regarded as successful by the urban system they found themselves living in: "I put a poker face on," said Malaka in Berlin, whose voice is often heard in the city's digital networks and beyond. Her words capture the anxiety of many others who, like her, feel that their presence in the city is a constant struggle to balance tenuous requirements and prove something. What is it that they have to prove?

> That we are not what the media here portray us to be. This is something facing Syrians in particular. We are not criminals. We are not here to take money from the state. The media here is full of those portrayals. Germans also look around and think we are using their taxes to eat and hang out in restaurants and have fun. We need to show them that we are not here to waste their money. That we have escaped war. That we are enterprising and will stand on our two feet, support ourselves. I am most proud of the fact that I have been able to show this. To prove this.

Malaka refuted media accusations of migrants as a threat ("criminals" who "take money from the state" and are "using . . . taxes to hang out and have fun") with an argument about Syrians as strong and resilient people (who "stand on our feet" and "support ourselves"). Her narrative, like that of many others we encountered in the three cities, reclaimed Syrians' extraordinary agency in the context of their life circumstances ("escaped war"), yet ultimately cast this agency within a discourse of entrepreneurialism: the self-reliant migrant committed to the dominant market ideal of individual success and its promise for self-worth and personal dignity. Even though Malaka's is a successful performance of self-responsibility ("I am most proud of the fact that I have been able to show this"), the anxiety evident in her emphatic formulations ("we need to show them," twice; "that we are not," three times; "that we are," twice) also demonstrates just how aware Malaka was of the fragility of this promise, while also revealing the emotional costs of performing the identity of the "successful" migrant.

The term self-responsibilization refers, in this context, to the requirement that state and non-state institutions place upon migrants to appear in charge of their own employment circumstances, either in justifying why they may have not found a job or in showing willingness to participate in ongoing training sessions or, again, in exhibiting business acumen in ways that satisfy the state's normative view of citizenship as entrepreneurial individualism—all the while ignoring the structural conditions of unemployment, migrant-specific and generalized, that migrants find themselves in upon arrival.[5] A key modality of neoliberal power, the self-responsibilization of migrants, is then not simply about attributing agency to them but about displacing responsibility for the inadequacies of urban employment markets from the state onto society's most vulnerable members, penalizing the latter for the failures of the former. By the same token, this mutation of migrant agency as self-reliance participates in the border regime of entrepreneurial securitization in that it elevates the norms of individualism and self-autonomy into a necessary condition for granting migrants legal status and treating them as legitimate members of their new communities.

The inner territorial border, in summary, is produced through urban networks of intermediation (Facebook and WhatsApp groups), where migrants need to perform as creative and resilient digital actors in the hope that their employment skills may translate into indices of esteem and formal recognition. In their capacity as techno-users, migrants are treated both as sources from which data, "biodata, registration details, job skills and spatial location" (Tazzioli 2020), are extracted and, at the same time, as performative subjectivities that are called to fit in to the normative entrepreneurialism of city life. And while the former inscribes migrants within the extractive biopolitics of the inner border, the latter mobilizes techniques of self-governmentality that construe people like Hadi or Malaka as ideal urban subjects—as productive citizens in the making within the nation-state.

Securitized Precarity

For many who are neither as visible nor as confident as Hadi and Malaka, however, pathways to recognition, socio-cultural or ontological, are more distant if not unreachable. Gloria, the coordinator of a Refugee Women's Center in an impoverished part of East Berlin, is one example. Gloria, herself a refugee, is well aware of the unrealistic requirements set for the women using the center—itself situated at the city's margins among ghettoized high-rise housing estates torn by poverty, polarization, and racism. She spoke to us about the multiple and conflicting pressures faced by the women using the center's services, first, to care for children and the elderly, and second, to swiftly integrate into a new city and its market economy. Newcomers, we heard and saw, are offered state-sponsored training in the Center in order to develop fast and effective linguistic and technological competences. Language and digital skills training, while not fully obligatory, as the coordinator of the women's center explained, is promoted by the German state as the evidence par excellence of its desire to integrate new migrants in the economy of the city. However, this kind of training appeared to us more as a "one size fits all" strategy for integration, which, precisely because of its inflexibility, is likely to fail those who need it the most: many of the women attending training lack basic literacy skills in any language, have received little if any formal education in their youth, and even during training classes, they have no choice but to care for their children.

As obstacles are raised by what are presented as opportunities but which actually exclude them, any form of recognition—from self-worth to developing skills—seems unattainable to many women, in the context of the Center's activities. As the coordinator, herself visibly upset and disappointed, further explains, as a result of the unrealistic expectations of entrepreneurship posed by the state, many of the women attending the center just resign themselves to a realization that their prospects of succeeding are slim, if not impossible. Dismissing the vision of integration that requires all newcomers—many deeply traumatized—to swiftly transform into resilient subjects, the coordinator speaks instead about an alternative project of self-making that takes into account not only the instrumental imperatives of the state but also the personal needs and skills of migrants themselves: "Slower is better. We need space and time for transition, to build that necessary peace, to have time to go back to ourselves." As employment databases code slowness as a delayed work timeline, however, migrant profiles are consequently registered as "low competence," cumulatively defining those falling in this category as failed potential citizens. There is, in other words, a state-sanctioned process of migrant control that, by combining regular surveillance with data extraction, shapes the conditions of migrants' involvement in urban markets in ways that make it impossible for them to participate. Under these circumstances, migrants fall into a vicious circle of surveillance that cumulatively marginalizes them further, either pushing them towards the precarious labor of the gig economy, where indeed the majority of them world-wide find work (van Doorn et al. 2020), or ultimately placing them in a trajectory towards deportation.

Even more precarious and marginalized in the life of the city is the category of people with disabilities. Fatima, in London, is an 18-year-old woman with no mobility in her body, who is looked after by her mother, and, until her wheelchair arrives, they are both confined indoors. While access to public space with a tailored wheelchair is necessary for her to gain mobility, have access to education, and work out a possible pathway to socio-cultural recognition, a data failing in the system's waiting list, where her personal information was wrongly recorded, prevented her from attending her long-awaited appointment and she was pushed to the bottom of the list. Five months after her arrival, Fatima is still restricted to a mattress on the floor, her only engagement with the outside world being her mobile phone that her brother helps her scroll through; this is all the digital engagement she can count on. Fatima, like many others, is fully dependent on databases over which she has no control over, bearing the consequences of a data-driven biopolitics that prioritizes its own systemic logic over her needs. While, in the context of pervasive datafication, this is a predicament for all, her example shows how the regime of datafied and market-oriented security ignores and ultimately harms primarily the most vulnerable.

The term securitized precarity, then, defines a sphere of the inner border that utilizes state-sanctioned networks of intermediation, for instance, training databases and data profiles on employment or health, so as to extract the data of precarious social groups in the name of their own benefit and protection. Such extractive data and their classification categories exclude by design the capabilities or needs that migrants may have and evaluate them in line with their own inherently biased logic, often trapping them in a spiral of failure. Given that work—with the esteem and financial benefit that comes from it—remains migrants' safest pathway to citizenship, securitized precarity, rather than a route to recognition, promises instead marginalization or even deportation. Malaka's performance anxieties and Hadi's desperate versatility, but also the Berlin refugee women's disappointment and Fatima's entrapment in immobility, all show the various positions that migrants may occupy within the entrepreneurial regime of the inner border. Together, what these positions point to, independently of their outcomes, is an overarching paradox that traverses the experience of securitized precarity as much as that of securitized self-responsibility. While many migrants crossed the outer territorial border and entered the city on the grounds of abject vulnerability upon arrival (which got them refugee or asylum-seeker status), this status swiftly switched to one requiring them to become competitive entrepreneurs, taking full control over their lives and performing competence for the state's data registers. And as this change reflects, what we earlier called, the impossible conditions for migrant recognition in the neoliberal city, the success of the few will always come at the cost of the many.

Conditional Conviviality

The city, however, is more than the datafied order we have so far described. It is also a space of conviviality and solidarity rooted in everyday encounters, civic life, and long histories of cities as migrant destinations (Georgiou 2018; Hall et al. 2016). Networks of intermediation, in this context, should not be exclusively understood as assemblages of control. Rather, such networks function as impure digital spaces where the border is affirmed but also contested, even if not always opposed. This is especially the case with digital initiatives for cooperation and innovation whose numbers have, since 2015, exploded across cities. Such initiatives reflect grassroots and institutional efforts, first, to extend welcome to newcomers in the city and, second, to use digital tools in support of their "integration." Integration in this context speaks to wider policy agendas that, informed as they are by dominant entrepreneurial discourses, define desired outcomes of welcome as contingent upon migrants' ability to secure economic independence and to actively demonstrate loyalty to the society that received them. This integration agenda, which spills across institutional and civic networks of intermediation, represents what Critical Migration Studies refer to as the deliberate depoliticization and individualization of migrant struggles to find security, by instead overemphasizing migrants' individual responsibility and civic nationalism (Larin 2020) as the main means to belong within a supposedly cohesive societal whole (Anthias 2021).

In this section, we discuss two main domains in which the requirement for integration is constituted digitally: networks that promote *work* and networks that facilitate *civic participation*. First, we examine how work-related digital innovation as evidence of entrepreneurship promises to open doors for work and recognition; we here focus on the case of the hackathons for refugees in Athens. Then, we examine how civic participation becomes equated to "integration," especially as performed and evidenced through the "interveillance" or mutual monitoring (Christensen and Jansson 2015) that citizens and noncitizens impose on one another through social media platforms; we here focus on the case of a particular grassroots network promoting urban conviviality in Berlin.

Hackathons are quintessential illustrations of *innovative entrepreneurship*. The dozens of hackathons for refugees organized across European cities, but also in other cities across the world since 2015, represent powerful cases of the convergence of the urban ethos of welcome with the digital promise for success through innovation. One of the most successful transnational initiators of hackathons is Techfugees (techfugees.com), established in 2015 by a group of IT professionals and having run more than 40 events by the end of 2020 (even during the COVID-19 pandemic). Set up in response to the publication of the Alan Kurdi images, as it notes in its website, Techfugees' aim has since been to support refugees in developing skills for employment in the digital economy; its "Who we are" webpage announces:

Techfugees is an impact driven global organisation nurturing a sustainable ecosystem of tech solutions supporting the inclusion of displaced people. Techfugees exists to empower displaced people whilst supporting tech innovations designed by, with and for them. (techfugees.com/about)

Using the language of empowerment and innovation, Techfugees, like other hackathon organizers, draw upon values of entrepreneurship, resilience, and talent to support migrant communities of expert conviviality and mutual recognition (see Perng et al. 2018 for hackathons' neoliberal rationality). They do so in three steps: first, the hackathon itself in which migrants compete with their own innovative ideas for access to expert support and investors' capital; second, a productive phase during which the winners, supported by the experts and investors, develop their projects in an "innovation impact hub" (i.e., an already-existing center of innovation and creativity within the city); and third, a dissemination stage, when they scale up beyond the nation and deploy their innovations for wider use and profit. In practice, this model is meant to catalyze brokering collaborations between migrants, impact hubs, and digital corporations that can generate successful and profitable innovations for both migrants and their investors—a model that has had significant appeal in Europe, not only among technologists but also among governmental and nongovernmental actors willing to invest in this vision.

In Athens, we observed how the promise of innovative entrepreneurship as a means to recognition, a hopeful opportunity as it may be, is nonetheless subjected to the security regime of the border. In 2016, a hackathon titled "Hack the Camp," organized by the US Embassy and supported by the Onassis Foundation, Microsoft, and the local Athens Impact Hub, gained significant traction on the city's remediation and intermediation networks, attracting headlines and public attention. The winners used their own experiences of migration to develop innovative designs, demonstrating talent that was celebrated in national media and granted them recognition by the organizers, the media, and audiences. This moment of success, however, turned out to be short-lived for most. As we found out through the Athens Impact Hub after the hackathon, the promise of crossing the border and competing at the European level never materialized as the migrants' asylum status forbade them to cross

EU borders. The forms of recognition they had already accrued, ontological and social, did not help them move towards the recognition that matters: legal recognition through the prospect of sustainable employment in the IT industries of Northern Europe. In fact, the brief success of most winners made no difference to their precarious ways of life: as asylum seekers, their subjection to transnational securitization meant that their future was determined by their right or not to freely move across Europe; as we were told by a contact in the Athens Impact Hub, they, like so many other newcomers, were to be lost in the city's underbelly with their prospects as digital innovators fading into further uncertainty. Convivial encounters that celebrate innovation appear thus to offer moments of hope and opportunity, but they are not enough to overhaul the structural inequalities of conditional conviviality that can, at any time, trump the promise of digital success even for the selected few.

Alongside projects focusing on digital work, there are those that celebrate *civic participation*. Since 2105, hundreds of welcoming initiatives have come to life on urban networks of intermediation with the aim to celebrate "integration" by recognizing migrants as active participants in the city's civic life. A powerful example is the active network Give Something Back to Berlin, which, as its name indicates, promotes "community integration, intercultural dialogue and participation"—a set of values also attached to the rhetoric of hackathons: "we work as a connector, creator and catalyst for all sorts of grassroots driven social impact work. We call it 'making worlds meet working together for a better city'" (Give Something Back to Berlin 2019).

Driven by a vision of connection across difference, Give Something Back to Berlin sees itself as an attempt to "nurture spaces where new and established Berliners work together to foster individual and collective creativity" (ibid.). In practice this ambition is realized in events that bring city dwellers together online and offline to "meet, mix, learn and share," and in a lively set of networked activities that emphasize the openness of the city. The Open Music School (where new and long-standing Berliners learn music together), Open Language (where language learning is made available to newcomers focusing on the dominant languages of the city—German and English), Open Kitchen (an invitation for conviviality through cooking and eating) and Open Hearts (a space of counselling and emotional support, with an emphasis on "intercultural dialogue" and "trauma healing"). The evidence of Give Something Back to Berlin's effort to mobilize civic participation around projects of creative learning and artistic expression is impressive. This is a digital space for doing things as well as for doing community, not least by promoting ideas such as "two-way integration" and an inclusive city for all.

Yet, as we just noted, inside these efforts for convivial collaboration, narratives of "impact," "creativity," and "innovation" remain as reminders of the neoliberal rationalities that regulate many of the digital attempts to share the city, including the hackathons (Cammaerts 2011). The discursive tropes of creative entrepreneurship and individual resilience are in fact ever-present across the network, showing how even everyday acts of cooking and making music together are not only occasions of conviviality but also opportunities of "interveillance," that is opportunities where digital sociality functions as a horizontal system of monitoring that subtly nudges one another's compliance with the ethos of integration (Christensen and Jansson 2015); for it is only when newcomers demonstrate certain values, such as business acumen, hard work, exceptional talent and creativity, that they can be seen as having "earned" their welcome (see also Archakis et al. 2018 and Tsakona et al. 2020 for a similar argument on migrants' linguistic "assimilation").

In Give Something Back to Berlin, then, we encounter the paradoxes of welcoming networks of intermediation. On the one hand, the initiative represents an assertive challenge to the communicative hierarchy of the border that divides citizens and noncitizens, as migrants are the driving force behind the project: they are the main narrators of the story of the city, seen and heard as talented and creative individuals, so their self-worth is set forward not only as a distant possibility but also as a claimed right. Yet, these same speakers are also enunciating their agency through an internalized voice that echoes (or ventriloquizes) the voice of their funders: a discourse of entrepreneurial determination and convivial celebration that, in its firm self-assurance, refutes the uncertainty and vulnerability, often trauma, at the heart of migrant experience. The "interveilled" agency evident both in these participatory networks of civic collectivities and, in fact, in the innovative collectivities of the hackathons, may support forms of socio-cultural and ontological recognition, at least ephemerally, yet the securitizing logics inherent in digital conviviality still trap them at the margins and can, as we saw, block the potential for legal recognition.

The Inner Border and the Tensions of Entrepreneurial Security

This chapter has offered a reconstruction of the inner border of Europe and its organization around intersecting networks of intermedation, and reflected on how such networks structured migrants' and citizens' contestations over work and civic participation within the border's regime of entrepreneurial securitization. As their attempts to gain access to urban markets, we argued, are inherently linked to their desire for recognition—for self-worth, belonging, and citizenship in their new communities—migrants are inevitably also caught up in the competing discourses of digital participation between creative agency and neoliberal entrepreneurialism that take place across three spheres of the inner border: *securitized self-responsibility, securitized precarity,* and *conditional conviviality*. Through these intersecting spheres, the border's two imperatives, to national sovereignty and to the biopolitical care for migrants, mix and fuse in ways that primarily safeguard national and European integrity over migrant lives but also, in the process, carve out contingent and fragile spaces of care and solidarity for them.

Our discussion of *securitized self-responsibility* highlighted the prominence of neoliberal notions of self-reliance in normative conceptions of migrant identity and demonstrated how such conceptions inform migrants' use of urban intermediation networks as a means towar legal recognition. While self-responsibility, we argued, works to individualize the burden of digital integration into labor markets upon migrants themselves and so to hide the structural deficiencies that keep them marginalized, the term also throws into relief internal hierarchies within migrant communities themselves. Related primarily to their digital competences (or lack thereof), these hierarchies are, in turn, integral to the neoliberal valuation of market skills (desirable for employability, visibility, and participation) that also divide and segregate migrants along the basis of class, age, education, ability, and, particularly, gender; we saw, for instance, how Hadi and Malaka, who are younger and better educated, benefit from digital work and visibility but also how others, mostly precarious categories of migrant women, stay behind. The hierarchies of the digital economy work here not only to reproduce the same social divisions as neoliberal markets do at large, but, in so doing, also to set in motion the classificatory function of the inner border for migrants in the city. For, depending on their ability to participate in intermediation networks, it is only for those who can "prove themselves" and persevere as digitally-skilled entrepreneurs that access to legal recognition becomes a viable, though far from guaranteed, achievement—with the rest facing an uncertain future (and see Lafleur and Mescoli 2018 for a similar hierarchy between "deserving" and "undeserving" among EU migrants).

Securitized precarity, refers to an adjacent sphere of urban intermediation networks with their own hierarchical system of migrant recognition that impacts the most vulnerable amongst them. Those precarious categories consisting of women, the less-well-educated, and people with disabilities suffer by the "one size fits all" approach to digital integration and its techno-utopian vision of professional and social success as access to the digital economy (see Bakewell 2008 for a critique of the harms of such as "policy worldview" of integration). As we saw, women who are caught in-between the conflicting demands of caring responsibilities and fast digital skill development become painfully aware that they are unlikely to perform the resilient self that is required of them in order to be able to claim any form of recognition. Disabled people, too, remain fully dependent on datafied systems that promise to open up opportunities for education, employment, and participation in public life. With such skills-development, employability and adaptability to market requirements coded in databases as competences (or lack thereof), migrant data profiles themselves simultaneously work as processes of "weeding out" those predetermined to fail: those who, in two or three years and depending on status, will be fully denied legal recognition and asked to leave.

The sphere of *conditional conviviality*, unlike *securitized precarity*, opens up opportunities for collaborative acts of welcome that bring together institutional actors, civic actors, and migrants. At the heart of this sphere is the tenuous ethos of integration that, on the one hand, opens up spaces for migrants to develop or benefit from their competences, yet only does so on the basis of entrepreneurial agency that render such recognition conditional upon migrants' compliance with this neoliberal ethos. We observed, for example, how innovative entrepreneurship is integrated into hackathon events and expanded across networks of intermediated conviviality; and we recorded how on digital networks of civic participation, such as Give Something Back to Berlin, migrants become the main actors that enliven the culture of the city—around music, cooking, language learning, and emotional support—while also themselves making sure that all members of the network comply with a limited sense of successful citizenship. In both cases, the common denominator is that migrant recognition remains conditional upon the deeply securitized requirements of the border, as, for instance, in the restricted mobility of hackathon winners.

In conclusion, the techno-symbolic assemblage of the inner border relies on digital urban economies that promote opportunities for work within the value system of neoliberal markets. By ignoring what Sandel calls, "the dignity of work" inherent in the full range of people's capabilities (2020), the inner border thus entails two sets of harm: first, even for "successful" migrants, the promise of recognition remains largely incomplete, potentially granting them ontological and socio-cultural recognition but hardly the legal recognition that matters for a secure future; and, second, it creates hierarchies within migrant populations as it marginalizes vulnerable groups, pushing the latter towards further precarity. Under these circumstances, as we discuss in the next chapter, recognition struggles remains an upward and often in-vain process that migrants, activists, and diverse urban communities take up through alternative practices of grassroots activism within the embryonic, and often fragile, networked commons of the city.

3

The Inner Border as Networked Commons

Entrepreneurial securitization is embedded in the techno-symbolic mediations of the inner border that benefit some migrants, those performing as entrepreneurial subjects, while condemning others, those living under conditions of securitized precarity, to the risk of further marginalization if not deportation. Is entrepreneurial securitization, however, a homogenous regime of power that reigns over the city? If not, which forms of agency are at play within this regime, and how do these negotiate the power relations of the inner border? How do migrants and other border actors, in other words, navigate the regime of entrepreneurial securitization, and how do they resist its practices of surveillance?

In seeking answers to these questions, we probe further into the elastic contours of the digital border by zooming into the context of the urban street in the post-"crisis" period of 2016–2020. As migrants' daily lives in their new homes rely upon multiple networks of mediation—from WhatsApp chats and Facebook groups to digital courses and offline get-togethers—the urban street, we argue, is more than simply a location of surveillance and control. It also becomes a site of coexistence, co-creation, and solidarity; or a site of possibilities for the realization of the *networked commons*: the digitally enabled, contingent, and political associations through which people generate meaningful community relations outside the remit of the state or the corporate sector (de Peuter and Dyer-Witheford 2010).

The networked commons of the urban street, we show, consists of plural spaces of connectivity that engage migrants with glimpses of everyday familiarity and experiences of social attachment but also with politicized claims to the city. This is important because, at the heart of the ambivalent experiences of the inner border we just examined lies migrants' own sense of "environmental unfamiliarity" in a context that "holds no memories and is uncertain in its affordances" (Rishbeth

2020: 28). Indeed, this sense of unfamiliarity and uncertainty, so central to migrants' accounts of their new cities, is informed by an experience of precarity; "precarity is at the core of their daily existence," as Trimikliniotis et al. say: "precarious labor, precarious stay and precarious lives" (2015: 1). Opening up a commons, in this context, means activating horizontal networks of digital *intermediation* and co-present *transmediation* in ways that bring people together in projects of education, self-expression, and mutual support with a view to forging a sense of confidence and bonds of familiarity or even intimacy amongst them.

At the heart of this generative process of the commons lies the urban condition of "throwntogetherness" (Massey 2005): a term that captures the emergent and creative confluence of bodies, technologies, and environments in shared spaces of publicity, in ways that make a difference in the daily lives of people within those spaces. The idea of the street as networked commons defined by the random throwntogetherness of those who inhabit it is instrumental to our argument on the politics of the inner border because, as Massey argues, it poses "that most fundamental of political questions," namely the question of "how are we going to live together" (2013: 15). Throwntogetherness resonates, in this sense, with our broader interest in how the city may generate hospitable encounters between residents and newcomers in ways that not only affirm but may precisely challenge the power regimes of the inner border. In our observations of the urban street, in particular, we identified an emergent commons that presents possibilities of collaborative practices and collective claims that go beyond the contingencies of conditional conviviality discussed in Chapters 1 and 2. Within this politicized understanding of the urban street, our analysis approaches the inner border as a *site of contestation*, where the encounters of its inhabitants, intermediated and transmediated ones, challenge the ever-expansive grip of entrepreneurial securitization; and the inner border emerges as a productive space not only of exclusion but also of struggle.

Based on fieldwork in Athens, Berlin, and London, which took place between 2017 and 2019[1] with follow-up small-scale research in 2020, we begin by theorizing the urban commons as networks of throwntogetherness grounded in the contexts of digitization, and we go on to explore three distinct, yet occasionally overlapping, spheres of networked commoning across these cities: *the commons through grassroots pedagogy, through cultural encounters,* and *through political activism,* as each works to reconfigure local communities beyond the familiar divisions of "we-ness" and "otherness" that dominate the inner border. Finally, we reflect on how the various practices of commoning across these spheres bring up tensions—affective, mediational, and political—which render the commons a vital but fragile dimension of the forces of resistance that traverse the three cities.

The Networked Commons as a Space of Struggle

The vocabulary of the commons is instrumental in theorizing the city as a political space where struggles over inclusion and participation take place, catalyzing what Caffentzis and Federici call "new forms of sociality organized according to the principle of social cooperation and the defense of the already existing forms of communalism" (2014: 96). Given the emergent nature of these spaces, literature in Urban Studies tends to conceptualize the commons not in terms of any formal, pre-existing properties, such as ownership or intended use, but inductively in terms of the bottom-up ways in which such spaces are shaped through the mobilization of the actors involved in them (Bradley 2015). Within this conception of the commons, the analytical task is to understand how urban actors intervene in the city and its technologies so as to generate various civic projects that can make a difference in migrants' lives— for instance, urban farming or gardening and street cultural events in deprived areas or actions associated with DIY urbanism (Finn 2014). What such grounded accounts capture is the capacity of local actors to catalyze what Chatterton (2010) calls a process of "radical commonization" of the city that helps redraw the divided lines of the border in ways that favor an inclusive relationship of conviviality between citizens and noncitizens.

While, however, some scholars use the concept of the urban commons in this broad sense to encompass any act that claims public space for the people by the people (Ostrom 1990), others prefer to situate politics and activist intervention at the heart of the urban commons. Conceiving of those spaces as transformative sites of claim-making, as was the case of Tahrir Square during the Arab Spring (Harvey 2012), such accounts do not simply highlight the transformative politics of the people but also address the role of digital infrastructures as emancipatory tools that give voice to the oppressed; as Lim argues, the 2011 protests in Egypt largely relied on Facebook and Twitter as "the means to shape repertoires of contention, frame the issues, propagate unifying symbols, and transform online activism into offline protests" (2012: 231). Skeptical of the political role of commercial platforms, others nonetheless warn against the surveillance regimes of social media and advocate instead for an alternative political activism of open-source technologies that enable knowledge-sharing and self-organization in fringe spaces. Inspired by the digital commons as platforms of resistance, for instance, Bradley (2015:102) suggests that the urban commons needs to be similarly understood as activism within "wider social movements of open-source 'commons-based peer production'; i.e. a form of production geared towards a more equitable distribution of power, knowledge and the means of production." While, as we shall see, the commons of our empirical narrative largely relies on commercial platforms such as Facebook and WhatsApp rather than open-source resources, the tactical use of intermediation and transmediation networks on such platforms—and their concomitant cautious switching between public engagement and disengagement—works to capitalize on these platforms' capacity to mobilize horizontal collectivities of support among marginalized actors while protecting those actors from the platforms' surveillance.

Despite their useful emphasis on alternative forms of social organization and activist practice, however, urban and digital commons literatures have not paid due attention to migrant populations as key agents in the "commoning" of the city (Harvey 2012). Yet, we argue, with Trimikliniotis et al. (2015), that the focus on migrants is key to understanding resistance in the inner border. Attending to mobility as an attribute of both technology (the mobile phone) and its user (the migrant), these authors' concept of a "mobile commons" draws attention to the ways in which digital networks put shared knowledge and community-making at the service of urban justice—what Lefebvre calls the "right of the city" (2010). Grounded on infrastructures of connectivity, the mobile commons, at the same time, also activates a whole range of bottom-up social processes that, as Trimikliniotis, Parsanoglou, and Tsianos (2015) contend, include migrants' own knowledges of mobility, the informal economies that support their lives, the diverse communities of justice that enable them to speak out, as well as the relationships of care that sustain bonds of trust amongst them. The mobile commons is, in this sense, best conceived as those informal spaces, online and offline, which encompass migrants' everyday struggles in and against precarity together with those who support them.

Infrastructures of intermediation and transmediation are core elements of the mobile commons as technologies of agency and struggle that are used tactically to configure communities of care and justice, sustained or ephemeral. It is, we propose, those informal infrastructures that bring people together in relationships of throwntogetherness, thereby animating new dynamics of cohabitation and collaboration in the city: for throwntogetherness occurs, as Georgiou et al. put it, "in the global city's multicultural neighborhoods, shaped and reshaped constantly through the mobility of new and old inhabitants into its territory" (2016: 6). Yet, even though literature on the mobile commons, as much as the urban or digital commons, has informed our own account, each one of these approaches is characterized by its own partiality. This means that each tends to single out one actor of the commons over others, be this the urban dweller, the political activist, or the migrant, rather than seeing how the throwntogetherness of the city is actually constituted through various intersections of these actors in different contexts and to different ends.

Our focus on the networked commons aims to address this gap and to highlight instead the coalition of technologies and actors as itself a generative conjuncture where intermediated and transmediated/embodied encounters with precarious populations take place in the urban street. As the regime of the inner border strictly limits migrant lives, the urban street, we show, opens up possibilities for participation that challenge the "otherness" of migrants in "our" midst and offers a glimpse of alternative modes of coexistence, collaboration, and resistance.

Reconstructing the Inner Border as Networked Commons

Our account of the networked commons as a space of contestation emerged inductively through research across our familiar cities of Athens, Berlin, and London, in 2017–2020. Partly drawing on the research project across the three cities introduced in Chapter 2,[2] and partly on follow-up observations of their networked commons, the illustration of the inner border and its networks in this section reflects the same structural inequalities between northern and southern European cities introduced earlier in this book; austerity policies, for instance, mean that public resources of healthcare, housing, and digital infrastructures were only scarcely available in Athens, conditionally available under narrowly defined criteria in London, and more generously provided in Berlin (Nienaber 2019; Rietig 2016).

These variations granted, the fusion of security with entrepreneurialism in the inner borders of Europe remains a central feature. We have already seen how EU states' neoliberal conception of work has been central to migrants' digital training, yet, we will here see how these states simultaneously also employ "universal" counter-violent extremism (CVE) urban policies to detect "pre-criminal" sites in need of counter-terrorist supervision (Kundnani and Hayes 2018). Within this dual logic, security no longer encompasses the domain of work only, but also increasingly that of social welfare in ways that articulate the two under the rubric of anti-terrorism prevention. Indeed, originally put in place to care for migrants as precarious populations and embed them into the market, the domain of welfare is today fully subordinated to a security logic that works pre-emptively to prevent "radicalisation processes" among migrant groups (Ragazzi 2017); as a result, "resources usually associated with social welfare policies (like mentoring, housing and education) are reframed as terrorism prevention assets" (Home Office quoted in Heath-Kelly and Strausz 2018: 89).

In the UK, for instance, the controversial *"Prevent* Strategy," which was quietly introduced as a counter-terrorism initiative in 2003 (Warrell 2019), has now saturated spaces of work, education, and worship, requiring from teachers, lecturers, and religious leaders to report those expressing radical and extremist opinions in the name of prevention of terrorist acts. Even though, as critics have claimed, the huge bureaucratic effort generated by the *Prevent* Strategy has actually distracted attention and resources "from the small number of people deemed to actually require de-radicalisation intervention," as Heath-Kelly and Strausz (2018: 107) put it, the act has, in fact, managed to turn security into a "banal" practice that permeates and regulates all aspects of migrants' everyday life in the UK. The UK is in no way unique in its security policies and, in fact, increasing numbers of European governments have introduced controversial regulations that seek to tackle terrorism through migrant profiling on the basis of colonial frames and their orientalist conceptions of religion, race, and culture. This is evident, for instance, in the requirements on civil society to report "suspicious" behaviors among migrants (Yuval-Davis et al. 2019), or in laws that allow states such as Germany, the Netherlands, and the US to monitor migrants' social media accounts without their consent (Privacy International 2019)—a measure that, as Miller claims, "vastly expand[s] the government's authority" raising "constitutional problems and privacy concerns" regarding migrants' rights (2018: 395).

Our reconstruction of diverse spheres of networked commons across cities is informed by these considerations. It is specifically motivated by the acknowledgment that migrants' urban experience is punctuated by daily reminders that they do not belong in their urban environments they find themselves living in. Beyond the larger issues of failed recognition we examined in the previous chapter, there are also the minor acts of banal xenophobia or racism that gesture, as Noble notes, "to the presence of suffering as a key aspect of the migrant experience" in western metropolises (2005). Communal tensions arising around such minor acts, for instance, migrant "smells" and "noises," should be seen as nothing less than "forms of public harassment—abuse, harryings and annoyances—that exist on a continuum of possible actions, ending with violence" (Noble 2005: 112, quoting the concept of "uncivil attention" from Gardner 1995).

Within this context, we next highlight the ways in which our three spheres of networked commons seek to open up alternative spaces of safe, creative, and engaged coexistence in the urban street: *the commons as a space of learning*, exploring bottom-up initiatives that bring migrants and local citizens together in a shared appreciation of reading, chatting, and language learning; the *commons as embodied encounters*, where online connectivity catalyzes face-to-face communities of artistic expression and mutual support; and *the commons as an activist space*, where grassroots groups address the needs and rights of the most precarious migrants, such as those who are sex workers or homeless, in the face of increasing policing measures.

Networked Commons through Grassroots Pedagogy

The city as a site of a pedagogic commons mobilizes networks of intermediation and transmediation to encompass digital and on-location initiatives that bring people together in communities of learning. In so doing, the pedagogic commons may appear to overlap with job training initiatives we explored as part of our entrepreneurial securitization analysis. Yet, the pedagogic commons goes beyond those both in that such initiatives are now not run by local authorities but driven by grassroots efforts and in that their learning content is no longer (fully) instrumentalized in the entrepreneurial logic of neoliberal markets.

Refugio is a typical example of a pedagogic commons: a social and cultural space of accommodation for refugees housed in the Berlin suburb of Neukölln—a buzzing and increasingly trendy neighborhood, since the early nineties reinvigorated mostly by Turkish and Arab migrants. Supported by the Berlin City Mission, Refugio nonetheless has an autonomous structure that combines housing for refugees with a communal space and a café run by noncitizens and citizens alike. It is, as its website puts it, a space "where new and old Berliners live and work together"[3] over a cup of coffee. One of its key functions is that of a "sprachcafé," or language café, which offers migrants "an opportunity to apply their newly learned skills in a friendly environment"[4] and encourages fluent German speakers to join and help "improve the skills of your new neighbours and future friends."[5] Planned and scheduled on social media but enacted in informal face-to-face exchanges between fluent and new German language speakers, sprachcafés have exploded in numbers across German cities after 2015 and have acted as an alternative or a complement to the official German language schools run by the state. Their principle is one of collaborative learning and convivial interaction, where newcomers and locals share knowledge and build collective capacities together.

Beyond the face-to-face, the commons of sprachcafés is organized through networks of intermediation, on Facebook and Instagram, which invite people to participate, comment, and interact online. We saw, for example, how a group of migrant musicians met on Refugio's Facebook page and ended up playing regularly together in performance spaces in Neukölln and beyond. Similarly, the Mobile Library in Athens, which we discuss in more detail in the next section, mobilizes networks of intermediation—for instance, their registration platforms for face-to-face learning and skills development: "We had a lot of Coursera [online learning platform] sign-ups last month . . . We have a collaboration with Coursera, if people want to do courses. Coursera has offered this to us. We sign them up and they get the courses for free." Meghan, one of the volunteers in the Mobile Library, further described how emotional support, care, and skills-development co-exist in the space around it: "Having qualifications and proof of their education is important to many people we speak to. Many of them are highly educated but have no papers to show for it, or their education means nothing here. So, this is important to them."

In these instances, we were able to record how local encounters among participants, some sustained and some ephemeral, operated as occasions of throwntogetherness that develop local cultural and social projects, including concerts and local farming. One example is London's Code Your Future, which opens its doors every Sunday in North London. A trans-urban, volunteer-run coding school offering free programming classes for migrants and those at the urban margins, Code Your Future was established by two migrants who themselves work in the digital sector and who wanted to support others' entry into the thriving digital economy of the city. Initially developed to support new migrants who were less privileged than them, Code Your Future's founders have in time expanded the school's reach to welcome other underprivileged actors who wish to develop digital skills and seek employment in the tech sector. Attracting dozens of students and hundreds of volunteers at any one time, Code Your Future is committed to teaching not only coding skills but also interview preparation and CV-writing as part of a broader project of nurturing a networked micro-commons of co-learning. As Max, one of the founders, told us, volunteers invite migrants and other learners from marginalized communities to become members of a supportive digital community that recognizes their capabilities and desire to seek a better future.

This space of co-learning, we were told, is, at the same time, a space of warm conviviality. The Sunday school, for instance, is performed within an atmosphere of informality as participants freely move around the school's areas, from the classroom to the kitchen and the chill-out area.

Their shared Sunday lunch stands out as a core element of Code Your Future's hospitality. For its founders, co-creating spaces and rituals that bring newcomers and locals together as a means of mutual recognition is just as important as preparing them for the job market through language and digital skills-training.

The pedagogic commons here reveals itself as a sphere, which grassroots-driven commitment to supporting newcomers through convivial experiences of education occurs nonetheless within the entrepreneurial premises of the neoliberal city and its preference for tech-professionals. Given that "almost half of the Member States," as the EU's Annual Report on Migration and Asylum 2017 says, have recently taken measures to "further attract and retain migrant entrepreneurs, mainly 'innovative' start-ups and investors" (European Commission 2017: 12), there seems to be little option for this commons of grassroots pedagogy but to prioritize the tech-market in its activism. As we shall see, however, this necessity simultaneously creates tensions within the networked commons between emancipation and co-optation—tensions that, as Ålund and Schierup claim, are "central to any movement of civil society, operating within the framework of dominant institutions—be they local, national, or transnational" (2019: 80).

Networked Commons through Cultural Encounters

The city as a site of cultural encounters mobilizes networks of intermediation that bring people into close-up, embodied interactions on topics such as books and the arts. Organized around libraries and performance scenes, the cultural commons overlaps with the pedagogic—for instance, in the activities of the Mobile Library in Berlin or the migrant-run cultural center Farzant Karmangar in Athens—but differs from it in that the cultural commons' focus falls squarely on the appreciation of intellectual and artistic expression as a means of urban connection where bordering divisions between "us" and "them" are temporarily blurred. *Farzant Karmangar*, for instance, an Iranian refugee initiative in downtown Athens, opens its doors to host cultural events that bring together newly arrived migrants and locals around their desire to explore Iranian literature and language, while, at the same time, it shares their experiences with a local, national, and transnational audience on social media.

The Mobile Library in Athens, with its van full of books and its free Wi-Fi connectivity, is another grassroots initiative that intervenes to revive and mobilize the most neglected neighborhoods of the city. Following a decade of financial crisis and austerity on top of a longer-standing neglect of the city center, parts of inner Athens, still struggling with impoverishment and hardship, have now become the precarious home for post-2015 newcomers. Caught in a limbo status of awaiting their asylum application decisions, these migrants have no choice but to occupy the derelict streets of the inner city and to depend on fragile and intermittent networks of intermediation to get access to the city's resources.

The Mobile Library compensates for these urban deficits as its van travels across neighborhoods, setting up a temporary base on the street for a few hours. When the doors of the van open, board games come out, books change hands, the Wi-Fi gets switched on and, for a few hours, the space around the van becomes an ephemeral commons: an urban street that enables reading, connecting, learning, playing, and socializing. The activists behind the project explained how the Mobile Library and the commons it supports emerged organically through the people in these city streets. "It [the Library] is like a pop-up; we respond to what people want in each space. In some spaces we provide a lot of language instruction, others are just board games and chatting," Meghan, one of the volunteers, told us. At the same time, she explained, the Library facilitates connections between migrants and other grassroots organizations and NGOs, for instance by referring people to Facebook groups such as the Mobile Info team, especially for legal advice relating to their status as asylum-seekers. Having started as a project to provide free access to books, the Mobile Library soon had to expand its services to provide the digital infrastructures that migrants desperately missed. By offering free connectivity, the Library enabled them to communicate with loved ones as well as with state authorities, on whom they depend in their efforts to obtain their legal documents.[6]

Another hopeful project is Baynatna,[7] the Arabic Library of Berlin, established when a group of young people, most of them from the Middle East, approached Berlin's City Library and received the support they needed to proceed with their vision: creating opportunities for showcasing Arabic culture in Europe through books and public events.

Rather than relying on volunteers and grassroot activity alone as the Athens Library does, Baynatna also benefits from public infrastructures that sustain the Library's vision to recognize the migrant as a central figure in the cultural life of the city. In this way, as Ali, one of the founders, explained to us, the Arabic Library contests the narrative of vulnerability and pity surrounding popular conceptions of the migrant in Europe. With its emphasis on migrant agency and creativity, as Dana, another member of the founding team, said, the Library is also inevitably a project of identity, a project of narrating the story of "newcomers"—a term the founders preferred over refugees or migrants—many of whom (including one of the founders) fled to Germany from wars in Syria and Iraq. A well-established cultural resource with more than 3,500 books, the Library is today more than a meeting point for migrants in the city. It is the stage for a range of performances, workshops, concerts, and get-togethers. Throughout the day, the Library invites people to browse through the books and magazines, while in the evening, Berlin's Arabic literary and musical scene transforms the Library into a convivial stage of artistic performance and sociality.

Digital connectivity may here be important as a tool for enabling transmediated encounters, yet it is people-meeting in physical proximity that really matters; as Ali, one of the team, has publicly put it, "we need an Arabic library in Berlin because we need a space where Arabic-speakers can feel welcome and comfortable. We need a place that can bring Arabic and German speakers together." Indeed, most of the twenty-something members of the Library team, highlighted the social and emotional significance of the face-to-face as a foundational dimension of its commons. In this respect, the Arabic Library represents a powerful example of open-source urbanism: a space of experimentation with arts, translation, and performance that, with its constantly repurposed spaces, challenges the hierarchical divisions of the inner border and celebrates the creative potential of urban throwntogetherness.

Part of a broader range of open-source urban spaces, this embodied and affective quality of being together has been at the heart of the cultural commons, across our examples. As Dana, one of the Berlin Library group, emphasized: "What comes after the welcome culture? The need to meet eye-to-eye. Creating a new diverse city culture together." In this respect, the networked commons of cultural encounters is driven by a productive tension between the necessity for digital connectivity as much as the values of physical presence outside of the digital; after all, as Natal and Treré note, "disconnection ... is closely associated and embedded in a deep engagement with digital technologies and platforms" (2020: 268).

Networked Commons through Political Activism

Alongside the pedagogic and cultural commons, urban communities also mobilize an activist commons which, unlike the previous two, adopts an explicitly political agenda in seeking to ensure that the most precarious migrants, that is, those without legal status, enjoy the benefits of digital connection while remaining protected from state surveillance. This commons is itself inevitably caught up in the power relations of entrepreneurial securitization and its biopolitics (Topak 2019; Yuval-Davis et al. 2019) in ways that oblige its NGOs and grassroots agencies to engage in forms of "guerrilla" activism so as to bypass or subvert the surveillance state. They do so by mobilizing intermediation and transmediation networks in ways that tactically combine public visibilities and necessary invisibilities at the service of migrants' protection, well-being, and rights (Tazzioli 2018).

In Berlin and London, we encountered grassroots organizations and civic actors that, while aware of the punitive force of the state, still worked to provide support for work, education, and housing for migrant families with no recourse to public funds (NRPF).[8] In so doing, they challenge state bureaucracies that deliberately delay or block asylum applications keeping migrants "without papers" in a state of long-standing indeterminacy and so forcing them to live under-the-radar lives of illegal labor and clandestine housing[9]: "We care about refugees from everywhere. Syria and African countries and Afghanistan. We care very much about refugees who have no documents. For them, this is a space without conditions. They have an open space to express themselves. It is important to have a place without conditions," says Omar, another grassroots activist in Berlin's Neükolln, whose organization, S27, did not set any document-related conditions to offer migrants access to online and offline infrastructures and resources, including free Wi-Fi and a communal, urban garden.

In Athens, a different commons was configured around Unmentionables, a project offering support for sexual safety among migrants, especially sex workers and other precarious groups. One of its key activists, Brittany, told us that the story of this commons began with her chance encounter with a 14-year-old boy selling sex to buy food; when asked whether he used protection, he had no idea what she meant. This realization that young migrants sell sex with no awareness of their risks and rights was the motivation for setting up, together with a group of activists, the Unmentionables as part of an international effort to support those workers and others with resources for sexual hygiene and reproductive planning. The Unmentionables, as its website reports, "is an organization that works to provide dignity to displaced people by providing a variety of personal hygiene essentials such as underwear, feminine and intimate hygiene products, sexual health products, and family planning related education."[10]

When we met the activist group, they had just launched an app that would allow people to attend sex education workshops without being physically present. This example illustrates a key media strategy of the networked commons, namely its reliance on the calculated use of intermediation and transmediation networks in order to both maintain the visibility necessary for their own legal status (and hence access to desperately needed funding) and, at the same time, protect the often undocumented people it cares for. By alternating between private, face-to-face or semi-private forms of communication, notably WhatsApp, these activist groups manage their public presence in ways that are both digital and pre-digital; in the words of Natale and Treré, "tactically choosing the best constellation of media technologies, formats and infrastructure that best suit their needs, social movement actors critically engaged with corporate social media, but also often disconnected from them" as they find appropriate (2020: 630).

This reliance on the pre-digital in the activist commons is rooted within the long histories of on-the-ground mobilization and resistance among left-wing and anarchist groups, in the context of the deeply unequal and racialized cities of the global North (Trimikliniotis et al. 2015). Their acts of solidarity never exclusively relied on networks of mediation but were built upon various situated and embodied trajectories of social justice movements across European cities; a similar trajectory can be observed in the context of the Arab Spring, where, as Lim has put it, "the Arab uprisings were built on years of civil society movements in the region, online and offline" (2012: 232).

Projects like the Unmentionables represent activism beyond humanitarianism in that they create spaces of protection for migrants not simply with a view to address their immediate needs but within a broader vision of social justice. If the territorial border prosecutes the illegal practices of the sex worker and banishes them to the city's underbelly, rendering them illegitimate and illegal, the politics of this activist commons speaks back by upholding a view of migrants not merely as ungrievable lives, powerless victims, or corporate workforce but as people with fundamental human rights. Solidarity with migrants for them is then a struggle against the racial, class, and gender hierarchies that traverse the city; as Walsh puts it, speaking of activism across the border, "more than just welcoming and caring for the other," activist interventions "promote forms of critical transnationalism and radically cosmopolitan models of political practice" (2013: 16).

A final illustration of the activist commons is the radical squat networks, mainly in Athens but also in Berlin and elsewhere in Europe, which offer migrants access to housing and education as well as communal life. Housing is, indeed, one of the most significant concerns for newcomers, as in cities like Athens and Berlin with housing crises of their own, it is all the more difficult for migrants to secure a home (Hersh 2018). Especially for those without legal recognition, and hence no formal and secure employment, the right to affordable housing is a distant possibility, thereby exacerbating their already risky existence as newcomers in the city. In Athens, for instance, with its unaffordable rents and house-ownership market bias, the process of receiving residential subsidies presupposes a bank account and a rental contract, making it too difficult even for regularized migrants to have access to such subsidies—by 2020, only 4% of migrants regularized in 2018 had received such support.[11]

Operating outside urban housing markets, the activist commons of squat networks disentangles housing from economic profit and so allows migrants with little or no income to enjoy a basic level of accommodation. This grassroots-led social welfare turns the commons of the migrant squats into urban gift economies, where shared living and an ethos of care directly oppose entrepreneurial securitization and the inequalities it reproduces. In so doing, radical squats are vital "strategies of struggle," in Raimondi's words, against the inhospitable if not hostile regimes of inner border, operating both as claims to the right to belong and to citizenship "from below"—understood as "subjectivities that choose to 'opt out' of citizenship as a legal status" (2019: 599). In light of their fringe operations, pushing the limits of law itself, urban squats are thus treading a fine line between the visibilities of intermediation, notably on the closed social media groups that coordinate its actors and practices, and the invisibilities of ground action materialized through transmediated encounters between activists and migrants in abandoned city buildings where free accommodation for hundreds of homeless newcomers is provided (Cossé 2020).

Despite its politics of solidarity, however, the activist commons is traversed by its own struggles. Operating within the dominant norms of entrepreneurial or humanitarian securities, some actors of the commons often voice the dominant discourses of care or the market, while others prefer a more radical visions of social organizing outside state law, thereby turning the commons into a tense space of competing visions and mutual suspicion; as Zaman's ethnographic research in Greek squats notes, "refugee squats in Athens are embedded in an almost ineliminable hegemonic humanitarian logic and are thus caught between hospitality and abject space" (2019: 129). Nonetheless, and despite their inner contradictions, in the context of rising racism, xenophobia, and hate speech, such grassroots groups are vital for sustaining collective bonds of migrant solidarity, activists told us during a workshop in Berlin. As repeatedly noted, their acts of resistance are a source of pride for many and a source of relief and optimism for those migrants left without hope in the midst of unwelcoming city streets. Basira's story is indicative of the impact of their work. A 21-year-old woman from Afghanistan, Basira, who was asked to leave her tent in Moria camp on Lesbos island after being granted asylum, told Human Rights Watch: "They cut the cash assistance and told me I have to go." And she continued: "They said that if they come again and find me [in the tent] they will take me by force. I felt fear and despair because I am on my own. I didn't know where to go." Without the commons' commitment to stand by migrants' right to the city, people like Basira would suffer the full brunt of nation-states' calculated indifference and their negation of any possibility for migrants to have livable lives in the cities of the global North.

The Power and Limits of Networked Commons

The networked commons, we argued in this chapter, yields a conception of the city as a political space of resistance and possibilities. Operating at the intersection of people, technologies, and places, this commons generates sites of connectivity and conviviality between citizens and noncitizens, imaginations of co-ownership of the city, and performances of collaborative and open access urbanism against the divides of the inner border. As newcomers and locals assemble in urban streets to voice claims and forge local cooperations, diverse spheres of commons come to life: pedagogic, cultural, and activist. While the pedagogic commons comes together through online and on-location learning experiences that promise to benefit migrants' entry into the labor markets, the cultural commons is about digitally-enabled, face-to-face encounters of reading, listening, debating, and playing; and the activist commons refers to guerrilla actions and voices that deliberately "mess up" the biopolitical surveillance of the state by protecting and supporting migrants in precarious circumstances.

These different forms of networked commons and their various politics rely upon throwntogetherness as a condition of urban life that can establish collectivities of support for but also collaboration *with* migrants as actors contesting inequalities in the city. Through mutual learning, cultural exchange, or political solidarity, these examples of networked commons simultaneously highlight the role of digitization in the making of these collectivities. For such commons, as we have shown, do not exist outside the border's networks of intermediation and its regime of entrepreneurial security. It is these networks' horizontality that reconfigures the urban street into a series of purposeful and meaningful, even if nonpermanent, affiliations that connect migrants and newcomers with one another and with the city itself. In the process, the city becomes an unstable and fragile space of solidarity and surveillance that is traversed by three ongoing and largely unresolved tensions, as we sum them up below. The first of these is technological, as the commons treads the line between digital and embodied encounters; the second, political, between resistance and security; and the third, affective, between activists' own exhaustion and perseverance.

The *technological* tension arises as the networked commons of the inner border cannot fully escape its power relations even as it tried to oppose them. This means that, as we have shown throughout Chapters 2 and 3, urban networks of mediation work as much through technologies of data extraction and surveillance—in sousveillance projects (such as the British case of *Neighbourhood Watch*) or job centers' employment profiles, to mention but a couple—as they do through grassroots activisms that forge convivial collectivities of mutual support. It is, at least partly, for this reason that such activism operates tactically within these networks, capitalizing on the capacity for intermediation to coordinate within and across communities but ultimately privileging offline, face-to-face meetings of learning, cultural exchange, and protection.

By building on established urban histories and their pre-digital experiences of activism, the networked commons thus combines a reliance on the mediation networks of the city with a bottom-up involvement with the actual experiences and needs of the people on the ground—what Sennett calls, the urban street's "experiences of the unexpected" (1992: 152). The sprachcafés of the pedagogic commons, the Arabic Library of Berlin in the cultural commons, or the Unmentionables of the activist commons, for instance, are all pre-digital forms of congregation that perform solidarity outside the intermediation networks of the city.

In this sense, the networked commons are inherently linked to what Natale and Treré call the value of disconnection-as-engagement (2020). Disconnection, the authors argue, refers to a form of critical engagement with digital platforms, which may appreciate online connectivity but remains skeptical of its social effects. The sprachcafé owners do have a website yet prefer the emotional significance of face-to-face conversations between migrants and locals, as these conversations can best highlight what happens when, to put it in their own words, "newcomers become hosts." Similarly, the Arabic Library founders have a strong online presence, yet they speak in admiration of the library's books and their "unique scent," which they prefer to the online experience of digital reading; and they also view the physical space of the library as much more than just a place to read. "We need an Arabic Library in Berlin because we need a space where Arabic-speakers can feel welcome and comfortable," says cofounder Ali. "We need a place that can bring Arabic and German speakers together" so that misconceptions of the "other" can be challenged: "There is no 'other,'" said Dana, another cofounder of the Library, speaking to Al Jazeera, "There is only us, and 'between us'" (Vidal 2018).

This suspicion towards intermediation as surveillance is further mirrored in the second tension of the networked commons, *namely the political* problem of how to resist entrepreneurial securitization while working within it. The possibility of becoming complicit to securitization means that the commons has to be alert to the risk of co-option by the state and the market, ultimately reproducing the same vocabularies of the migrant as entrepreneur or victim as the border's security regimes do (Caffentzis and Federici 2014). While it makes sense to approach this antagonism between participation in and co-optation by platformed activism as a stake in the ideological struggle between left-wing fractions of the commons, we argue that this tenuous predicament of working-against-from-within is, in fact, more than this; it is the very condition of possibility for the existence of the networked commons in the first place (see also Ålund and Schierup 2019). For, as urban activists emphasized (but also as the Chios volunteers said, in Chapter 2), how their acts of solidarity are formulated and what they aim for are often conditional upon the strict requirements set by the state and the market. Indeed, for those working at the grassroots, securing funding in support of migrants is often shaped by the narrowly defined integration policies that require applicants to show how their support for migrants enables entrepreneurial agency and an "innovative," tech-oriented workforce. As they need to reproduce this discourse to sustain infrastructures of care and solidarity, activist vocabularies of migration tend therefore to operate as discursive mechanisms that legitimize dominant conceptions of what migrant support means, and what appropriate "market training" for migrants is; in this sense, as further research has also shown, networked commons can and do themselves reproduce the binaries of well-meaning citizens and needy migrants (Squire and Bagelman 2012).

The technological and political tensions of the networked commons intersect with a third tension related to the *emotional* labor of the commons. Even though the question of emotion—of how activists manage the affective costs of their engagement with the inner border—has so far remained implicit in our own narrative, it nonetheless constitutes an important undercurrent in urban migration activism. In the context of neoliberal austerity, public resources are only scarcely available to citizens and noncitizens of Athens and London and only available under narrowly defined preconditions in Berlin, thereby threatening the commons' sustainability everywhere.

In the three-year period (2017–20) that this chapter focuses on, we witnessed a radical change in the landscapes of the networked commons we just discussed. Unmentionables in Athens ceased to exist due to lack of funding, the grassroots S27 has lost its Neükolln garden and access to urban farming, the Arabic Library of Berlin has been temporarily (the founders hoped) shut due to the COVID-19 pandemic, and the network of squats hosting migrants in Athens was almost fully dismantled by riot police. So, predictably, speaking to migrants and activists during fieldwork and while writing this chapter, we heard stories of exhaustion and despair stemming from their painful awareness of the unequal struggle they were engaged in. Meghan from the Mobile Library in Athens told us: "I do feel exhausted now. I was doing too much for too long I think. And I think that I hadn't learnt to put up enough emotional barriers . . . I didn't draw any boundaries and I was trying to do anything I possibly could for anyone who asked me anything. I stretched myself too far for too long. It is exhausting." Meghan's words are far from exceptional; her words reverberated in Michael's testimony, a legal information resource officer from Greece's networked commons, who similarly spoke of his struggles to manage the emotional pressure when working with people who experience extreme precarity and who often cannot be supported in any meaningful way. Migrant activists' own words reflected a similar sensibility. "I am just tired now," Ali says in Berlin, while Ahmed, an Iraqi-Kurd homeless man in Athens, speaking of the grassroots support by the Mobile Library and the Mobile Laundry, noted how tired he was of waiting for real change in his life. Putting his finger on it, he said that solidarity is not enough and it cannot replace the needs for sustainable infrastructures of care: "I really appreciate these initiatives, I do, but, really, we need a different kind of support. We need jobs, employment."

The networked commons as collective acts that challenge the inner border carry with them the border's constant pressures: emotional pressures that have to do with the invisible labor that goes into sustaining the networked commons, while knowing that such labor is always bound to be subjected to, if not co-opted by, the biopolitics of the border; political pressures that put activists in a difficult position of balancing the clashing requirements of solidarity and security; and technological pressures that are about maximizing the potential of intermediation to connect people while doing so through the securitizing mechanisms of these same networks. As we now move from the territorial to the symbolic border, we will return to the tensions of the commons in two further chapters: in Chapter 6, where we explore the symbolic performances of agency and contestation among citizens and noncitizens, and in our Conclusion, where we come full circle to reflect on the ambivalent and often heart-breaking dynamics of the digital border.

SECTION II

The Symbolic Border

4

Narrative and Voice in News Stories

While in the first section of this book our attention fell on the territorial border and its entanglement with the technologies, bodies, and power relations of migrant reception at the edges and the heart of Europe, in this section we turn to the symbolic border: the narratives of the media, whether in language or image, that circulate within and across national territories. Part of the broader techno-symbolic assemblage that routinely produces divisions between "us" and "them," the symbolic border highlights how humanitarian security is not only embedded in the state infrastructures and local actors at work at national entry points, but is also enacted through practices of representation across space and time. By focusing on journalistic storytelling and social media feeds as they circulate within the urban environments of reception, this section shows how such symbolic enactments of the border "other" migrants but also how they offer opportunities for migrant voice to be heard in western media spaces.

This section's three chapters offer, thus, a comprehensive look into the narrative struggles of the symbolic border, with each chapter attending to a distinct trajectory of migrant voices within and across national media. Chapters 4[1] and 5[2] draw on a rich body of news remediations, collected and analyzed within the LSE study on *Migration and the Media*,[3] while Chapter 6 expands our analysis of intermediation and transmediation by illustrating how narratives of migration are also shaped digitally through international and national institutional initiatives and grassroots networks of migrant voice. Specifically, the current chapter focuses on the remediation of the migration "crisis" in online news stories at the peak of migrant arrivals in 2015, whereas Chapter 5 engages with photojournalism, the visual remediation of the "crisis" on western news platforms. Chapter 6, finally, turns to the digital spaces of websites and social media, where migrant voices are represented by intermediational and transmediational interventions initiated by organizations and activist groups in local, national, and transnational public spheres. Together, the three chapters and their text analyses (content, visual, thematic) offer an account of the symbolic border that encompasses all three dimensions of its techno-symbolic assemblage: its networks of mediation, whether in institutional journalism or social media user-generated content; its temporal and spatial malleability, tracing the shifting dynamics of mediation at and after the "crisis" moment; and its dialectics of resistance, capturing the border's symbolic exclusions as well as its moments of struggle.

This chapter focuses on remediation understood as a platform-driven symbolic process that produces and disseminates meanings about migrants and migration to mass publics. While remediation has multiple dimensions, from the technological (the appropriative logic of all media; Bolter and Grushin 2000) to the institutional (journalism and digital reporting; Deuze 2006), we are here primarily focusing on remediation as storytelling, that is on the narrative strategies and language patterns that regulate the representation of migrant voices in online news (Chouliaraki 2013). Language here, we argue, is not simply a means of communicating the "crisis" but a technology of power that constitutes the arrival of migrants as a "crisis" at the very moment that it claims to simply communicate it. This is because, as we discussed in the book's Introduction, the function of the journalistic language of migration is not simply to impart information about migrants but, in so doing, to simultaneously offer the conceptual resources within which migrants are constituted as subjects of western knowledge. This performative view of language as discourse (Hall 1997) lies at the heart of our content analysis of front-page online news in eight European countries at the peak of the "crisis," and guides our investigation of how migrant voice figures within those news: how exactly does the language of the news distribute the capacity to speak among the actors of the border? And how, in so doing, does it establish hierarchies between those who name migrants as "legitimate" or "illegitimate" and those who bear the consequences of this naming?

We demonstrate that, national differences notwithstanding, the question of migrant voice is regulated by "universal" textual strategies, which prioritize "our" protection over "theirs," and produce migrants as subaltern: silent or irrelevant and undeserving interlocutors of western news publics; these are the strategies of *silencing, generalization*, and *de-contextualization*. The symbolic border emerges here as the linguistic effect of these strategies of remediation that, by organizing the content of national media, lend legitimacy to the exclusion of migrants' voice from western news stories and misrecognize their humanity as citizens with political and personal stories to tell.

Voice and Narrative in Migration News

In the second half of 2015, all online news platforms under study narrated the "crisis" through a dual focus on how "our" borders are kept safe *and* on how "we" care for the suffering of arriving migrants—a focus that reflects the continent's response to the 2015 migration flows in terms of a geopolitics of humanitarian security. Suspended between the positions of the threat that needs to be kept at bay and the victim that needs to be protected, the migrant is consequently seen to emerge within an orientalist imagination of "otherness"; an ambivalent figure of pity and fear that is radically different from "us" (Malkki 1996; Berry et al. 2016). This construction has been nuanced, for instance through the identification of an additional, albeit lesser, neutral news "frame" of "management" in migrant reception (Mancini et al. 2019), yet the critique of the migrant as a linguistic signifier subjected to the epistemological colonialism of western broadcasting—through the victim/threat binary—remains, nonetheless, dominant here, as also demonstrated widely in the fields of migration and media studies.[4] While these two linguistic tropes have been central to the representation of migrants in western discourse, we propose, however, that they should best be seen not as static terms but as an internally diverse field of meaning, or a discursive formation, that variously configures the semantic patterns wherein migrants appear as subjects across narrative contexts (see Benson 2013 for a similarly dynamic, albeit distinct, approach towards the "humanitarian" and "threat" frames of migration). On the one hand, research on *victimhood* encompasses two patterns of migrant representation: passivity and generality. Passivity is reflected in portrayals of the migrant as a body-in-pain that awaits to be rescued—not a social being with their own will but what Agamben (1998) calls "bare life" or "humans as animals in nature," in Owens' interpretation of his use of the term, "without political freedom" (2009: 567). Generality is manifested in portrayals of the migrant as a statistic, a mass of unfortunates in which one is indistinguishable from another. If presenting human frailty as the migrants' form of life or essential identity robs them of their agency as social beings with the capacity to speak (Hyndman 2000), grouping them together as a number, a mass of bodies, erases their individual histories and personalities (Nyers 1999). Both linguistic patterns, theorists argue, are characteristic of the logic of humanitarianism, which employs what Malkki calls a "philanthropic universalism" to convey the ethical obligation to do something about the migrants' predicament: "such representations, however, often end up portraying an undifferentiated 'raw' or 'bare' vision of humanity which works to mask the individuality of refugees, as well as the historical and political circumstances that forced them to take this identity" (1996: 288–89). As a result, these patterns end up situating migrants outside the realm of history and rationality inhabited by western humanity and render migrants less-than-human (Rajaram 2002).

On the other hand, the two main linguistic patterns identified within the critique of *threat* are: agency and malice. While the former projects the migrant no longer as a passive body but as a sovereign being, malice restricts their agency exclusively to their potential to do harm—the migrant as terrorist (Camaüer 2011). Despite their contrasting features, this construction of the agentive, malevolent terrorist is, like that of victimhood, also criticized for de-humanizing the migrant in the news. The attribution of agency gives the false impression that the migrant enjoys full autonomy when they are, in fact, largely defined by their circumstances rather than being able to make sovereign decisions: "there is," as Sandvik (2010: 294) puts it, "something unsettling about the manner in which individuals in arguably desperate or dangerous situations are attributed agency . . . as token participants performing for a global audience." The further ascription of malice simultaneously construes the migrant as a menacing stranger who puts "our" communities at risk (Moore et al. 2012). Unlike victimhood, the threat critique argues, malevolent intentionality breeds suspicion and legitimizes discourses of fear in which migrants are seen to deserve encampment and deportation (Bleiker et al. 2013). Indeed, insofar as such representational patterns establish the conditions of possibility for public discourse on migration, the trope of threat works to circumscribe this discourse within the logic of securitization, where, as O'Connell, drawing on Farrier, puts it, "the refugee and the terrorist are competing but twinned tropes that link the refugee to a 'spectral double' and legitimise or mitigate acts of violence towards non-citizens" (2020: 172).

Migrant Humanity and Journalism's Economy of Voice

While we agree with this critique of dehumanization, our own particular interest lies in the ways in which the linguistic terms of this binary work less as antithetical poles and more as complicitous equivalences. As a discursive formation, victimhood and threat do not simply substitute for one another in an either/or way but tactically alternate or co-exist with one another in ways that systematically prevent alternative vocabularies from articulating the multiple and diverse experiences of migrants as human beings: who they are, what they do, what they want, believe in, or hope to achieve. By this token, the twin notions of victimhood and threat also work to regulate our own collective response towards migrants; in Butler's words, they help shape not only "whether and how we respond to the suffering of others" but also "how we formulate moral criticisms" and "how we articulate political analyses" (2009: 64).

This performative volatility of the victim/threat binary in the news remediations of the migrant "crisis," we show in this chapter, is made possible by a journalistic *economy of voice* that organizes the news text around the question of who speaks and, in so doing, differentially distributes the capacity to speak within such a text. A common feature of western news, the absence of migrant voice from media texts, has long been a key point of criticism in relevant scholarship; as Smets and Bozdağ remark, "studies on media coverage in diverse countries show that, despite contextual differences, immigrants and refugees are mostly not allowed to speak for themselves, but are rather represented by others" (2018: 295; see also Horsti 2016; Thorbjørnsrud and Figenschou 2016). And while migrants can, in different contexts, enjoy more complex media representations (Mancini et al. 2019), we argue that, in the context of the 2015 migration "crisis," in particular, victimhood and threat work as a formation of muteness: a linguistic arrangement that, by reducing migrants to the couplet of non-individuated passivity or malevolent agency, misrecognizes migrants' as voiceless but also, because of this, as devoid of the legal, social, and historical status required to belong to a political community. Theorized through Gayatri Spivak's concept of the subaltern (1996), this linguistic muteness is tightly connected to the historical relations of colonial power that still underpin contemporary structures of global governance and is systematically expressed in the silencing of the migrant in western public discourse—a theme we will be returning to throughout this section.

For now, this relationship between voice and humanity, as we introduce it here into our analysis, relies on what Cavarero (1997), echoing Arendt, calls the "originary practice of storytelling." Narrating one's story in public, Cavarero explains, constitutes us all as "narratable selves": members of a public discourse that recognizes us as its members precisely because we are able to share our stories with others within this discourse. "Who somebody is or was," Arendt herself argues, "we can know only by knowing the story of which he is himself [sic] the hero" (1998: 186). Voice, in this account, goes beyond notions of talk as the content of speech or as a semantic event and foregrounds instead the *act of speaking* as political praxis in its own right. As Arendt again puts it, "in acting and speaking, men [sic] show who they are, reveal actively their unique personal identities and thus make their appearance in the human world" (1998: 179). It is, in other words, in the performative act of bringing people together in public space that voice becomes responsible not only for simply representing a person but also for endowing this person with the quality of humanity in the first place.

Our study of news remediations in the migration "crisis" focuses precisely on this journalistic economy of voice as the single most important mechanism of migrant misrecognition; that is, of the collective failure of western media to acknowledge migrants as worthy interlocutors of the communities those media address. Our analytical assumption is that, while misrecognition presupposes a normative conception of voice as the social capacity to speak out in contexts that validate one's narratives—what Couldry (2010) calls "voice as value"—voice in fact becomes empirically available to us (as members of the community being addressed) only through the tangible traces of the act of speaking in the surface of public discourse (Chouliaraki and Fairclough 1999; Chouliaraki 2008). Misrecognition, in this sense, leaves its semantic traces in what we call, "voice as narrative": the linguistic organization of news stories that delimits how migrants are portrayed or who speaks about/for them.

The social significance of "voice as value," that is, in Phillips' words, the "right to speak on [one's] own issues and concerns" (2003: 264), has already been widely theorized as a "fundamental human right" that requires the "voices of the voiceless" to be included in public discourse (Fraser 2010). However, our own point is that "voice as narrative" also needs to be seen as equally necessary for any normative vision of pluralist discourse to materialize. This is because it is only through the linguistic choices of speech attribution, performed as this is within the journalistic economy of voice, that speech assigns human agency to its subjects. It does so by designating not only who is a narratable self but also in what capacity the self speaks and which environment it speaks within; that is, how the self is oriented towards the publics it addresses and to what effect. Speech attribution, in this sense, contributes to sustaining the symbolic border by seeking also to control who responds and how in public discourse, rather than simply who speaks within it; not only the conditions of speaking, in other words, but those of listening, too. In our analysis of the economy of voice as a boundary-creating process, then, we draw attention to the language of journalism[5] as itself a border technology, where "others" are imagined in discourse before they appear in flesh; and in the process, we further highlight how journalism handles the most profound moral and political challenge that the symbolic border poses to western nations: our relationship to non-western "others."

Voice as Narrative: A News Content Analysis

Throughout our data collection period, which was organized over three distinct "moments" in the "crisis" of 2015 (July, September, and November),[6] news platforms across Europe, particularly those that witnessed the arrival of migrants first-hand on their soil, reported on the "crisis" daily and intensely. Our study encompasses a cross-national analysis of the online press in eight countries, plus the two main

Europe-based Arabic language online newspapers.[7] All but one of the national samples included two major online broadsheets, one representing a left-leaning and the other a right-leaning editorial stance to capture the key ideological positions of the coverage; and we looked at four newspapers in the case of the UK, two from each side of the political spectrum. Four of the countries in the study are geographically positioned along the migrant route from the Southeast towards Central and Northwestern Europe (Greece, Serbia, Hungary, and Czech Republic) and the remainder are preferred migrant destinations (Ireland, France, Germany, UK). While this choice of countries allowed us to capture a wide range of discourses on migration among national publics directly involved in the crisis, our interest here is not differences across cultures. Rather, it is the *common patterns of voice* underlying such variations that we focus on (Tesch 1990; Boeje 2002). This means that, given differences between national news cultures, newspaper affiliations, and business models, our study is about whether and how dominant narrative patterns of speech attribution appear across national platforms and in what ways they shape a shared European response that resonates with and further consolidates the logic of humanitarian security.

We use a content analytical framework on three catalytic moments of the "crisis," from June to December 2015, each of which defined public debate at its time—though not always policy-making.[8] Exemplified in detail by Georgiou and Zaborowski's thematic analysis of the news in this same period (2017), these are the moments of "careful tolerance" (early phase, July 2015), "ecstatic humanitarianism" (September 2015) and "fear and securitization" (November 2015) (Georgiou and Zaborowski 2017)[9] and, for each moment, we sampled twenty articles per newspaper—a 1,200-article data bank in total. The analysis of this material in terms of its speech attribution patterns—"voice as narrative"—is subsequently organized around the *subjects of voice* (absence or presence of migrant voice); the *status of voice* (how migrants are named and what they are characterized as); and the *context of voice* (the justifications and consequences through which we are to understand the migrants' plight).[10] Operating, as we shall see, on the basis of three common speech strategies, *silencing, collectivization,* and *decontextualization,* news narratives across Europe seriously restrict "voice as value," and produce forms of misrecognition that are key to the formation of the symbolic border, as they work to remediate and legitimize not only geopolitical hierarchies of voice but also orientalist hierarchies of human life.

The Subjects of Voice

The question of who speaks in European press stories about the migration "crisis" in Europe has one unequivocal response. It is politicians. Quotes from politicians (national or EU) were present in 66% of our 1,200-article data bank, as opposed to migrant quotes, present in only 16.6% of the articles. Despite differences among newspapers, the minority status of migrant voices compared to politicians was consistently present across all countries (Figure 4.1), appearing particularly stark in the western European press, where national politicians enjoyed a remarkably higher presence (39.2%). Even though left-wing news was more inclusive (containing 20.4% of migrant quotes compared to right-wing papers' 14.1%), thereby illustrating key differences in conceptions of democracy and civic dialogue within Europe's political spectrum, the main insight here remains the persistent gap between "our" and "their" voice, across these divisions (Mancini et al. 2019 for national/institutional differences in the study of migration news). The temporal dimension of reporting complicates this gap without fundamentally challenging it. The humanitarian phase of reporting, following the tragic news of Alan Kurdi's death (September 2015), was characterized by a 4% increase in migrant quotes, pushing their percentage from 17% to 21% during this phase.[11] Predictably perhaps, the emotional charge of the news also turned more positive, with feelings of "solidarity" rising by 2.2% (from 12.5% earlier to 14.7%) and attitudes of "understanding" increasing by 2.5% (from 7.5% to 10%; Figure 4.2). Politicians nonetheless continued to dominate: 41% of articles contained quotes from national politicians (see Benson 2013 for the link between politicians' voice and national belonging in migration news), 34% had quotes from politicians coming from other nations, and 30% had quotes from EU officials. The security phase of reporting, however, following the Paris attacks in November 2015, triggered a 9% drop in migrant quotes (from 21 to 12%) within our sample. Defined by the sharp shift in the language used about migrants from a discourse of victimhood to one of threat, this phase is marked by the silencing of

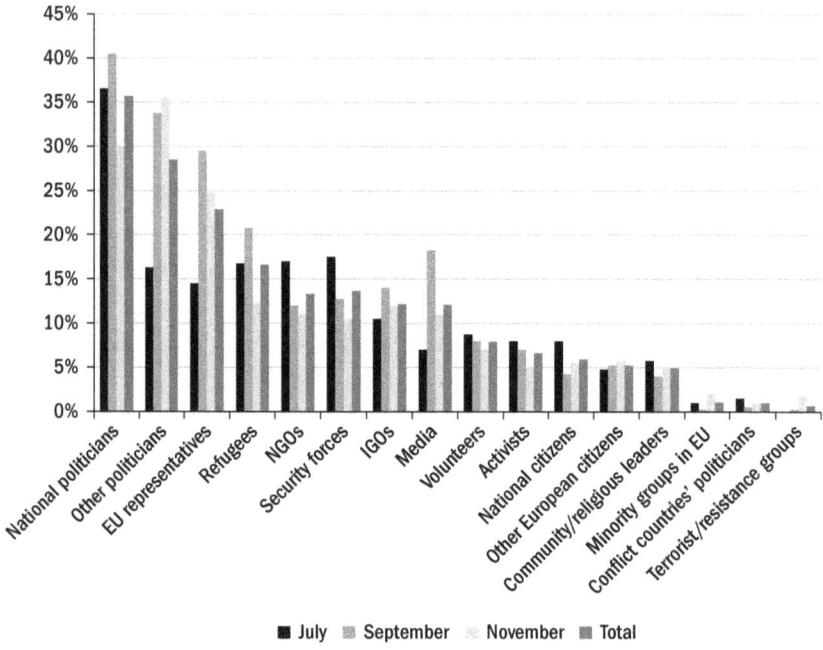

Figure 4.1. Actors quoted in articles, by period.

migrants (Figure 4.1) and a concomitant increase in negative emotion: "frustration/concern for possible security risks" rose from 10.7% to 18% and "fear" from 4% to 10%, while "solidarity" halved (from 14.7% to 7.7%; Figure 4.2). Even though this drop is explicable in light of the Paris terror events, what is most striking is a persistent chasm between elite and migrant voices that occurs regardless of the latter's naming as victims or assumed perpetrators. However migrants are characterized, in other words, they remain largely marginalized in western news. As victims, migrants are defined exclusively by their basic human needs and, as such, they are seen as unable to speak for themselves; while, defined as a threat, they are enemies of national security and hence do not deserve to speak. Either way, their exclusion from news stories confirms criticisms of the media vocabulary of migration for "othering" migrants; for misrecognizing their status as human beings.

Beyond this consistent rupture between "us" and "them," however, there is a further division within "us" between members of the elite and ordinary citizens. Together with migrants, the voice of civil society in the news was also marginalized across Europe in our database of articles (Figure 4.1). While volunteers and activists were quoted in 7.9% and 6.7% of articles respectively, NGOs were present in 13.3%. Ordinary citizens were also quoted sporadically, with 5.9% of all articles including quotes from national citizens, 5.3% the citizens of other European nations, and 1.1% minority group citizens. Despite this marginalization of civic voice, however, news stories did make regular appeals to "ordinary people" and "their emotions." Low intensity negative feelings in particular, such as "frustration" and "insecurity"—rather than the "grand" emotions of anger or fear—dominated our news articles both in the early, tolerant and late, security moments of the crisis, with "frustration" at 18%, "uncertainty" at 12.6%, and both emotions scoring lower during the humanitarian moment (Figure 4.2). This overall marginalization of citizen voice not only reduced the visibility of citizens and their views in the news, it also allowed the authoritative voices of politicians (through their direct quotes) and journalists (through their general references to

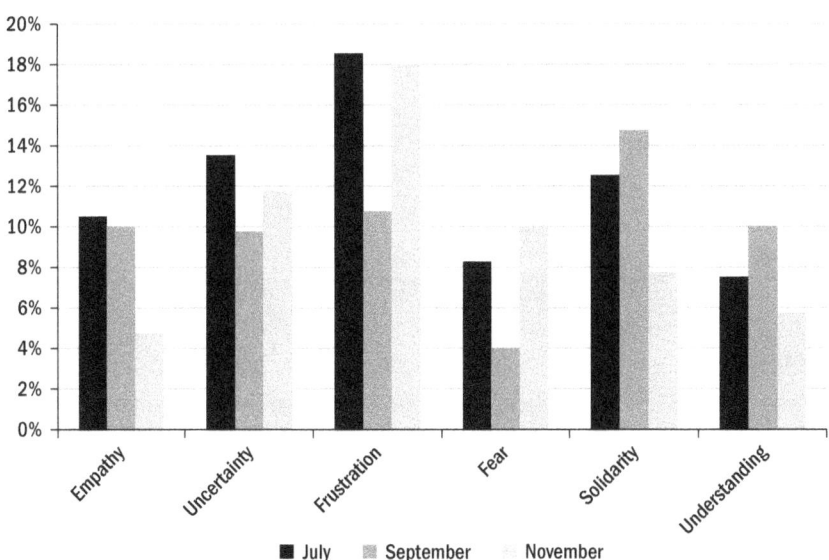

Figure 4.2. Most frequent emotions attributed to citizens concerning the refugees and the future, by period.

public affect) to control the public narrative through which western audiences made sense of the "crisis" and of new arrivals.

Even though such hierarchies of voice are more systematic features of political reporting that go beyond migration news (Benson 2013), nonetheless, this double silencing across European news in the context of the "crisis" misrecognized both migrants *and* western public as political subjects with a right to speak that could have, at least partly, challenged the status quo—for instance, by including civil society voices (such as NGO representatives) that advocate the cause of migrants. At the same time, as a result of this double silencing, the voices of the political establishment and their concomitant emotions of frustration and uncertainty assumed a naturalness that turned the migration "crisis" into an issue of technocratic calculation, while the arguments and emotions of other actors were ignored (see Georgiou and Zaborowski 2017 for national differences on this point).

The news' allocation of voice, in conclusion, was largely regulated through linguistic strategies of *silencing*, which sidelined migrant voices as well as those of European citizens and favored the voices of political elites. Even though there were gradations of silence with certain moments of reporting granting more voice to elite actors than other moments did, ultimately, this persistent hierarchy privileged arguments of the establishment and legitimized emotions of frustration and uncertainty, while squeezing out bursts of empathy and alternative stories of solidarity by or with migrants. The silencing of migrant voices is, then, the first linguistic strategy of news remediation—a strategy that excluded migrants by misrecognizing their identity as political actors. If, as Arendt argues, people assume a political status when they appear in public "in the unique shape of the body and the sound of the voice" (1998: 179), then those who remain voiceless are by definition exiled from the political sphere. They are denied the right to participate in the public debates of European publics as voices worthy of attention—if not respect or understanding. As a journalistic economy that excludes the voice of others in favor of decision-makers, the news stories of our analysis consequently also favored the phobic imagination of Eurocentric communities that neither challenged the limits of humanitarian security nor acknowledged migrants as rights-bearing actors with a story to tell.

The Status of Voice

Who are those who arrive on our shores? And what is it that they bring to European societies? Important as these questions of identity are, we hardly get to know anything about migrants through western news agendas and newsmaking. They were largely portrayed in terms of their group membership, namely their nationality (in 62% of all articles) but also, to a lesser extent, age (27%) and gender (24%). Individualizing specifics such as names and professions had the lowest frequency, included in 16% and 7% of the articles respectively (Figure 4.3).

This depersonalizing tendency towards generality persisted throughout the key moments of our study, albeit with slight variations. During the security moment, for instance, this tendency was intensified by speculation that one of the Paris killers was a just-arrived migrant, thereby highlighting a link between migrant status and terrorism while sidelining (accurate) accounts of the aggressors as home-grown terrorists. During the "ecstatic humanitarian" moment, in contrast, there was an increase in personalization, as 25.5% of articles included migrant names and 32% age. Coinciding with Alan Kurdi's death, however, this shift towards specificity might not have reflected a broader trend towards humanization but simply indicate a steep and brief rise in references to this victim's name and his family—a hypothesis supported by the lack of correlation between increase in name/age and increase in profession-related references (the latter remaining relatively stable at 7.7%, 7%, and 6.5% respectively across the three moments of the study).

This personalization of the migrant was further accompanied by an intense emotionalization in storytelling, as reflected in a significant increase in the language of solidarity (from 17.5% to 25.2%) and empathy (from 17.7% to 22%) (Figure 4.4). While this emotional peak endowed Alan with iconic status as a martyr of innocent suffering and a sign of "our" own failure to care (Ibrahim and Howarth 2016), it paradoxically did so at the expense of misrecognizing him. On the one hand, Alan's iconic status came at the cost of muteness: the absolute silence of the dead. Even though his father sought to voice the family's tragic fate, he was swiftly challenged as fake in news stories that identified him as a "human smuggler"—an accusation that discredited his story and led to his eventual silencing. On the other hand, the promise of Alan's death

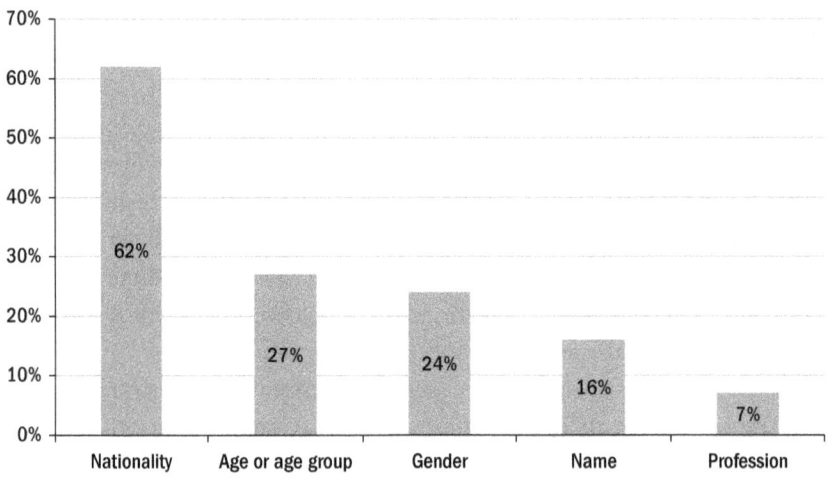

Figure 4.3. Refugee characteristics identified in the press.

to highlight the plight of migrants, denouncing Europe's "death-by-indifference" tactics on its sea borders (Basaran 2014), remained unrealized, eclipsed by the dominant voices of elite actors who, in expressing sorrow and empathy, attained their highest audibility at 40.5% in this news moment alongside Alan. Rather than rendering Alan's death a poignant occasion for European self-criticism over the continent's deadly border politics, this coupling of elite voice with empathetic emotion replaced the potential for a critical re-evaluation of Europe's border politics with sentimental pity.

The status of voice in European news narratives was, in sum, controlled by linguistic strategies of *generalization*, where migrants were narrated not as individuals but as a group. Misrecognition in the status of voice enacts the symbolic border by portraying migrants as massive flows of people rather than distinct beings and displacing responsibility for their tragedies onto the voices and emotions of selected western actors. While silencing deprived migrants of the right to speak as equals in public and resulted in their misrecognition as political subjects, here, in the status of voice, migrants were misrecognized as *social* subjects. Not only were they spoken about rather than speaking out themselves, but they were also reduced to nameless and jobless figures without "personhood"—the symbolic marker of humanity inherent in the figure of the singular and autonomous actor (Rose 1998: 2).

Unable to invite western audiences to contemplate the migrant as an ordinary person whose earlier life is now shattered by war or abject poverty, this journalistic economy constrained its publics' "imaginative mobility," a characteristic that, in Arendt's words again, offers us *"the capacity to represent the perspective of others"* as similar to, even if separate from, our own (Villa 1999: 96). Rather than turning the global shock from Alan's death into an occasion for critical reflexivity over its own responsibilities for the Mediterranean deaths (see Albahari 2015; Basaran 2014, 2015), European news reproduced narratives of migrants as pitiful but radical "others" that consolidated a predominantly Eurocentric ethos of community.

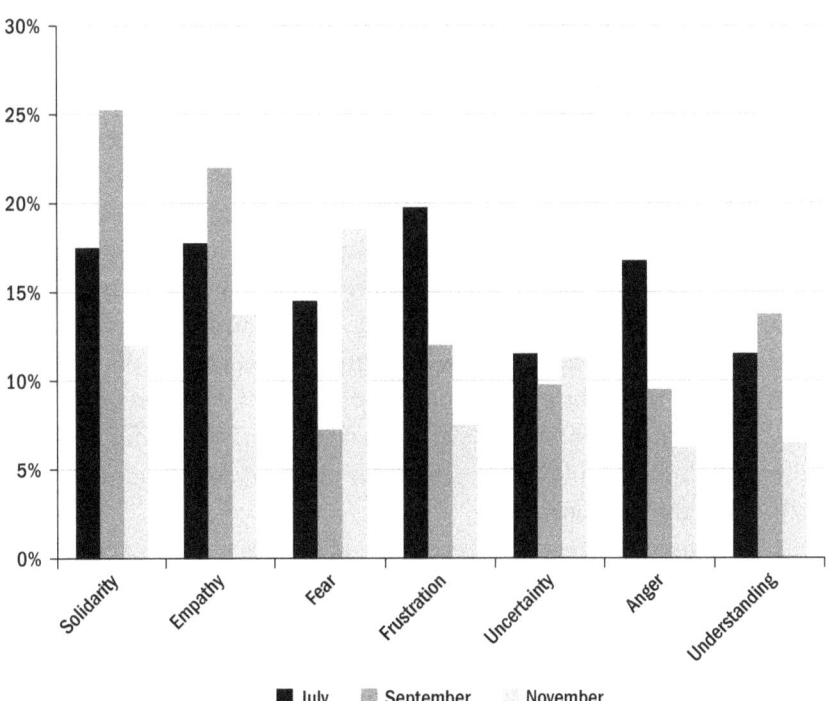

Figure 4.4. Most frequent emotions attributed to the citizens concerning the refugees' arrival and the current situation, by period.

The Contexts of Voice

Why is this migration peak taking place? What are its implications for European national communities, as well as for the migrants? These questions about the contexts of migrant voice are crucial in situating the "crisis" in a broader interpretative framework and in inviting news publics to make sense of it. Context in this news topic is, in other words, about *explanation* of the reasons why migrants were arriving on our shores and about *discussion* of the consequences of their arrival, positive as well as negative. Across the news, there was little by way of explanation as to what led migrants to leave home and endure life-endangering journeys to reach Europe: 49.4% of all articles mentioned either none or only unclear underlying reasons for the inflow. As a consequence, news stories consistently scored low in rational arguments as opposed to emotional ones expressing "solidarity" or cultivating "uncertainty" throughout the three moments of reporting—with emotional orientation appearing in 11.5% of articles (solidarity), 13.7% (uncertainty), and 6.5% (understanding). Despite passing references to the geopolitical reasons for Syrian arrivals (for instance, "fleeing war") in 43.9% of the articles, a more explicit and systematic explanation was absent. Typically, migration news and war reporting were assigned to separate news sections, thereby removing the possibility of easily providing explicit and sustained links between, say, chemical gas attacks in Syria and Syrian families' desire to flee the death zone. This failure to provide an explanatory narrative in European news might have informed the relatively low and largely unchanging percentages of empathy—the feeling for the pain of others as if we could be in their place—which remained stable at approximately 10% throughout the crisis, with no peak in the humanitarian moment, and plummeting to 4.75% after the Paris attacks.

Any discussion of consequences was, at the same time, overwhelmingly biased towards the negative, privileging notions of potential harm. A remarkable 58% of all stories employed one of four arguments against hosting migrants: geopolitical (terrorism), economic (economic crisis), cultural (antipathy towards Islam), or moral (deceit or crime) (Figure 4.5). The dominant argument referred to geopolitical consequences concerning the spread of terrorism (in 28.5% of articles in total), with

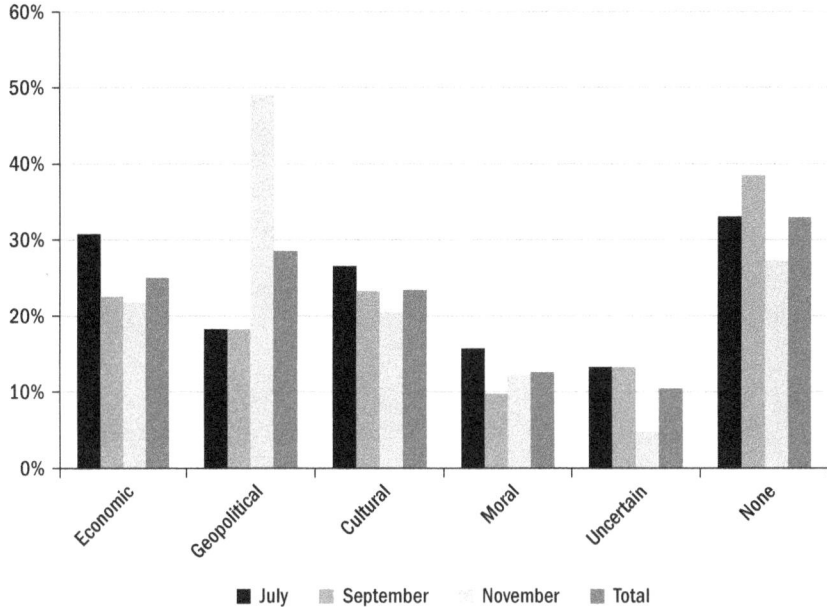

Figure 4.5. Mentions of negative consequences of refugee arrivals, by type and period.

the sharpest peak occurring after the Paris terrorist attacks (49%), while economic consequences (25% in total) were highest in the first stage of the event, July (31%). Instead of fear, however, which peaked at 10% in the security moment, this persistent negativity was accompanied by low-intensity emotions, such as "frustration," stable at 18% with a predictable fall to 10.7% in the humanitarian bracket; and "uncertainty," fluctuating between 13.5 and 11.7%—and again slightly dropping to 9.7%, after Alan's death. This consolidation of negative consequences and affects in the language of the news legitimized and reinforced a logic of symbolic bordering that construed the "other" as either an economic burden or a terrorist threat.

Positive consequences of migrant arrivals, whether geopolitical, economic, or cultural, were hardly mentioned, appearing in 8.8% of articles in total. In the context of an already information-poor narrative on the status of migrants, this proliferation of uncertainty-driven, negative language consolidated a thoroughly dehumanizing image of migrants as "only trouble."

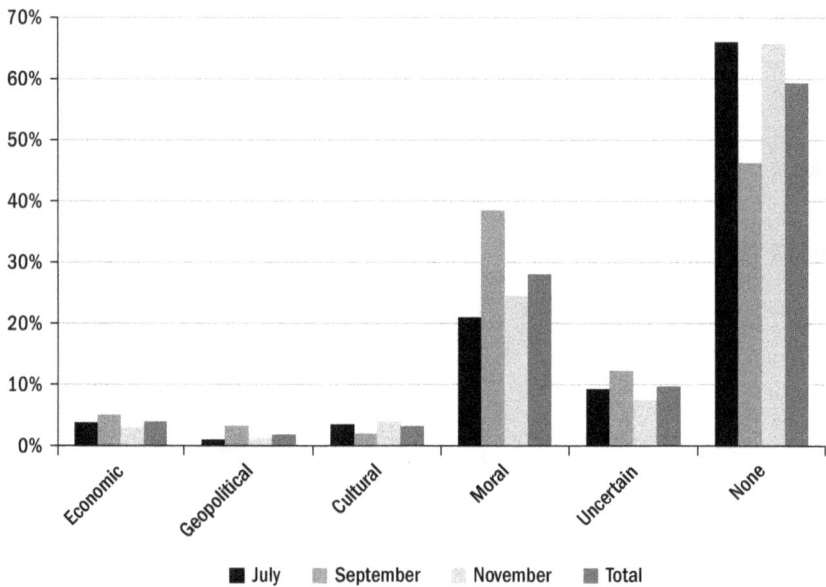

Figure 4.6. Mentions of positive consequences of refugee arrivals, by type and period.

In the absence of more complex arguments that could have demonstrated how migrants might productively become part of the workforce of European societies, the only support for a positive reception was the exclusively moral argument of European solidarity—a deontological rhetoric of "obligation to receive" that spoke of hospitality as a historical legacy of the continent: 28% of articles reproduced this rhetoric, with the percentage shooting up to 38.5% in the "ecstatic humanitarian" moment (Figure 4.6). This upward trend further correlated with news discussions about *measures* of reception, that is, specific activities of rescue and accommodation, where the European obligation to saving lives was present in as many as 71.7% of all September articles compared to 55.4% in July (Figure 4.7). While, in this Eurocentric language of benevolence, the news framed migrants as victims, the security moment of November 2015 replaced rescue with a militarized narrative of migrants as malevolent actors. Moral narratives thus dropped from 38.5% to 24.5% (Figure 4.6) and proposals for self-protective rather than life-saving measures soared: 60.7% in November as opposed to 47.2% in September (Figure 4.7).

Complementing our findings on the subjects and status of voice, our analysis of its contexts illustrates a final linguistic strategy that is at play in the symbolic border: *decontextualization*. This served to sever the connection between the migrants' arrival and their historical circumstances, thereby discouraging public discussion of the reasons for and implications of migrants' arrival. They were only rarely represented as civilians fleeing from death zones in the conflicts in Syria, Afghanistan, or Iraq, while the consequences of their arrival in Europe were almost exclusively discussed in negative terms. Lacking explanation of the causes of or benefits arising from their arrival, news stories across Europe further suppressed emotions of understanding or empathy, resorting to an abstract rhetoric of solidarity that proved unstable and short-lived in the face of complex and challenging events.

Silencing and generalization are part of a western economy of voice in that they misrecognize migrants as political and social subjects; decontextualization, we argue, operates as symbolic bordering because it misrecognizes migrants as *historical* subjects. In other words, news stories did not simply construe them as lacking personhood, or life stories like "ours," but further stripped them of the historical contexts that might

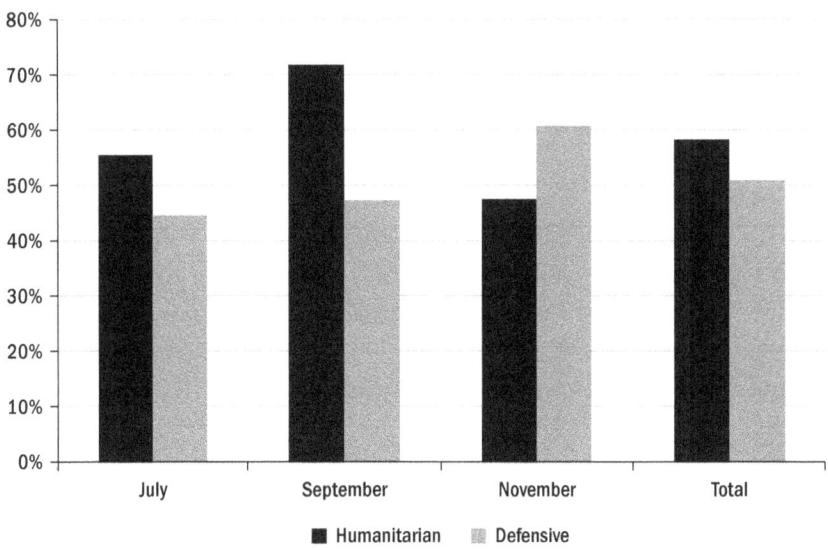

Figure 4.7. Humanitarian versus defensive actions mentioned or declared, by period.

have explained why they fled their homelands and found themselves on "our" shores. If, as Arendt puts it, having a history means that "every individual life . . . can eventually be told as a story with beginning and end" (1998: 184–85), then depriving migrants of the narrative space to tell their own stories also cuts them off from their own historical predicament and individual biographies.

The News Economy of Voice as Symbolic Border

Instrumental to the performance of both the territorial and the symbolic border is the question of voice. While, as our Chapter 1 showed, the territorial border mobilizes its techno-symbolic assemblage to establish a hierarchical ordering of voices in the site of migrant reception, the island of Chios, the symbolic border, we have argued here, is constituted through the linguistic performativity of news storytelling. It was, in particular, an orientalist economy of voice that decided who spoke in the news and in what capacity and, in so doing, regulated whether and how the actors of the border might have been listened to in public as voices of equals. Our study focused, in particular, on voice as narrative—that is, how the language of news regulates patterns of speech attribution and how, in the process, it mobilizes "voice as value," endowing migrants with audibility and "recognizability" (Butler 2009). Concentrating on the similarities rather than differences across our 1,200 articles in our cross-national analysis, we made two key observations about the nature of voice as an orientalist device of news storytelling. First, the distribution of voice in European news on the "crisis" followed a *strict hierarchy*—one that relied on specifically journalistic *strategies of bordering*, yet reflected and reproduced broader hierarchies of life in European political spheres. Second, this hierarchy of voice led to a *triple misrecognition of migrants* as political, social, and historical actors, and it is these subtle forms of misrecognition that mundanely sustained their subalternity, that is their symbolic exclusion from "our" communities of belonging.

The first significant, albeit perhaps predictable, insight of our analysis is the use of silencing as a strategy for legitimizing a particular *hierarchy of voices*, whereby political voices dominated news journalism at the expense of those of citizens and migrants. National politicians, followed by

European and international leaders, were the most audible voice in crisis news. While this supports the claim of existing research that "in institutionally driven news, political institutions set the agendas of news organizations" (Lawrence 2000: 9), it also thematized the moral function of elite quotes in the news, namely to maintain a sense of control and normality in the midst of crisis (Pickering 2001). The cost of normalization, however, was that it collapsed public discourse to the voice of its ruling actors and squeezed out alternatives, in this particular instance marginalizing the testimonies and emotions of citizens and migrants.

The marginalization of *citizen* voice points to long-established deficiencies in the structure of broadsheet news, which, as Ross puts it, "privileges elite and other (white) male voices" that, in turn, "appear to exert a greater influence and conformity over who 'counts' as an authoritative voice" (2007: abstract). The marginalization of *migrant* voice reflects a similar narrative structure of exclusion, which worked by simply ignoring the stories of those it did not already regard as part of "us" while, in doing so, it consolidated their exclusion. Despite sharing a common exclusion from the news as non-elite voices, migrants nonetheless differed radically from citizens in that the latter are a foundational component of the west's liberal democratic polities, while the former remained alien—they are the west's "other." The distinction is succinctly captured by Arendt's critique of human rights as comprising the rights of citizens only, so that, for those who become stateless, as she puts it, "the abstract nakedness of being nothing but human was their greatest danger" (1976: 300). At the heart of the dehumanization of the stateless, Arendt continues, lies precisely this structural failure to be seen and heard in public as actors with a voice. It is, we claim, because of its failure to represent migrants' voice "in public" and so to establish potentially humanizing, even if fleeting, encounters between "them" and "us" that European news journalism operated as a symbolic border.

Indeed, this failure of the journalistic economy of voice was not simply a matter of silencing. It was, as we have established, a matter of a more complex linguistic dynamics, involving strategies of generalization and decontextualization. *Pace* relevant literature—which presents this vocabulary of victim/threat as responsible for the "muteness" of migrants, showing them as always silent in the media—our own analysis started from the discursive volatility of the migrant as victim or threat in order to unpack muteness as a broader problem of voice in the context of the migrant as subaltern: a social position from which the post-colonial subject cannot be heard. Our interrogation of the textual properties of "voice as narrative," namely subject (who speaks), status (with what authority) and context (in which circumstances), aimed to demonstrate precisely how these three linguistic strategies worked to regulate the distribution of migrant voice in the news in ways that led to this muteness, and so to what we have identified as a *triple misrecognition of migrants*.

It is, as we saw, either by way of subordination to elite voices (subjects of voice), denial of their individuality (status), or emptying out their biographical continuity (context) that these stories denied migrants the capacity to speak to audiences that might listen to and value their claims. By being deprived of this capacity, their "voice as value," migrants were also further denied the possibility to be seen and validated as political actors, for they did not speak in public; as social actors, for they were not seen as having "our" familiar webs of social relationships; or as historical actors, for they are cut off coherent life narratives with a beginning and an end. If, to recall Cavarero (1997), the fundamental question of recognition is "Who are you?," then, the response of "our" media is "nobodies": mute groups of "others" devoid of personhood or history.

By the same token, "we" become who we are through "our" encounter with those "others." Our identity depends in part on how we respond to the existential question that this encounter poses to us: "Who are you?" Confronted with "them," European news responded to this question by abruptly shifting from pitying the victims to denouncing the terrorists. Despite the spike of tender-heartedness, which reflected a moment of grief and guilt over the death of the Syrian toddler, Alan Kurdi, western newsmakers overall were reluctant to encourage their audiences to engage in open and curious encounters with migrants and their predicament. Instead, this contingent expression of empathy, combined with increasing uncertainty (Gottlob and Boomgaarden 2019) and ongoing campaigns of ethnocentric fear (Wodak 2015; Krzyżanowski et al. 2018), sustained an erratic emotional orientation towards migrants that gravitated towards a Eurocentric ethos of introverted defensiveness. As Leurs and Smets put it, despite images of sinking ships and drowned bodies, where "Europeans occasionally get confronted with the spectacle of human tragedy," ultimately, "there was limited attention for the background story" (2018: 4).

This chapter has offered an insight into how the symbolic border emerges as a linguistic effect of news storytelling in the 2015 migration "crisis." The language of the news, we demonstrated, is not disengaged from the territorial border. Rather, the journalistic economy of voice reproduces and consolidates the same geopolitical logic of humanitarian security that we had encountered in the Greek island of Chios; in the online national press and on screen, we identified a similar framework through which the voices of the already marginalized were suppressed or fully excluded, reproducing orientalist hierarchies of human life. Just like the language of journalism, its imagery also participates actively in the remediations of the digital border and so in the reproduction of the symbolic boundaries between "us" and "them." How news images do their own bordering work; how, that is, their performativity works as a practice of exclusion across national news sites is the question we answer in the next chapter.

5

Visibility and Responsibility in News Imagery

This chapter continues to investigate the question of how processes of journalistic remediation enact the symbolic border by switching its focus from news stories to news imagery. The two, language and images, work always together as the multimodal semiotic repertoire through which the hierarchical distinctions of "us" and "them" are produced and amplified across media pages and screens. But each semiotic mode has its own particular economy of representation—that is, its own way of organizing the meaning-making practices of journalism around certain normative discourses about who migrants are and how we should respond towards them.

Our contention is that, while language was organized around an orientalist economy of voice that regulated how, if at all, migrants might be endowed with the quality of humanity, imagery operated through an economy of visibility that enacts and so proposes normative relations of western responsibility towards them. It is this performative norm of responsibility that forms the conceptual center of this chapter. The question of humanity, as before, continues to inform our analysis of how photojournalistic and social media imagery operates, in that relations of responsibility always rely on some conception of who is human enough to deserve the responsive action of others; the vocabularies of victimhood and threat, for instance, are criticized precisely on the grounds that, by de-humanizing migrants, they also prevent the question of what action could make a difference to them from being posed (Berry et al. 2016; Georgiou and Zaborowski 2016). Entitled "A Conspiracy of Neglect," Amnesty International's 2015 annual report similarly raised this question of humanity, when it castigated "the neglect of the international community in the face of this human suffering" (that is, the migrant "crisis") and urged nation-states around the world "to renew their commitment to international responsibility-sharing" (Amnesty International 2015). While the question of responsibility is officially resolved in Europe's discourse of humanitarian security by offering care yet ultimately keeping migrants outside the continent, our main concern is with the news representation of responsibility in the visual practices of journalism as a key remediation platform of the digital border.

The main question within the economy of voice was "who speaks" but within the economy of visibility the question we identify instead is "what to do" in the face of images of precariousness and suffering. As migrants find themselves sea crossing in fragile dinghies or confined in squalid camps at the outer edges of Europe, we ask how the visual practices of news photography, in representing the migrants' plight, enact performances of responsible agency—of whether and how we may care—but also how such performances, amplified by social media, make proposals of ideal citizenship to their viewing publics (Chouliaraki 2006). As before, we view visual texts as constitutive dimensions of the symbolic border, yet we avoid clustering their meaning-making patterns in binaries of "empathetic" or "fearful" imagery and instead concentrate on pictorial representation as a discursive formation: that is, a fluid, albeit always regulated, space where the migrant appears as an ambivalent figure and where competing ethico-political proposals for civic responsibility for the migrant's plight also emerge. While, as seen in our previous chapter, such proposals inevitably orientalize and "other" migrants, our focus in this chapter shifts from the condition of the depicted towards the politicizing impact that they potentially have on the publics that view them. How are "we," western viewers, invited to relate to migrants? What normative dispositions of responsibility towards migrants do these images articulate? What do such dispositions tell us about the ways in which news imagery operates as a pedagogy of responsibility? And how, in so doing, does it reproduce or challenge the symbolic border?

Our analysis draws on the same data pool as Chapter 5, but we now focus on newspaper front-page images from five European countries (Greece, Hungary, Italy, Ireland, and UK). We use these to construct a typology of migrant visualities, each of which performs a different form of responsible citizenship towards migrants, from monitorial (just watching) to empathetic (feeling for) to self-reflexive (what could I have done?). Yet, we argue, none of these tropes enables "us," news publics, to engage with migrants as actors endowed with their own humanity. Those depicted, we conclude, remain subaltern within a symbolic border that acknowledges their existence in various ways yet denies them the possibility to appear as fully human. In order to represent these people with humanity and voice, we conclude, news images need to shift the way they conceive of and perform responsibility. They need, we suggest, to move beyond a notion of what Silverstone calls, "formal" responsibility, that is "the responsibility I have for my own acts, those aspects of life and deed which I can be held accountable for" (2006: 152), towards the notion of what he, after Jonas (1984), refers to as "substantial" responsibility: "responsibility for the condition of the other" (2006: 152). While the former enables action at the cost of depriving migrants of humanity and voice, the latter bears the potential for migrant "narratability": visual representations that enable migrants to appear with their own life contexts, past and present, and so connect their lives with ours.

News Journalism and Its Economy of Visibility

The economy of visibility, just like that of voice, has also been criticized for representing migrants through the binary of victimhood and threat. Collective and anonymous representations of migrants as either young Black men or as precarious families emphasize their racialized and gendered "otherness" as intimidating enemies or needy sufferers (Bleiker et al. 2013). There is, within this binary, no subaltern discursive space for contemplating a more complex, even if still constrained, civic role for the viewers of news; for, as Chouliaraki has argued, "the agency of spectators to engage in public speech about the suffering [of others] depends on the humanization of the sufferers" (2006: 88). While this argument is central to critiques of the news' economy of visibility in the relevant literature (Wright 2002; Krzyżanowski et al. 2018; Wilmott 2017), we here contend that the negative rhetoric over the role visual representation plays in journalism is not simply a matter of the western economy of visibility (Gynnild 2017; Ilan 2018) but lies at the heart of broader legacies of western theory, in both Photography and Security Studies—legacies upon which the news' economy of visibility itself has come to rely.

We begin with the canon of Photography Theory, which theorizes the represented and their spectators as existing in a relationship of passivity or suspicion (Barthes 1977; Berger 1973). This static conception is grounded in the context of late nineteenth-century photography and its uses "for the purpose of surveillance, regulation and categorization" (Sturken and Cartwright 2009: 106), but this discourse of distrust remained prevalent throughout the twentieth century in dominant understandings of the gaze itself, the act of looking at images, as an act of control: "not something one performs but a relation in which one is caught up" (Sturken and Cartwright 2009: 442). Sontag's influential argument asserts, for instance, that photographs of suffering work to either numb our sensibilities (1977) or incite sentimental emotion (2004) and that in both cases they do little to enable their publics to act on the predicament of the depicted; in Hariman and Lucaites' critical account, "photographs" for Sontag, "either beautify and thereby 'can bleach out a moral response' or uglify and thereby can at most be provocative [. . .] in any case, they 'cannot dictate a course of action' and instead 'supply only an initial spark'" (2016: 8). Despite a recent shift towards more agentive conceptions of photography (Azoulay 2008), digital photojournalism is, nonetheless, still predominantly seen to participate in a global market of visual consumption, which delivers "naked humanity": "images of suffering" as Ibrahim claims, "are being calibrated through the act of sharing and gaining attention through networks which recommend and tag posts" (2019: 3).

At the same time, Visual Security Studies, a field that engages with the link between aesthetics and politics (Bleiker 2019), focuses on the role of images in shaping processes of securitization on a national and global scale: "such practices," as Vuori and Saugmann say, "attempt to direct understandings of security through the manipulation of what the security apparatus looks like, and by controlling representations of it" (2018: 11). Whereas images are also seen to be always polysemic and intertextual, encompassing a range of possible meanings (Hansen 2011), nonetheless, the hegemonic understanding in the field remains that the political function of the visual is a more negative one—as is also the case within Photography Studies. Photojournalism participates here in the symbolic construction of threats and dangers by the "others" of the nation-state and, as Axel Heck says, in this way enables "extraordinary political measures (from public surveillance to so-called enhanced interrogation techniques and military interventions) to secure the endangered referent object" (2018: 1). Exploring the visual representations of migrants in the Australian press, Bleiker et al. similarly conclude that their "visual patterns reinforce a politics of fear that explains why refugees are publicly framed as people whose plight, dire as it is, nevertheless does not generate a compassionate political response" (2013: 398).

Even though we partly concur with this criticism, we also depart from it, claiming rather that the discursive formation within which visual representations of the migrant emerge is governed neither by the singular logics of passive spectator or security-driven imagery, nor by binary structures of victimhood/threat. Instead, it is the relatively fluid coexistence and substitutability of different signifiers (including but not fully reduced to the above) that regulate the boundary of inside/outside and, in so doing, variously invite the addressees of the visual discourse to engage with its meanings across the space-times of the symbolic border. The news' economy of visibility should in this sense be seen as "inherently ambivalent," as Chouliaraki puts it: "it is positive because we can only relate to the 'other' on the condition that we are already constituted as free subjects," and so we consciously and selectively draw on our existing visual resources; and "it is also negative because the systemic 'bias' across types of news ultimately reproduces an exclusively western sensibility" that may reinforce the "othering" of those depicted (2006: 66). The possibility for some form of conditional agency within this regulative discourse, where news publics may navigate their own position as responsible citizens vis-à-vis the migrant's plight, lies precisely in this ambivalent conception of visuality as a discursive formation.

Azoulay's theorization of photography in terms of "civic duty" (2008) relies on this ethical and political potential of photography as a form of "social contract" between those who are depicted and those who witness them. News publics, as Azoulay (2008: 93–4) puts it, have a "civic duty toward the photographed persons," which does not pre-exist the image but is constituted through the photographic encounter itself. As Carville explains, civic duty emerges "because of the active address towards the spectator by the represented that Azoulay identifies in photography as a political space through which the recognition of citizenship takes place" (2010: 357). This performative understanding of civic duty as a tension between pictorial address and spectatorial agency fully resonates with our own approach to the symbolic border as an assemblage of mediations that entails forces of both domination and active resistance. We thus approach the journalistic economy of visibility as a relatively open political space which, in communicating news about migration, also performs a pedagogy of civic responsibility that raises questions about who the migrant is and what "we" can do about them. What conceptions of responsible action informs this approach?

Responsibility: A Conceptual and Analytical Vocabulary

In assessing the moral significance of the imagery of migrants, literature on the visual representation of the migrant as a sufferer is largely negative. It rightly assumes that the dominant visual tropes fail to make proposals of responsible agency to their audiences, yet it does not go further to explore the conceptual connections between visualization and responsibility, nor does it appreciate the historicity of this relationship as the symbolic properties of the visual transform across time. The current literature thus is unable to help us think through how the visualization of responsibility is performed and what it might achieve in the context of the migration "crisis." Despite this under-theorization of responsibility within Visual Studies scholarship, the concept, in fact, figures prominently in literature on Media Ethics (see Keane 2003; Silverstone 2006; Tomlinson 2011).

It is, in particular, Silverstone's account of "mediated communication" as a space within which "an ethics of care and responsibility is, or is not, enabled" (2002: 761) that thematizes the relationship between responsibility and the media. Developing a normative account of ethics, Silverstone draws attention to two pathologies of responsibility, both of which suppress the potential for civic agency towards those who are vulnerable: complicity, which is about "us" taking for granted, rather than problematizing, media representations of human vulnerability; and collusion, which is about "us" treating the predicament of those others with complacency or denial. Collusion locates responsibility for in/action in the "active audience" and its practices of forgetting, while complicity focuses on "the vocabulary and discourse of representation, narrative and report" (Silverstone, 2006: 131)—including, of course, visual discourse. Even though the two pathologies are interrelated, Silverstone insists on the importance of recognizing complicity as the specifically symbolic work of dehumanization performed by the media, in their effort to manage their audiences' vicarious trauma as they witness the pain of "distant others." As they encounter mediated scenes of suffering, then, complicity here works by helping audiences to "translate the properly challenging other both into the comforting frames of the familiar and into excommunicated banishment" (2002: 777).

Silverstone's moral frames of "the familiar" and of "excommunicated banishment" are clearly associated with our binary of dehumanization: victimhood, which brings the suffering other close to "our" heart, and threat, which places them at maximum distance. Silverstone goes further, however, in explaining the moralizing function of these claims in terms of the media's psychological mechanism to protect audiences from emotional trauma. Using the reductive figures of victim and evildoer, he claims, media representations fulfill "our" "desire for simplicity, comfort and order in our everyday lives" (Silverstone 2002: 777). The dehumanization of migrants is, thus, causally connected to a conception of responsibility as "working through"—responsibility that, in its care to protect "us" instead of "them," subjects migrants to a "process of repression . . . not eradicating them but placing them elsewhere" (Ellis 1999: 58).

While Silverstone's critique of mediation rightly focuses on "complicity and collusion" as failures of responsibility, it stops short of opening up two key dimensions of performative visibility: one, conceptual, and the other, methodological. First, his critique does not explicitly establish the conceptual connection between these failures and the embeddedness of mediation in the historical power relationships of viewing. In turning the (relatively) safe west into the object of protection and treating suffering "others" as hurtful spectacles, media visualities construe the depicted into a visual subaltern and perpetuate an ethnocentric ethics that keeps "others" outside of "our" sphere of responsibility (Chouliaraki 2006). Second, despite its appreciation of representation, Silverstone's critique does not engage with the meaning-making function of the image. In so doing, it fails to appreciate what in the Introduction of this book we theorized as the malleability and historicity of the symbolic border: its potential to go beyond dominant visual tropes to offer alternative options for responsibility.

Unlike this approach, which relies on pre-existing suppositions about what responsibility might look like or how it works, our approach turns the concept on its head. So, instead of defining responsibility in terms of given pathologies of mediation, we mobilize responsibility as a heuristic term that enables us to explore how the concept is discursively used to invest the various visualities of the migration "crisis" with distinct moral claims to action. We argue that it is these performative claims to responsibility that, in turn, cumulatively work to establish the normative horizon of the symbolic border, that is the horizon within which we are invited to make judgments (collusive, complicit, or other) on what we see and how we relate to it. Our analysis again goes beyond the binary tropes of victimhood and threat, subsuming photojournalistic representation within a broader economy of visibility through which the actors of the border are variously constituted in the media as subaltern or responsible citizens—what we refer to as migrant "visualities." If we use the term *visibility*, then, to refer to the normative horizon that regulates what we see and how we relate to it in news photojournalism, *visuality*, as Mirzoeff puts it, is the empirical domain of images wherein the "struggle over who is to be represented" and how, is played out (2006: 76). From this perspective, regimes of visuality constitute our principal analytical unit in that, as we show just below, they provide the organizing frames through which migrants emerge as objects of civic responsibility for western audiences—though how exactly these audiences engage with such frames or not remains a distinct empirical question.

Visualities of Responsibility

Informed by the same empirical study of migrant news across Europe as the previous chapter, our analysis of online front-page imagery from the two dominant broadsheets of five countries (Greece, Italy, Hungary, UK, and Ireland), 51 images in total, keeps its focus on the same three key moments of the "crisis" as before. Employing a semiotic analysis that was guided by questions of how migrants are portrayed in these images and who or what appears to act with or on them, we proceeded by mapping out the meaning-making patterns, or regimes of visuality, through which relationships of responsibility are enacted in each one of the front pages. Our analysis progressed in an iterative movement of reading, provisional image classifications, and further refinement to the point of data saturation. In the process, we came to develop insights about associational patterns and significant relationships, which we eventually crystallized around five visual frames: what we discuss below as monitorial, empathetic, securitized, hospitable, and posthumanitarian responsibility.

The assumption behind this five-part typology is that its empirically grounded frames stand in a relationship of tension to theory; they are not reflections of a universal norm of responsibility, but neither are they random singularities. They are typifications of dominant visualities, which work to collectivize, victimize, or vilify migrants and, for this reason, stand as illustrations of broader strategies of representation across the national press cultures under study—strategies that, as we saw in the previous chapter, echo and perpetuate the geopolitics of humanitarian security. In this sense, our categories have the status of what Flyvbjerg calls "paradigmatic cases" of research: "cases that highlight more general characteristics of the societies in question" (2005: 16). It is to these paradigmatic visualities of the symbolic border that we now turn.

Monitorial Responsibility

Images that depict people on fragile dinghies or in humanitarian camps situate migrants within a visuality of biological life—a field of representation that, let us recall, reduces their human life to corporeal existence and the needs of the body (Agamben 1998). This biological subjectivity entails a thin notion of humanity as an "anthropological minimum" (Mehta 1990), a subaltern humanity reliant on western emergency aid or rescue operations to survive and so dispossessed of will and voice. Insofar as migrants are portrayed as life to be governed, this visuality can be thought of as biopolitical: a form of symbolic power that produces human bodies as "living matter," subject to the humanitarian benevolence of the west. Even though these bodies are deeply political, in that they emerge at the intersection of corporeal and geopolitical relations of power between the west and the global South, they lack civic status; their dehumanization can, in this sense, be seen as an effect of these very power relations that claim to sustain them as human bodies, in the first place (Ticktin 2011a).

Which proposals of responsibility does biopolitical humanity articulate? This visuality of long-distance shots and collectivized representations situates migrants and their news viewers in a relationship of what Boltanski calls "generalised pity"—a relationship with human suffering "from the standpoint of distance, since it must rely upon the massification of a collection of unfortunates who are not there in person" (1999: 13). Characteristic of international news, in the imagery of UN camps and/or boats floating in the Mediterranean, this visual distance of the audience from migrants invites a "monitorial" relationship with those it depicts. It simply registers the facts of their existence and offers minimal context for their suffering. The news narratives that frame them, for instance, hardly connect the exodus of Syrian migrants from their country with the escalation of the Syrian conflict.[1] With no causal link between these two, the "crisis" is, as in our content analysis, decontextualized and so portrayed as a sudden event that simply fell upon the continent, as a humanitarian emergency (Calhoun 2004), rather than as a failure of long-term international politics and western wars in the broader Middle Eastern region. Schudson's concept of "monitorial" citizenship that, as opposed to fully informed citizenship, refers to ". . . the obligation of citizens to know enough to participate intelligently in government affairs," captures this sensibility of light-touch scanning through the news that enables a vague awareness of the plight of migrants but invites no reflexive engagement with the contexts and conditions of this suffering.

Empathetic Responsibility

In contrast to biological life, empathetic responsibility is about intimate snapshots of individuals or couples, such as a crying child, a mother with her baby, or a rescue worker in action. While, in the previous category, collectivization takes the perspective of distance and ignores the uniqueness of people as persons, this is a photojournalism of individuation that adopts a close-up perspective and has the potential to offer a more humanized representation of migrants.

It is the imagery of the child that above all figures as emblematic of the individualized visualities of empathy (Al-Ghazzi 2019). The epitome of innocent vulnerability, the child has historically operated as an instrument in mobilizing tender-hearted care and parental love in particular: "children dramatize the righteousness of a cause," Moeller claims, "by having their innocence contrasted with malevolence (or perhaps banal hostility) of adults in authority" (2002: 39). The photograph of the lifeless body of toddler Alan Kurdi, the Syrian boy who drowned on the coast of Turkey in September 2015, gained iconic status precisely as a signifier of paradigmatic adult failure, the failure to offer protection to a child (El-Enany 2016). It is this sense of failure that challenged the western self-description of the caring parent and, let us recall, shifted the news narrative of the "crisis" towards sentimental pity—a self-oriented emotion that both castigates "us" for this exceptional tragedy and celebrates "ourselves" as a benevolent public showing empathetic emotion for a distant victim (Mortensen and Trenz 2016: 350).

Despite the humanizing potential inherent in the individuation of suffering, however, child imagery is at the same time held accountable for infantilizing migrants: depicting them predominantly as distressed, clueless, and powerless. "Children," as Burman puts it, ". . . plead, they suffer, and their apparent need calls forth help," echoing "the colonial paternalism where the adult-Northerner offers help and knowledge to the infantilized-South" (1994: 241). Infantilization may thus aim at mobilizing empathy in the name of "our" common humanity, yet, in portraying migrants as children-in-need, it ultimately deprives them of their complex and often tragic biographies and their social positioning within global geopolitics; as al-Ghazzi (2019) observes, casting adults in the figure of a child works to establish ahistorical subjects that "speak beyond the complexities of geopolitics; war, and ideology." What form of responsibility does this visuality make possible? This is the responsibility of charity, which encourages dispositions of compassion, yet, in doing so, also signals the "otherness" of migrants—their subalternity captured in the lifeless body of the young boy, fleetingly heart-breaking yet not "ours" to grieve and memorialize. This ambivalent agency ultimately constitutes a moralizing response towards migrants, which can momentarily inspire affective responses of guilt but ultimately remains ephemeral and unstable, swiftly shifting into the rival affective moods of indignation or fear.

Responsibility of Security

Visualities of threat, peaking after the November 2015 Paris attacks, consist of masses of migrants walking along motorways on the Balkan route or squeezed in rescue boats; and of Black and Brown young men wearing balaclavas and participating in riot scenes. Characterized by both collectivization, as in biological life, and singularization, as in victimhood, this category nonetheless differs from the previous two in thematizing not empathy but fear—anxieties that "our" social order is disturbed by racial and cultural "others" (Gale 2004).

Instrumental in the mobilization of fear is the shift from imageries of the child towards what Buchanan et al. call "threatening young males" (2003: 9) who appear to trespass "our" own safe space. In contrast to portrayals of bodies-in-pain as signifiers of common humanity, visualities of threat rely on the racialization of migrants, where skin color and clothing operate as signifiers of evil "otherness" in "our" midst—also reflected in animalistic references to "swarms," "flocks," or "cockroaches" in news narratives (Balabanova and Balch 2020). These visualities reproduce what Willoughby-Herard calls "racialised knowledge of the non-white/western/European, Black African 'Other'" (2015), in that they constitute those "others" as deviant from the implicit norm of whiteness behind western economies of visibility. While, in sum, the emotional proximity to crying children casts migrants as objects of care, the physical proximity of dark-skinned men turns them into what Boltanski, after Arendt, calls "les enragés," intimidating "others" who threaten "our" safety (Boltanski 1999).

What form of responsibility does this visuality make possible? This is a responsibility of security: a form of responsibility that prioritizes the wholesale closing of borders over acts of hospitality for victims of war. While military security is a constitutive dimension of the sovereign power of the nation-state, we can here see how, by producing biopolitical distinctions between the human and its "others," news narratives also participate in the sovereign politics of security. They do so insofar as their visualities recurrently legitimize collective dispositions of "permanent vigilance" against what Chandler calls "global insecurities" (2010: 296) and sanction policies of lethal sea patrols and barbed wire along the coast of Europe.

The implication of this form of responsibility is thus not only the vilification of those who are not like "us" but also our own subjection to a regime of self-responsibility, where "our" well-being cannot co-exist with the safety of migrants but is fully antithetical to it. The popularity of visualities of threat and their populist "stop migration" politics, for instance, relies precisely on this biopolitics of responsibility as a zero-sum game of incompatible options, where the crying child is swiftly replaced by "the bearded male migrant" and so "rather than compassion, ... elicits feelings of apprehension and fear" (El-Enany 2016: 14).

Responsibility to Hospitality

In direct contrast to the visuality of threat, the visuality of hospitality involves imagery of pro-migrant protests across Europe, notably the "Migrants Welcome" marches in September 2015. Images of these depict masses of citizens marching across city centers, holding banners or placates with messages such as "migrants welcome here," "migrants are human beings," "let them in," "be human," "20,000? Are you joking?" etc. Such images of concerted action represent acts of hospitality, defined by Silverstone as acts of "welcoming the other in one's space, with or without any expectation of reciprocity" (2006: 139). In combining the affirmative posture of conviviality–"let them in"—with the critical spirit of denunciation against "our" decision-makers—"are you joking?," a reference to the UK's low quota of migrant admissions—visualities of hospitality, we argue, work through a reversal of humanization. In contrast to threat, which sets "us" up against evil "others," visualities of hospitality place "us" in the position of the evil-doer; it is now "our" politicians who harm migrants rather than the other way around. The redistribution of the figures of pity and its concomitant problematization of the victim/threat binary are typical of activist agency: a form of civic agency that criticizes the establishment and aims to "help create visibility for the perspectives and experiences of marginalised groups" (Polletta 2006).

At the same time, however, even though the physical presence of migrants may occasionally figure in these visualities, for instance marching along wearing an "I'm a migrant" T-shirt, migrants are themselves largely absent. They may be linguistically recognized as human on protest banners, but their humanity is undermined by their invisibility as political actors. Despite having important stories to share, they are deprived of what Arendt calls "the relevance of speech" (1968/1998: 297) and have become interchangeable and unseen. Mediated hospitality is, in this sense, primarily symbolic; it is enacted through the portrayal of discursive claims to the humanity of migrants while reserving the humanizing capacity of public visibility to local actors.

The form of responsibility that the visuality of hospitality proposes is, consequently, an ambivalent responsibility of transnational solidarity; one that, as Harney puts it, temporarily "resolves the moral ambiguity of this threatening encounter through the welcoming performance" (2017: 236) yet, at the same time, takes place within the securitizing framework of the nation-state. In other words, even though the visuality of hospitality, by drawing on the repertoire of civil society, is indeed the only politicized form of solidarity present in the news, its grammar is not without its own tensions. Insofar as it occurs on behalf of rather than together with migrants, this visuality subjects the latter to the subaltern condition, where the defense of their rights takes place at the cost of marginalizing their presence and voice. Thus, despite its public intervention in favor of international law and in support of migrants, the responsibility of transnational solidarity may nonetheless be subjecting migrants to what Paik (2016) calls "epistemological violence": in the name of politicizing their case, marginalized groups are inevitably entangled with western practices and discourses that tend to perpetuate their own exclusion.

Post-Humanitarian Responsibility

Two different types of imagery participate in this visuality: *celebrity benevolence*, which is marked by a "show business" aesthetic, and *social media graphics*, characterized by an inventive reflexivity. The former involves images of celebrities in support of migrants—for example, Angelina Jolie, Vanessa Redgrave, or Susan Sarandon visiting the Greek islands. These images are characterized by a focus on the celebrity figure surrounded by migrants, in camps or beaches, hugging, helping, or talking to them. The images thus capitalize on the representation of co-presence so as to transfer symbolic capital from the famous and prestigious celebrity to the anonymous and precarious migrant, with a view to raising awareness for their predicament and claiming recognition for their cause (Sandvik 2010). Embodying an "aspirational" form of agency, these images perform solidarity not only by giving voice to the suffering of migrants but also by routinely educating "us" into compassionate ways of feeling and acting at a distance (Chouliaraki 2013). By depicting the physical performance of such dispositions of compassionate care, celebrity visualities act as metonymies of empathetic publics at large, inviting their viewers to engage with those held at Europe's borders.

The imagery of social media graphics, on the other hand, forms part of a distinct network of remediated intermediations—in particular, news reports on Twitter users' posts on the death of Alan Kurdi. These news pieces present us with re-visualizations of the original death scene, the boy's body on the beach, in a range of imaginary contexts—Alan in heaven or in a beautifully decorated child's bedroom. Characterized, on the one hand, by the substitution of photographic realism with the artistic aesthetic of cartoons or drawings, and, on the other, by a register of confessional intimacy that expresses shame or guilt, these remediated posts establish a relationship of reflexive guilt with their topic. This is the case, for instance, in a drawing of Alan's body on the shore and an adjacent one, subtitled "Europe," showing Alan's clothes hung out to dry—the ironic message being that Europe cares more about procedures than human life itself.

Despite their different aesthetic properties, these two visualities, celebrity and aesthetic playfulness, converge in their attempt to humanize migrants through acts of co-presence and confession aimed at validating their predicament of suffering. Yet, both imageries ultimately displace the presence of migrants, who are either overshadowed by the glamorous presence of celebrity or fictionalized by the digital drawings of Twitter. This viral displacement of the "other" is also a feature of the imagery of hospitality, but the difference between the two lies in moral claims. Images of protest combine empathy with denunciation, critiquing the exclusionary politics of European elites; in contrast, images of famous actors' encounters with migrants or artistic compositions on social media tend to replace critique with the self-oriented and depoliticized affectivities of celebrity and Twitter culture.

In both cases, echoing earlier pictorial patterns, an ambivalent form of migrant humanity traverses the visualities of self-reflexivity: spoken about, rather than speaking, their case is made, but they are not the ones in control of it. Visually marginalized as part of a glamorous spectacle featuring what Mostafanezhad (2016: 28) calls the "aestheticized cosmopolitan celebrity care," or idealized in the amateur illustrations of Twitter, the irreducible humanity of migrants fades in the background. The form of responsibility that emerges out of these visualities is what Chouliaraki calls "post-humanitarian" (2013: 3): a responsibility that retains an ethics of solidarity towards vulnerable others yet, deeply suspicious of politics, turns to the self as the key source of this ethics. Be this the celebrity performance or the self-reflexive tweet, it is because "we" feel this way that migrants are worthy of "our" attention. In replacing the politicized responsibility of the protest with the post-humanitarian "narcissism" of celebrity news and tweets, these visualities tend to privilege pleasurable and fleeting forms of consumerism while ignoring the de-humanizing effects inherent in their Eurocentric voices. As a consequence, migrants ultimately become the subaltern in a conversation that takes place exclusively among "us" and about "us."

The Economy of Visibility as Symbolic Border

The symbolic border is constituted not only in the remediation of news narratives but also that of news images. Indeed, the visual remediation of migrants, we have argued in this chapter, does not simply communicate the migration "crisis" but, to recall Azoulay (2008), establishes political encounters that bind the represented and their viewing publics in a "social contract" of responsible action. It is in this sense that we approached the above visualities not as binary vocabularies but as discursive formations of the symbolic border—that is, as historically situated practices of meaning-making that, in variously portraying arriving migrants, also articulate ethico-political proposals of responsibility as to how "we" should respond to their plight. The news imagery of migration, in this account, participates in the symbolic border insofar as its performances of responsibility occur within a western economy of visibility that centers not on "them" but "us": our empathy, security, hospitality, or reflexivity. But how do these multiple visualities engage "us" in various kinds of political encounter with migrants? And what versions of civic responsibility does their economy of visibility make possible in western public spheres? It is these two questions that we next explore, in conclusion to this chapter.

Our response to the first question of *problematizing migrant visualities* begins by re-emphasizing that victimhood and threat are by no means a straightforward representation of binaries in the empirical pool of our study. Biological life and empathy, for instance, share the moral claim that the vulnerable "other" requires our care. They differ, however, in their portrayal of the "other's" agency and the meaning of care they invest in it: the body-in-need appears as an anthropological minimum, in biological life, and as an anthropological maximum, in empathy. This distinction between a mass of destitute bodies and a crying baby's face is here not only a matter of emotional distance or proximity to the migrant but also, importantly, a matter of ethical commitment to their plight: to a latent form of responsibility, in the case of the massed bodies, where care is about the monitorial action of "registering the news," versus a charitable responsibility, in the case of the crying baby, where care is about shedding a tear, signing a petition, or donating goods for the innocent sufferer. While, therefore, their shared emphasis on the body-in-need evidently situates both categories under the theme of victimhood, their dispositional topologies introduce nuance into this visuality.

The visualities of threat and hospitality, in a parallel move, work on the assumption that migrant imagery is not only about who we care about or who we denounce. For even though, on the basis of their structural similarity around protest, both categories could be thought of as visualities of threat, their proposals for responsibility differ drastically. The distinction between a mass of threatening young men approaching "our" borders and a mass of protestors carrying "migrants welcome" banners is here not only a matter of vilifying or humanizing the imagery of migrants but also, again, a matter of ethical commitment: to a responsibility of security, which is about protecting "ourselves" from "them," in the case of the threatening young men, versus a responsibility of hospitality, which recognizes the political and moral obligation to protect "them," in the case of the pro-migrant protest.

Our analysis, at the same time, identified an emerging category that interrupts the polarity of victimhood and threat and the ethical commitments of responsibility that these entail. In the visualities of remediated intermediations—for instance, Twitter graphics that circulate in the news—it is neither the precarious body of the migrant nor the presence of Black men as terrorists that mobilize moral engagement with migrants through empathy or fear. It is, instead, "our" own representations of them, in drawings, collages, or retouched photographs, which become the vehicles for "our" agency. Even though this imagery still belongs to the traditional visualities of the body-in-need, it breaks with the previous ones in that it appropriates such images in a new aesthetic and mobilizes this to digital practices of moral self-expression. Its aim is online connectivity with others like "us" rather than connectivity with the migrant either as victim or as threat. This post-humanitarian visuality is, from this perspective, a platform-driven regime that, by relying on the virality of likes and shares, tends to avoid questions of political causality and facilitates a self-centered form of civic agency (Chouliaraki 2013; Rosamond 2016).

By complicating the symbolic economy of visibility during the migrant "crisis," our typology not only problematizes traditional representations of the migrant but further contributes to ongoing debates on its *pathologies of civic responsibility*. Complicity and collusion, to recall Silverstone, are here shown to be just two of the many types of relationships that "we" are invited to practice, as we encounter images of migrants. Our engagement, in other words, with the news' proposals for action, is not reduced to those two inherently deficient options: comfortable familiarity with the migrants' sameness or fear of their radical "otherness." Instead, as we saw, there is a wide range of performances for civic agency that the migrant visualities of the news articulate for "us"—monitorial citizenship, tender-hearted benevolence, vigilant nationalism, cosmopolitan activism, or self-reflexive confession. The key question is whether this diverse range of proposals manages to redeem the notion of responsibility from a pathological practice of "othering" to a practice that humanizes migrants and recognizes their cause.

To this second question, then, that of *problematizing responsibility*, our analytical insights converge with previous literature. In line with existing scholarship in Photography Theory and Security Studies, we, too, have established that, despite the range of proposals of responsibility available in news imagery, the news' economy of visibility systematically employs symbolic strategies of dehumanization. Whether these are strategies of collectivization, vilification, infantilization, marginalization, or aestheticization, the migrant who appears within this economy is a deeply ambivalent figure: a body-in-need, a powerless child, a racial "other," a celebrity token, or a sentimental drawing.

We argue that, at the heart of this "crisis" of humanity in the visualities as much as the narratives of the news, there lies not a crisis of migration but a crisis of responsibility itself. More specifically, it is a crisis of the notion of responsibility that informs western understandings of visuality as a civic pedagogy of action, namely "formal" responsibility: "the responsibility I have for my own acts, those aspects of life and deed which I can be held accountable for" (Silverstone 2006: 152). Even though formal responsibility, the obligation to ourselves for our acts, is important in that it gives rise to a plurality of proposals for civic agency, it ultimately fails to grant migrants the opportunity to also "be seen and heard as [. . .] equal," as Arendt (1968/1998: 50) would put it, in public. This is because, due to their lack of civic status, migrants are structurally unable to claim voice and agency in spaces of western publicity; they lack, to reiterate, "the relevance of speech."

In response to this limitation of formal responsibility, we propose the notion of substantive responsibility, as "responsibility for the conditions of the other" (Silverstone 2006). Building on Silverstone's own utopian account of substantive responsibility as "unconditional hospitality" for the "other" (see Dayan 2007 for a critique), our own approach emphasizes instead the relational and discursive character of this form of responsibility—a responsibility that inevitably concerns not only images and their regimes of visuality but also narratives and their strategies of language as in the previous chapter. Rather than the self-oriented focus on "my" actions characteristic of formal responsibility, substantive responsibility begins from the human capacity to establish communities of belonging through what we earlier discussed as "the sharing of stories" (Cavarero 1997).

Drawing on Arendt's normative argument that the public performance of voice is a world-disclosing practice, where narration "enable(s) individuals and collectives to experience—and not just intellectualize—th(eir) responsibility" (MacPhee 2011: 178), we thus propose that "our" visualities treat the journalistic economy of visibility as, in principle, open to all. Substantive responsibility does not, in this sense, necessarily mean that migrants are *de facto* treated as equal participants in this economy, but rather that the boundaries around who speaks or who appears in it become permeable and open, thereby enabling a plurality of voices to claim social and political recognition.

It is precisely these boundaries, impervious to outsiders in the economy of visibility, that we have explored in this chapter, as migrants have been consistently excluded from or marginalized within the images we have discussed. To be substantially responsible, in this context, does not only mean to stop silencing others in order to speak for or about them; it also means to stop speaking about them through "our" own stories. Substantive responsibility presupposes, instead, that we consider the lives of migrants are worthy storytelling material where they, too, appear as reflexive Twitter users, political activists, or caring citizens[2]: for instance, in images that they have photographed themselves; through actions that portray them as creative and knowledgeable actors rather than as victims or terrorists; or through their own views on the causes of the "crisis" as professionals with expertise and aspirations. It is to these performances, as they appear on the intermediation networks of social media platforms, that we next turn to.

6

Subaltern Voice and Digital Resistance

If mainstream news media silence or displace the voice of migrants, where are migrants' voices heard? Where, if at all, do migrants become agentive participants in the spaces of western publicity? In this chapter, we address these questions by arguing that the symbolic border is constituted *both* through the exclusions of migrants' voice and visibility from western public discourse *and* through the migrants' own narratives as these emerge outside the mainstream media and within institutional (NGO) and grassroots social media spaces. The border emerges here, more than anywhere else, as a site of contestation and, at times, resistance. It also appears as a historical site that is defined both by the temporality of "crisis," as we examined it in the previous two chapters, and also by that of post-"crisis." Indeed, developing further our analysis of the border's historicity, we here compare narratives of migration within two different temporal frames: the peak moment of 2015 and its aftermath in 2016–20. By adopting this temporally comparative lens, we produce an account of the digital border's techno-symbolic mutability and narrative elasticity, and we argue that these qualities lie at the heart of the border's efficacy, as they allow for various reconfigurations of its regimes of power and potentials for resistance to play out across different times ("crisis" and post-"crisis"), spaces (outer border and inner border), and assemblages of power (symbolic and territorial).

Our working assumption is that this elasticity of the border is expressed in three ways over time: (i) the diversification of narratives of migration, (ii) their expansion beyond institutional media and across digital networks, and (iii) the re-centering of migrant narratives and voices. Our focus falls on the networks of intermediation that are developed over time by non-governmental/international agencies and by grassroots activists in order to challenge the migrant as a subject who is spoken about and, in this way, enable them to communicate and connect with policy makers and wider audiences on social media and the web. As, in the past five years, migrant voice has been increasingly but unequally integrated into such networks, in ways that both resist and regularize the border's hierarchies of voice, our focus sheds light on the forms that these integrations take outside the mainstream media and the extent to which they enable migrants to claim their right to speak as social and political actors.

Starting from our interest in *voice as resistance*, we draw on Spivak's (2010) notion of colonial subjectivity as a predicament of constitutive voicelessness and use this to frame our understanding of urban networks of intermediation that, in time, both enable migrants to speak out and subject their voice to the narrative order of the symbolic border. In the discussion that follows, we illustrate how the border emerges here as a more unstable process that we have seen so far, as it is reconstituted over time through fragile but sustained acts of migrants' speaking out. We do so by analyzing and comparing two case studies of *institutional* "positive representations" of migration (AwareMigrants.org; #Iamamigrant) and two cases of *grassroots* "positive representations" (Refugee Radio Network; *Migrant Voice*), in 2016. As nodal points in broader networks of migrant intermediation, these cases enable us to map out the politics of subaltern voice as a politics of struggle around who speaks and who is silenced, which actors are heard and which are ignored, which voices actually resist and which legitimize the border.

Subaltern Voice

Voice as the capacity to speak is a practice of world-disclosure, let us recall, where speech works as a political act in itself: an act by which individuals announce their presence in a political community and use their voice as a form of public intervention. The requirement for recognition, where speech is not only articulated but actually heard and acknowledged in public, lies at the heart of this politics of voice—what, as noted in Chapter 3, Couldry calls "voice as value" (2010). Yet we have seen how western economies of voice and visibility prohibit migrant speech acts from appearing in public discourse and how, in so doing, such economies dehumanize migrants as un-narratable selves. Indeed, as we discussed in Chapter 4, the systematic representation of migrants as voiceless occurs within an environment of hypermediated migration where other actors speak about or for them, namely western political elites. Reflecting on this voiceless hypervisibility of migration, Horsti (2016) points to its core contradiction, namely how such silence is not only incompatible with migrants' own digital agency (Diminescu's [2008] "connected migrant"), but further situates them within a hierarchical order of humanity, wherein their lack of voice is misrecognized as lack of humanity.

This form of misrecognition occurs because, despite the affordances of mobile phone apps widely used by migrants (Wall et al. 2015), the global flows of voice are still subjected to historical relations of power that locate human lives within orientalist hierarchies of remediation (Chouliaraki 2013). Whose voice deserves to be amplified beyond their own intimate circles and onto western news platforms, in other words, is not a matter of access to technology but of access to power: "voice," as Tacchi (2012) argues, "is inadequate unless there is also a shift in the hierarchies of value and attention accorded different actors and communities" (2012: 7–8). In the same spirit, Gajjala (2013), in her study of the relationships of resistance and complicity in South Asian women's use of digital media, locates such media "in a field of power (the West) and in the production of a particular knowledge (about the East)" and contends that, within these contexts, it is not enough to listen *of* poor people, but it is necessary to listen *to* them.

From this perspective, techno-determinist approaches that overemphasize migrants' use of social media as evidence of their agency and voice ignore the structural constraints within which such use takes place: what Wall et al. call the circumstances of "information precarity" that migrants are subjected to "in terms of technological and social access to relevant information; the prevalence of irrelevant, sometimes dangerous information; inability to control their own images" (2015: 240). Rather than simply giving them voice, such technologies enable selected intermediations within migrants' communities that simultaneously subject them to repressive practices from silencing to surveillance.

Postcolonial critiques, informed by Spivak's "Can the Subaltern Speak?" (2010), address this condition of systemic voicelessness by locating its roots in the reproduction of colonial power that sustains itself in contemporary structures of mobility and mediation. Such structures, including the practice of journalism, work by keeping subaltern voices outside the decision-making spaces where their lives and livelihoods are narrated. Colonial discourse, Spivak argues, does this by not necessarily silencing but by accommodating this voice in ways that reaffirm differences between the "civilized" west and the "barbarian" east. Spivak's argument places at the center of colonial critique the impossibility of an uncontaminated subaltern voice, problematizing the vision that there can ever be "a pure form of consciousness," articulated outside western discourse. Given, she says, that colonial subjects "never themselves had agency within the traffic of imperialism" to begin with (1996: 100), any process of translation (or indeed mediation) is inevitably also a return of the colonial voice to the position of the subaltern: a voice silenced or, when spoken, unheard. Understood as a form of violence—epistemic violence—this series of silences, omissions, and reformulations turns the colonial subject into an "other," precisely by containing its meanings within the logic of western discourse. Referring to Spivak's paradigmatic subaltern, the woman in an Indian immolation ritual that is reinterpreted by western discourse as the savage habit of a patriarchal society, Birla explains how "the subjectivity of the woman is not only read as a violent and unstable effect of an agency not her own, but she is revealed to us as the instrument of that agency" (2010: 89).

The theme of the subaltern has implicitly informed our own analysis of migrant silencing in European media, where the migrant appears in news discourse as an abstract figure existing outside history. Various forms of subalternity naturally also occur elsewhere, too—when, for instance, migrants are framed as "problems" within technocratic, "problem-solving" discourse (Nyers 2013) or as the product of exceptional circumstances and thus as an "anomaly" that needs governmental solutions (Andersson 2019). Both these representations speak about migrants by quoting their own words but leave little space for their own voices to be heard and understood (Schwiertz and Schwenken 2020). In the process, migrants are silenced or ventriloquized, and it is western "experts" instead, whether politicians or support organizations, who become the voice trusted to speak on their behalf. In so doing, such voice simultaneously subsumes migrants' lives into western ways of knowing (Sigona 2014).

Drawing on the problematic of subalternity, our analysis of migrant-inclusive websites represents an attempt to understand the opportunities and constraints for the subaltern to speak within a symbolic border that silences their voice yet, at times, also invites them to become authors of their stories. In this context, we approach the category of the subaltern not as an empirical figure with a pure consciousness, as Spivak cautions against, but, just as we did in Chapter 4 with voice and Chapter 5 with visuality, as a heuristic device that enables us to ask pertinent questions about the contexts within which migrant voice is articulated (or not) and the conditions of possibility under which it can be heard, if at all: whether, as Dreher would put it, they are "granted an audience" or not (2010: 99). This focus enables us to pay attention to and interrogate those digital spaces that promise "partial structured participation that allows networked agency . . . in the public sphere, albeit constrained" (Gajjala 2013: 13).

Migrant Voices and the Dialectics of the Symbolic Border

The case studies we focus on here consist of two institutional (NGO-related) digital projects associated with migration governance and two digital grassroots projects associated with migrant rights activism. The aim of this analysis is to understand how migrant voices are channeled through networks of intermediation and how, in so doing, they confirm or challenge the symbolic border. The institutional initiatives are: (i) IOM (International Organization for Migration)'s project #Iamamigrant. This project was originally established as the refugeemigrants.org portal (which has since ceased to exist in this form) leading visitors to two different spaces, #Iamarefugee and #Iamamigrant, but was soon transformed into the single and combined project of #Iamamigrant; and (ii) *Aware Migrants* (awaremigrants.org), an Italian government and IOM collaborative project, which came to life in the midst of the 2015–16 "crisis" and continued developing with the aim to reach (potential) migrant audiences in 2020 and beyond. The grassroots initiatives include two migrant-led projects: (i) the Hamburg-based digital Refugee Radio Network (RRN), which produces programming for local, national and transnational audiences and streams on the web; and (ii) the UK-based *Migrant Voice* (migrantvoice.org), an activist project campaigning for migrant rights, which primarily focuses on British politics and policies, but which also engages strategically with transnational migration governance matters.

We selected these specific cases on the basis of their three commonalities. First, they represent examples of "best practice," where migrants are seen and heard. Second, they reflect practices that aim, or claim, to put in action some of the liberal west's most celebrated values: equality, integration, and respect for human rights. Third, these are projects that, for different reasons, attracted wider attention among supporters and critics (Carling 2016; de Jong and Dannecker 2017; Musarò 2019). At the same time, even though both types of initiatives put migrant voices at the center of their narratives, their points of departure and aims are different. Digital institutional initiatives are the result of formal decision-making that deems certain representations more effective than others in meeting institutional aims; thus, their images and narratives are means to an institutional end, namely, as we shall see, the promotion of security discourses. Grassroots initiatives, on the other hand, are forms of claim-making, of *voicing*, that seek to intervene in the public sphere. Rather than mere means to an end, they are ends in themselves, performing voice-as-resistance in broader networks that intermediate migrant experience in the global North.

Intermediation in NGO Governance: Institutionalizing Voice?

#Iamamigrant

IOM's digital campaign #Iamamigrant is a fascinating project of intermediation that captures both the persistence of institutional narratives of migration and, at the same time, their reconfiguration across time. This is a project of storytelling, which at the time of writing included approximately 1,200 stories narrated by individual migrants in eight languages (though mostly in English). Originally signposted with a hashtag, the project clearly defines its success in terms of amplifying the intermediations of migrant stories on the web and social media and among audiences that include not only western publics and policy makers, but also, importantly, potential migrants. The aesthetics and narratives of this international project offer personalized narration, which is carefully curated and presented within a visual and textual frame of communicative fluency. Storytelling is here represented within the linear trajectory of origin-travel-destination and is illustrated by high resolution close-up portraits of individuals directly facing the camera. These linguistic and visual features seek to nurture a sense of narrative intimacy which serves as an intentional attempt to tackle "hostile public discourse about migrants" (IOM 2020) and to invite more migrants to join in: that is, to contribute to a user-generated-content (UGC) project by telling their stories through prompt-questions. While, thus, #Iamamigrant is presented as a UGC project, the content seems carefully curated, both aesthetically and ideologically.

Within this context, voice is represented as the driving value of combatting hostile discourse about migrants. As noted in the "About" page:

> "i am a migrant" allows the voices of individuals to shine through and provides an honest insight into the triumphs and tribulations of migrants of all backgrounds and at all phases of their migratory journeys. While we aim to promote positive perceptions of migrants we do not shy away from presenting life as it is experienced. We seek to combat xenophobia and discrimination at a time when so many are exposed to negative narratives about migration—whether on our social media feeds or on the airwaves. (IOM 2020)

Speaking directly to discourses of anti-racist and migrant rights' activism, this is a well-crafted statement, which identifies the value of voice as a catalyst for their recognition (Honneth 2007). The entry page to #Iamamigrant includes a number of featured stories that are regularly updated, alongside a set of keywords to help users navigate the hundreds of stories; keywords include gender, name, profession, current country, and country of origin, a set of identifications that directly contest the nameless, jobless representation of migrants in the mass media. Stories come from across the world in a deliberate attempt to globalize migration and voices represent all different kinds of migrants: from refugees to expert migrants, from white to non-white, from privileged to marginalized ones. The temporal trajectory of voice in the project from 2016 to 2020 further reveals some of the fundamental representational struggles that shape the symbolic border in terms of the dominant socio-political logics of migration, namely humanitarian and entrepreneurial security, and in the institutions that articulate them—such as IOM.

In 2016, when our analysis began, #Iamamigrant was conceived and configured in the context of wider international institutional responses to a "crisis." The project's original online space, which directed users to either #Iamarefugee or #Iamamigrant, separated vulnerable migrants (labeled "refugees") in need of support, from entrepreneurial migrants (labeled "migrants"), whose mobility revealed determination and resilience. This divide was short-lived but reflected the institutions' ambivalence when attempting to balance urgent need for care with political and economic pressures for secure borders and controlled migration. In the days of #Iamamigrant/#Iamarefugee's early development, positive representations of migration were carefully curated to recognize those different narratives.

For example, #Iamarefugee projected stories of uprooting and resettlement out of need, such as in the case of Malakeh, a Syrian journalist in her thirties living in Germany. Malakeh is a veiled but apparently "modern" Muslim woman who is visually represented through a close-up shot with eyes facing directly into the camera, projecting a confident but unthreatening presence that directly engages with the viewer's gaze. The professional photo shows Malakeh on a rooftop of an unidentifiable location: it could be in the Middle East or in Europe. From her longer narration, these words are selected and superimposed on the picture: "In Germany the old cathedrals remind me of our churches in Syria . . . There are no words to explain how much I miss my country." This curated narrative emphasizes Malakeh's universal humanity with cross-border links sustained through Christianity and reaffirms her positioning as a legitimate participant in the western public sphere. This unthreatening familiarity, together with Malakeh's repeatedly declared commitment to return to Syria, renders her worthy of recognition, on the grounds that she is "here" for a limited time only—a gift of hospitality granted to her by the benevolent west. Many other profiles on #Iamarefugee similarly appeared to balance securitization with hospitality, opening up aesthetic spaces of western generosity towards foreign but familiar "others."

#Iamarefugee's humanitarian securitization, as we repeatedly saw, co-existed with #Iamamigrant's entrepreneurial securitization on this digital project even back in 2016. What this suggests is that entrepreneurial securitization is not a new regime of power but one already rooted in the longer-term governance of migration and in international organizations' mission to manage migration on the basis of business productivity and technocratic rationality (de Jong and Dannecker 2017). Early profiles on #Iamamigrant, like the 2016 profile of Carlos, an Indian man in his fifties who has lived in Italy for the past thirty-five years, support this point. The photographic profile that accompanies his personal story shows him in the middle of a street between two houses, possibly in Italy. He is well-dressed, has a gentle smile, and faces directly into the camera. Above his head, circular streetlights softly illuminate the street; one of the lights is positioned directly over Carlos's head, giving the impression of a halo. The phrase superimposed on the photo is: "In Italy I always felt more than welcome. People were intrigued by my differences, I was 'the Indian,' a mythical figure." As in the case of Malakeh, the speaker's foreignness is emphasized alongside his gratitude for Italy's hospitality, while the exoticization of "a mythical figure" is represented as a positive feature that helped his integration rather than as a feature of "othering" and exclusion—an example of what Iwabuchi would call "complicit exoticism" (2009). Narrated as a case of a financially successful, resilient, and documented migrant, Carlos, like others, fits the wider frame of entrepreneurial securitization, according to which migrants have to work hard to earn their recognition. At the same time, his curated voice plays out as much on entrepreneurial recognition as it does on the racialized frame of humanitarian ambivalence, which recognizes in him an unthreatening, even if inferior, humanity.

What becomes strikingly visible through the temporal development of the project is the gradual retreat (though not disappearance) of such narratives of ambivalence and the intensification of increasingly more assertive frames of entrepreneurial securitization. Gradually, post-2015, voices heard on #Iamamigrant articulated confident migrant agency by combining discourses of resilience and determination with horrific references to migrant failure and death as obstacles that had to be overcome. For instance, the main profile featured for most of 2020 was that of Souleyman, a Gambian man who speaks of his horrendous trip towards Europe from northern Africa. He explains how, unlike many friends who died, he survived after experiencing slavery, imprisonment, and torture in Libya. The superimposed quote on this portrait reads: "My fellow brothers need to know that this route is one of sacrifice. You don't know how you will die, but chances are it will happen." Under the video frame, we read that "Souleyman has benefited from the voluntary return and reintegration program under the EU-IOM Joint initiative funded by the EU and implemented by IOM." This is a controversial and highly contested program of migrant returns to their country of origin or to a neighboring country; the program does not allow settlement in a western country. The story of Souleyman is very similar to those narrated by many other Black participants in the #Iamamigrant project in 2020: Souleyman, like others, takes responsibility for his failings and speaks in a voice of caution to an assumed audience of uninformed or naïve African (prospective) migrants who (may) put themselves through the deadly experience of migration. Their testimonies, in other words, may be used to publicize their tragic experiences, but they are also acts of warning aimed at keeping others like them outside the boundaries of Europe. Within this securitized narrative, the socio-economic context of migration and the brutal western policies of externalized and outsourced bordering security across Africa (Andersson 2019) are absent from #Iamamigrant storytelling.

In contract to this securitized narrative, the entrepreneurial narration of resilience in the face of adversity works to confirm the legitimacy of the symbolic border in different ways. Mama Jackie's story is one among many similar ones, where Black Africans describe success in Africa against the potential lethal failure of (attempted) migration to the global North. Mama Jackie, from Chad and now in Cameroon, reflects on migration, describing "the desire to go to Europe in the quest for well-being, regardless of the sacrifices that must be made." "But the West is not an Eldorado," she adds. For, having lived over a decade in Europe, Mama Jackie says that "you can live better in Africa. One can undertake in one's country with the limited means at one's disposal" (IOM 2020).

While #Iamamigrant remains a complex and often contradictory space of voice, enabled through the digital expandability of representation that integrates 1,200 migrant stories, the project increasingly contains voice *within* the symbolic border and its security imperatives. Specifically, the hierarchical appearance of migrants who speak is a stark reminder of the orientalist order of migration governance, that is "premised upon race as a mode of governing and knowing" (Moffette and Vadasaria 2016: 294). Speaking in their own words of punishable mobility, migrants appear to normalize this racialized order of the symbolic border and to sustain the geopolitical arrangement of the digital border, in the first place. Their institutionalized and performative acts of agency work less as acts of recognition and more as confirmation of the regime of entrepreneurial securitization as a desirable and beneficial-to-all regime of power.

Aware Migrants

Our discussion of a second institutional case—that of the *Aware Migrants* digital project—illustrates, alongside #Iamamigrant, a key iteration of the paradox of voice: while, over time, migrant voices have increased in institutional networks of intermediation, their spaces of recognition have shrunk.

Aware Migrants, an online project established by the Italian Department of Civil Liberties and Migration with IOM's support, was, from the start, conceived as a project of using migrant stories to deter primarily African travelers from setting out for Europe. Like #Iamamigrant and activist networks of intermediation, *Aware Migrants* communicates the border through social media aesthetics and narratives, most importantly the individualized narration of migration by (would-be) migrants themselves—mostly Africans (potential) migrants who also constitute the primary intended audience of the project.

The main page includes eight tabs: one of them offers information about "Alternatives"—that is, legal channels to enter European countries, which would exclude most African migrants. The remaining seven tabs focus on different elements of the dangers involved in "illegally" migrating to Europe, with the vast majority of speakers being Black men and a small number of speakers being Arab men and women. In 2016, a music video with African speakers titled "Be Aware Brother, Be Aware Sister" spoke of migration risks, sending a clear message to avoid the journey because of the risky Mediterranean crossing. In 2020, another music video titled "I Remember" replaced the original one, but focused on one particular crossing: in this video, a dead person narrates his story of drowning in the Mediterranean after believing the myth of European paradise that other migrants (deceptively) share on social media. The website's dominant format is video testimonies, usually narrated in English or in French with English subtitles. Each photo is accompanied by the first name of the individual and a blurb; all stories describe despair, regret for migrating, and, increasingly, death. In Cesar's story, alongside despair, we hear that migration deprives subjects of agency, learning them to face a fate of death: "We were lost in the sea and there was no hope. I stayed three days without eating . . . those who succeed to come here . . . it's a destiny. It's a tombola. You may arrive in Italy alive or rest in the sea forever."

More recent storytelling focuses on harrowing testimonies of women describing in detail the sexual violence they experienced in the course of their journeys and of men recounting similarly horrific instances of suffering and torture. The only glimpses of hope come from those who did not attempt to migrate. "I never thought of migrating because I believe in myself," Yaye says, countering the bleak narrations of most others on *Aware Migrants*. The message becomes even clearer as she adds: "Staying in our country, being proactive, working, even being successful. This is what I believe in."

An initiative project that already in 2016 appeared as an exceptional case of institutional securitization developed in time into a cynical project of routinely publicized thanatopolitical narratives of deterrence and threat—punishment and banishment for the "others" who decide to make the trip to Europe. Black subjects speak, and in fact their voices drive the content of this digital project, but they only do so on the condition that their voice warns others away or they talk of success when remaining away from western lands and of failure when they don't. Even though such warning-based information campaigns are known to be ineffective as strategies of persuasion (Oeppen 2016), their narratives not only incorporate migrant voices in their deterrence strategies but do so in the name of humanitarian care. It is because they care for migrant lives that governance organizations warn potential migrants of the risks of human smuggling, rather than because they want to keep new migrants away from their territories—such stories, as Oeppen argues, "make for a compelling policy narrative, allowing European policymakers to position their actions as controlling migration, whilst being seen to meet their humanitarian responsibilities" (2016: 65).

Representations of the subaltern in online institutional media have been the focus of our two previous chapters, and now this one shows how subalternity works by means of digitized institutional campaigns as they enter intermediation networks and their promise for virality and interactivity. Uploading, sharing, or forwarding messages of professionally curated Black voices can now reach and engage local populations in their countries of origins in ways that were impossible for earlier mass media campaigns or public space messaging. Yet, as such networks integrate migrant voices only to place them at the service of the border's power relations, they also, in so doing, reconfigure the processes of migrant (mis-)recognition. First, migrants speak as humans with a performative agency, but with voices that are amplified on the condition that they either remain territorially distant, or, when proximate, that they affirm the unthreatening narratives of entrepreneurial individualism. While, that is, they speak with their own words, such subaltern voices respond and correspond to western imaginaries, reiterating entrepreneurial stories of success: individual resilience, a business-like ethos, and punishment for illegality. Second, and while speaking with the authority of their own experience, migrant voices remain inferior to western ones; for example, they are all identified through first names only, which implies a misplaced sense of intimacy and ultimately reduces their social status to private persons not worthy of western modes of public address. Moreover, Malakeh's account of her amazement at the sight of Germany's Christian cathedrals remains a dominant reference in her narrations, while Carlos is grateful for Italian hospitality and fully embraces his orientalization as a "mythical" subject. Even more compelling are the words of male migrants like Cesar who speak of their destiny of violence and torture as a consequence of their own wrong decisions, and the voices of many women, like Blessing and Jessica, who seem to submit to the identity of self-blaming victims through the ways they narrate their traumatic stories of rape and sexual exploitation. Third, migrants who speak on such institutional networks are denied political agency: the actor/narrator is a smiling or crying adult, who speaks of thankfulness towards Europe, or of the painful costs of their journey always associated with their undeserved access to the continent. These representations of migrants consistently emphasize emotions of gratitude, yet no one asks questions about Europe's border policies or contests the violence of the border itself. On the contrary, the anger—appearing in early *Aware Migrants* testimonies and increasingly on #Iamamigrant too—turns inwards as personal frustration for their own failures. Refracted by western discourse, migrant sea emergencies and deaths are, in this way, disconnected from the thanatopolitics of European borders and recast in terms of personal recklessness or naivete. What we encounter in institutional activism, in summary, are cases of voice without recognition. For, insofar as the audibility of these migrants' stories rely on their own "self-orientalization" (Zia-Ebrahimi 2011), mirroring or echoing dominant rationalities of security, these voices ultimately remain subaltern: formulated within and subordinate to western discourse.

Intermediation in Grassroots Activism: Resisting Voices?

Alongside, and often against, such institutional initiatives, a series of grassroots projects have emerged across networks of intermediation to contest the symbolic border and the reproduction of migrants' "otherness" as undeserving of access to western territories and systems of rights. These projects use the web and social media as oppositional to the institutional ones so as to mobilize voice in the political sense we encountered in Chapter 4: as an act of speaking out with a view to be heard and gain recognition. Such grassroots projects of voice are usually perceived and activated as nodes of wider networks of activism that join up in their efforts to resist the border, and we here show how these networks work, and when they don't, through two powerful cases—the transnational Refugee Radio Network[1] and the UK-based *Migrant Voice*.[2]

Both are aesthetically and technologically simple digital projects, unlike the professionalized ones of *Aware Migrants* and #Iamamigrant; Refugee Radio Network and *Migrant Voice* are obviously functioning with limited funds and with little, if any, support from professional web designers. As networks of intermediation and transmediation, they address a range of audiences: activists, migrants, policy makers, and wider national and transnational publics. From refugee testimonies to music productions, from online rights' campaigns to offline media and political action, these activist projects bring forward a multiplicity of voices that aim to disrupt assumptions of a united Europe (Ponzanesi and Leurs, 2014) and of a white, homogenous west.

Refugee Radio Network

Refugee Radio Network (RRN) was established in Hamburg by Larry Macaulay, himself a refugee. Its programs are streamed online and are also available on SoundCloud, Mixcloud, and popular social media platforms, such as Facebook, Instagram and YouTube; at the same time, some of RRN's programming is rebroadcasted on FM across a number of German cities and some programs are collaborations with those local stations. Under the banner of "Refugee Radio Network: The voice of freedom, equality and justice," this digital project broadcasts in two languages (English and German; originally also Italian), and its primary audience, according to the project's aims (RRN 2020), are refugees located in Europe, the Middle East, and Africa. At the same time, RRN has been engaged in a range of national and transnational networks that involved co-production and collaboration with German radio stations, international broadcasters such as NPR, Deutche Welle, and Al Jazeera, as well as collaborations with other migrant networks such as *Are You Syrious?*[3]

Migrant voices are here heard through a collection of diverse radio programs that target different collectivities: from established migrant communities to newly arrived refugee ones, and from diasporic groups to multicultural urban audiences. Streamed programming deliberately contests singular identifiers, such as that of "the refugee," and rejects vulnerability as a singular frame of refugee experience. Similarly, its programming attends to different identities, desires, and needs, including political and international newscasts and debates, music, and light entertainment targeting children, families, and cooking enthusiasts. *The Refugee Voices Show*, for instance, brings on air issues "affecting . . . the refugee community," while another program, *Letters from the Voiceless*—as its name indicates—sets the stage of bottom-up conversation with subaltern voices claiming center-stage in public debates that usually exclude them. Programs such as these perform voice in the sense of constructing a narratable self that, rather than being contained within western frames of representation, owns its own voice, and can talk about migrants' ordinary experiences and everyday desires. The *Migrantpolitan Music Show* is a similar example that "contains the trendy current music types, both African and International," a description that puts African music rarely ever heard on western "airwaves" at the core of its radio experience. Finally, *Evening Drops* is described as a "potpourri of songs and poetry, a virtual lounge for the radio listener," which produces spaces of collective enjoyment by highlighting the personal taste of its listeners: it is "a personality-driven program."

Established in 2014, before Europe recognized migration as a "crisis," RRN nonetheless gained its prominence during the "crisis." In 2015–16, international broadcasters, policy makers, and foundations turned to RRN not only because it represented an established project of migrant voice, but also because it provided an invaluable resource for many European and international media that lacked understanding of the refugee experience. At that peak moment, the voices of Refugee Radio Network gained wide attention and funding. A year later, RRN received the Alternative Media Award and, between 2015 and 2017, it was invited to numerous educational and cultural events across Europe and beyond, attracting charitable funding in support of its "education and integration understanding" (RRN 2017). It was within this same temporality of "crisis" that RRN established most of its collaborations with German radio stations and international broadcasters.

Despite having systematically spoken out and against border violence, however, the network also, at times, implicated grassroots networks in the securitizing dynamics of the symbolic border. In 2017, for instance, RRN launched an anti-terrorist campaign under the banner: "If you see something, say something . . . We must keep vigilant against terrorism. It is everyone's duty to do so." The message was printed on top of a black and white close-up photo of a man's face, a dark figure that looked straight into the camera with half of his face hidden behind his hands. Even though the appeal sought to promote a conception of the migrant (viewer) as a dutiful and law-abiding citizen, it ambivalently also evoked a securitized image of the migrant as terrorist, thereby mirroring the western imagination of the threatening other onto its own pages. As in previous cases of digital activism we examined, this example similarly illustrates how for migrants to be recognized as equal interlocutors in public spaces they first need to acknowledge and address western imaginations of otherness and often to comply with the requirements of surveillance inherent in the symbolic border.

Unsurprisingly, the wider, if tenuous, interest in RRN's migrant voices was short-lived. When the "crisis" subsided and media attention turned elsewhere, migrant voices became yet again marginalized within mainstream media. In fact, the collaborative projects and transnational media coverage of RRN between 2015 and 2017 largely faded out, and there is little evidence that the Refugee Radio Network currently sustains active connections with the major national and transnational institutions it once did. Post-"crisis," and as the symbolic border was gradually established as a space of rigid surveillance, migrant voices also became increasingly framed within discourses of entrepreneurial security and so narratives of forced migration, uprooting, and resettlement became weaker and weaker.

The case of RRN has exemplified, we hope, how the temporality of "crisis" and post-"crisis" shaped migrant (mis)recognition in the longer term, as grassroots migrant projects, initially welcomed within broader networks of the intermediation and remediation of migration, subsided in time. Nonetheless and against the odds, spaces of migrant voice do not cease to exist: RRN is still going strong, even if with less mainstream appeal and with even fewer funds. The Refugee Radio Network is still today a fascinating case of resilience and claim-making that recognizes migrants as narratable selves, speakers of their own stories, leaders of their own communities, and legitimate participants in public life.

Migrant Voice

Alongside Refugee Radio Network, we here also discuss the case of *Migrant Voice*—a node in the activist networks of intermediation that throughout the period of our analysis positioned itself in clear opposition to mainstream media and securitized border policies. *Migrant Voice* emerged within the networks of activist intermediation in 2010, and its aim has since been to contest migrant misrepresentation and misrecognition: "We started *Migrant Voice* because there was a huge debate taking place about us, without us. We were scapegoated and faced hostility. We wanted to speak for ourselves and to support other migrants to speak out too" (*Migrant Voice* 2020).

Indeed, *Migrant Voice* defines itself explicitly as a project of resistance to border policies and to exclusionary media discourses. In its brief history, it has also contested the humanitarian logic of emergency care that took place during 2015–16. Its communication strategy is instead anchored in a long-term commitment to digital mobilization for the advancement of the right of subaltern migrants to speak openly and to converse with institutions and other citizens as equal partners. The concept of voice, in this sense, could not have been more central to this project, though voice is here articulated differently to the curated and aestheticized visuality of *Aware Migrants* and #Iamamigrant. As is evident in the temporal development of the site, its storytelling has in time shifted from individual portrait-driven narratives, as the previous ones, towards more raw-looking and politicized content. In 2016, for instance, the curation of online testimonies was oriented towards more confessional stories, but such stories are now placed firmly within a critical policy discourse. A case in point is the story of Daniel Debessai, a statistician from Eritrea whose torturous "journey through the UK job system," as he calls his struggle with the UK employment bureaucracy, is recounted as the most difficult part of his journey, including his crossing of the Mediterranean. His profile photo accompanying the story lacked the visual gloss typical of mainstream NGO sites but offered a portrayal of Daniel as a professional, sitting by his computer, possibly in his office.

Another portrait was that of Roza Salih, a Kurdish Iraqi refugee, whose story "Education—Application Denied," described her struggle to get access to education as an asylum seeker in the UK. Her story concluded with the introduction of an NGO Roza co-founded—Glasgow Girls—campaigning against deportations of vulnerable asylum seekers. Visually, her selfie, itself an instance of agentive self-representation (Chouliaraki 2017), accompanied a story of contestation and resistance. Even though it lacked the gloss of #Iamamigrant's visuality, it did convey a strong sense of immediacy and passion, as Roza appeared in a close-up shot looking directly into the camera and the viewer's eyes.

By late 2020, *Migrant Voice*'s content has become less dependent on individual storytelling and more focused on collective initiatives. The first story on its front page, in November 2020, shared resources to help those impacted by COVID-19, with a primary focus on Black, minority, and migrant communities that had been most severely affected. The second one was a report from Libya's horrendous detention centers where migrants are imprisoned and tortured. While these stories foregrounded collective struggles for freedom and equality, individual storytelling still had a role to play, albeit now explicitly driven by the border's injustices.

The story of Dickson Tarnongo, a disabled asylum seeker crowdfunding to cover his Ph.D. fees, also figured on the main page, alongside the case of Gurmit Kaur, a 75-year-old undocumented migrant from India threatened with deportation. Dickson's story was framed as both an individual project of self-realization and a commitment to fighting injustice, and was visually accompanied by an image of him at his graduation in a wheelchair: "As a person with a disability who has experienced discrimination on the basis of my disability, I intend to use my PhD research work to advocate for the rights of persons with disability," he says. Similarly, Gurmit Kaur speaks as a person experiencing injustice, explaining why she should not be deported: "Being here in Smethwick is my true home, it's where I work to help the community, it's where I give back." Other individual stories appearing across *Migrant Voice* send similarly strong political messages.

The story of Syed, originally from Pakistan,[4] describes his fear of deportation because of the strict regulations on sponsoring for international students: "I used to stay awake at night because I was scared that immigration enforcement officers would raid my house and arrest me." The voice of Syed frames a much bigger message; as the story describes a flawed system of migration control, it also explains that Syed is not alone but instead one of many in a similar situation: "over 34,000 international students were wrongly accused of cheating [in their English language tests] by the Home Office and a further 22,000 wrongly labelled possible cheats." These voices contest the decontextualized migrant storytelling we saw in government-sponsored web projects, where migrants' voices remain subaltern—that is, they speak but only when their stories are deeply individual and detached from the politics of the border. For projects such as *Migrant Voice*, in contrast, individual voices constitute what Couldry calls "political acts (not just moments of spectacle)" (2010: 148) and, as such, they always connect the individual to the collective.

Even so, however, *Migrant Voice*, as with the wider networks of urban intermediation wherein it is embedded, cannot exist outside the assemblage of the inner border and its dominant economies of voice and visibility. While government-sponsored projects have the resources to compete for attention on digital platforms, for activist projects, the aesthetic and ideological appeal of mainstream hyper-individualized visibilities is a real challenge. The balance is always hard to strike and, as we saw, these projects are constantly suspended between advancing personal storytelling (with all the benefits this accrues in terms of audience reach and funding) and confrontational narratives of collective resistance to the violence of the border. What both these grassroots projects illustrate is the difficult space that digital activism against the border occupies as it seeks to retain its ethos of inclusiveness and allow the subaltern voice to be heard in its own terms. Even in such cases, as we saw, voice cannot but remain impure and porous, shifting in time as it partly absorbs and partly resists the aesthetics and discourses of the symbolic border.

Subaltern voice, in summary, emerges from within the intermediations of the symbolic border, even if in fragmented and contained forms. This is manifested in the spaces of digital activism in three ways. First, migrants appear as human beings through an aesthetics of unglossy ordinariness yet, at the same time, as social actors with professional identities and skills—for example, as radio producers or as campaigners. Second, they appear as vulnerable yet also agentive subjects with their hopes, struggles, and aspirations: they may be suffering but they are not objects of pity. Third, they are political agents: they speak out as citizens to share their stories and expose the violence of the border; each one of them is, to use Arendt's (1994) formulation, being "the doer of deeds . . . and the speaker of words." This last point is important in that it illustrates how migrants can and do speak as citizens, with full names and professional attributes, even if they lack citizenship rights. They can and do, in other words, make claims for self-worth and social belonging even if not legal recognition. Their claims to voice, however, as we also saw, are inevitably always subordinated to the power relations of the inner border. This becomes apparent, for instance, in the selective voices we heard here: those who appear and speak online already hold a certain symbolic capital through their educational background or class habitus—they are the ones that have managed to contest injustice, and, on occasion, have succeeded in resisting it.

The Power and Limits of Subaltern Voice

Using Spivak's notion of the subaltern to capture the radical ambivalence of colonial voice in western discourse, we have here explored how migrants speak in the intermediation networks of the symbolic border. Throughout the five years covering the 2015 European migration peak and its aftermath, we have observed how migrant voice has been reconfigured in different online networks and how, in the process, over time, voice has become a value to be celebrated, denied, incorporated, and reclaimed.

In 2016, networks of intermediation mobilized those voices to debate the conditions of migrant recognition. Over time, and through 2020, these networks have diversified, embedding migrants in different projects of voice: to deny recognition on the one hand (governmental) and to contest misrecognition on the other (grassroots). At the same time, while at the moment of "crisis," the institutions of migration governance spoke through tenuous voices of securitization and humanitarianism, this ambivalence has, in time, been replaced by a more rigid, albeit still unstable narrative of entrepreneurial securitization. Within this process, activist networks moved through different positions of ambivalence and resistance in their attempt to find their place in and against the wider assemblages of the border. Intermediating voice thus became in itself a learning experience of how to do digital activism; in practice this meant that grassroots networks mobilized migrant voices to partly engage with humanitarian securitization and partly to contest it through narratives of aspiration, or, sometimes, through the familiar narratives of hyper-individualism.

This long-term trajectory of voice has highlighted a key shift that has occurred in the past half-decade, namely the move away from the silent migrant towards the more agentive figure of the migrant who speaks out. In examining this shift, we have also drawn attention to the complex politics of recognition that is involved in the digital representation of migration. At the heart of this complexity lies, we suggest, the subalternity of the migrant as a condition not only of linguistic muteness but also of subordinate speech that is, for Spivak, characteristic of historical hierarchies of representation and human life in the global North. Two major modalities of subaltern voice have emerged in the course of our study: *ventriloquized* and *articulated* voice. Ventriloquized voice refers to contexts where migrant voice was appropriated within western discourse, echoing, mirroring, and legitimizing its securitizing agendas, and articulated voice is about contexts that attach value to migrant voice enable it to be heard as equal in public conversations. While articulated voice fosters forms of social and political recognition, we have here shown how ventriloquized voice offers visibility but no recognition.

Ventriloquized voice became apparent in the integration of migrant speakers into institutional networks wherein they speak within the narrowly predetermined frames of the victim, the threat, or the entrepreneur. These networks create symbolic conditions of speaking out that offer membership to public discourse without guaranteeing inclusion. We saw how this works in the visualities of #Iamamigrant and *Aware Migrants*, where migrant voice was put to the service of border surveillance, justifying the discourse of deserving migrants in terms of business success or the violence of the border in terms of self-blaming stories, for instance, in the vulnerability of the African migrant who has no control of his fate and the Indian migrant who is grateful for Italians' fascination with his "otherness." Through these personal confessions of entrepreneurial success, self-learning, and regret, the human hierarchies of the inner border are also reconfigured and expanded in that, what initially used to be the pitiful figure of the vulnerable migrant is gradually replaced by the naïve migrant who brought pain, even death, to themselves. The surviving migrant similarly morphs into the determined entrepreneur, while the threatening migrant now turns into an all-encompassing racialized, cunning, and devious outsider who will stop at nothing to reach western shores.

Consequently, and inevitably, such digital narratives further nurture a narcissism of ignorance, as the selected few publicize familiar stories for western audiences and migrants "back home," while keeping more complex trajectories of migration out of view. And while this visibility has certain conditional benefits of recognition for some newcomers, what Georgiou calls "membership without inclusion" (2018: 55), there are also those whose voice remains not only unrepresented but unrepresentable—as, for instance, the women refugees, people with disabilities, and young sex-workers whose stories we heard in Chapter 3.

Articulated voice is evident in activist websites where migrants claim a more engaged role for themselves in their new societies. Two characteristics of articulated voice stand out. First, the source of voice, the migrant speaker, is an active figure who still relies on the symbolic border's existing networks of intermediation, yet does so by rejecting the sleek aesthetics of individualized storytelling in institutional spaces and allows for an alternative social media aesthetics of amateur ordinariness to be deployed—and so for a different kind of authenticity to be articulated through the story. Second, the enhanced visibility of the migrant as speaker in both intermediation networks, activist and institutional, is tied up with histories of protest and activism, as these latter have long problematized the misrecognition of migrants in the public sphere and advocated for alternative, more inclusive portrayals of the migrant experience, portrayals that, in the words of Leurs and Ponzanesi, "could offer migrants alternative means to assert their voice, stake out their identity, and engage in community formation" (2018: 14; see also Downing and Husband 2005; Titley 2019; Trimikliniotis 2019). The changing status of migrant voice in networks of intermediation today is, in this sense, deeply implicated in those longer-term contestations around the humanization of marginalized populations, involving a range of actors from media to policy makers to activists to migrants themselves. The use of articulated voice in activist websites needs to be seen, from this perspective, as both a reflection of the asymmetrical histories of speaking and hearing within western and global public spheres and of the ongoing digital struggles of the symbolic border over migrant agency and recognition. Through these struggles, activist networks of intermediation not only remind institutional actors and the media of their own accountability in narrating migration but also offer alternate options of representation that go beyond the tropes of misrecognition that we scrutinized in Chapters 4 and 5. These struggles finally also offer a glimpse of a different, inclusive public sphere and a promise of a commons beyond the hierarchical and racialized divides of the symbolic border.

Conclusion

The Crisis Imaginary: The Digital Border and Its Crises

An Overview of the Border Assemblage

"Who are the rightful inhabitants of this earth?" asks Achille Mbembe, quoted at the start of this volume, and "What do we do with those who do not have a claim to earth?" Our book has been an attempt to address this question. Within the dominant epistemology conceiving the earth as a space of national territories and borders, we have argued, the question of who can inhabit our planet becomes a question of who has the right to cross the border, claim protection, and settle in the territory of a nation-state beyond that of one's birth. Our notion of the border not as a fixed line but as a process that draws boundaries of inside/outside in order to selectively exclude and include those who reach it captures the border as an act of power that separates "us" from "them": western citizens from their "others." Written upon historical structures of colonial violence and a deeply unequal distribution of resources, this process of boundary-drawing ends up systematically excluding and "othering" those who arrive from the global South seeking safety and a better life. In so doing, the border reproduces in the figure of the migrant the same racialized representations and structures that have haunted the western imagination of the South since western powers' colonial hegemony over the rest of the world.

The Workings of the Digital Border

Our approach to the border complicates this foundational understanding of who can inhabit the earth by integrating the digital into the process of boundary-drawing. It does so by theorizing the border as an assemblage of techno-symbolic networks of mediation, where boundary-drawing takes place through convergent platforms of data extraction, as much as through narratives of migration on mass and social media—Silverstone's double-articulation of technology and meaning (Silverstone 1994). Specifically, three key networks of mediation across the contexts of migrant reception are responsible for this complication, as they operate not only on the ground, in the territorial border, but also on page or on screen, in what we call the symbolic border.

Such networks, we have argued, draw boundaries between "us" and "them" by relying on multiple trajectories of connectivity that intersect with, overlap, and reinforce one another. Remediation works by reverberating news from migrant crossing points onto global broadcast platforms. Intermediation is about data processes of tracking and surveillance as much as it is about the horizontal connectivities on social media or the web that bring citizens and noncitizens together in online meeting points. And transmediation occurs when these online networks morph into offline action and become communities of face-to-face conviviality and cooperation.

These vertical, horizontal, and trans-contextual connectivities of the digital border variously configure the places, bodies, and voices of migration around the inside/outside boundary in ways that reproduce but can also challenge the power relations of the border. The outer territorial border, for instance, was drawn unevenly and discontinuously around the Eurodac data identification technologies at the Registration Center of Chios, the WhatsApp messaging among major humanitarian actors in the UN camp, or the Facebook groups around the volunteers' kitchen of the island (Chapter 1), while the divides of the inner border were reaffirmed but also contested around online networks of job-training, social media groups of co-learning, as well as through "guerrilla" interventions for activism and the protection of the most vulnerable (Chapters 2 and 3). The symbolic border was first and foremost constituted through linguistic strategies of marginalizing or silencing migrant voice and through visual strategies of Eurocentric migrant representation in online news narratives (Chapters 4 and 5), both of which "othered" migrants as figures of pity, fear, solidarity, or self-reflexivity, never totally reduced to victimhood and threat yet never fully human either. At the same time, the symbolic border was negotiated through online storytelling: while the institutional initiatives we analyzed reaffirmed the narrowly conceived figure of the migrant, this conception was contested, we found, by activist online projects that asserted migrants' own agency as political subjects speaking out on their own desires and aspirations (Chapter 6).

Across these contexts of mediation, the border as process also extends not only in space but also in time. It is about the "crisis" moment of 2015 as much as about 2020 and the years in between, what we call the temporalities of post-"crisis." It is precisely this spatiotemporal elasticity of the digital border that enabled us to analyze its mediations not as a totalizing space of power, focusing exclusively on biopolitics and datafication but also as an assemblage: a hybrid terrain of techno-symbolic contestations where security, care, solidarity, and activism co-exist. As this terrain shifts and mutates at different scales, its primary function of security comes together with other political imperatives of the liberal west and the neoliberal market—namely the imperative to care and the imperative to profit—and these imperatives complicate the border as an always unstable site of shifting regimes of power.

The Politics of the Digital Border

The regimes of humanitarian and entrepreneurial securitization, central to our analyses throughout the volume, reflect this mutability of the digital border as a process that both defends territorial outposts and protects those it treats as a risk, or seeks to integrate them into its urban markets. The *humanitarian border* operates across dispersed spheres of action from the militarized security of the Registration Center to the securitized care of the UN camp, and to the compassionate solidarity of local volunteering and transnational activism. Manifested through an assemblage of remediations and intermediations, the territorial border organizes the digital, that is, datafied, interactive, or transmediated/embodied encounters of reception, into particular relationships of power and hierarchies of voice, while also producing new tensions at the intersection of protection and protest. At stake here is the western politics of the human, which variously situate migrants within a continuum of over-politicization as potential terrorists or de-politicization as vulnerable victims, but hardly ever address them as rightful actors seeking a better life and citizenship rights.

The *entrepreneurial border* similarly consists of distinct but interconnected networks of intermediation, mobilizing data-extractive and socially connective networks, and transmediation, configuring situated communities that work within or against the marketized and datafied security of urban labor markets. The self-responsibilization of migrants in search of job success as a marker of their worthy inclusion, the securitized precarity of grassroots online job training, or the conditional conviviality of face-to-face groups appear here as digitally enabled spheres of action where diverse forces struggle over migrants' civic status. At stake in these struggles is recognition not only as a legal attribute but as a social and ontological need; as legal precarity is an inevitable condition of city life for many, these other forms of recognition—that is, the basic acknowledgment that, independently of their formal status, they are worthy and desirable members of society—are key stakes in migrants' sense of belonging.

While the power relations of these two border regimes, whether they operate through the hierarchies of voice in the camp, the data surveillance of urban life, or the discursive choices of online journalism, ultimately work to reproduce the border, these relations also mobilize resistance. Rather than outright challenge or subversion, often resistance here refers to minor acts of re-subjectification, for example, through attempts to performative refugeeness at registration de-briefing sessions and through creative digital work; through online storytelling that unsettles the order of ventriloquized, institutionalized voices; and through the grassroots pedagogies of urban solidarity in the networked commons. Such acts move migrants from the domain of bare life or urban subalternity to that of a politically qualified life, one where migrants take some control over their identity, speak out in public, and make a difference in the communities in which they participate.

Our analysis of these regimes also demonstrated not only how the border's networks of mediation reconfigure the power relations of their contexts in different ways but also how each performs a distinct function in doing so. Processes of remediation largely work to normalize the border, by selecting, ordering, and framing the voices, visibilities, and claims of the actors involved in it. In this sense, remediation, related as it is to the powerful networks of global broadcasting, primarily operates as a symbolic border. News stories, for instance, repeat familiar linguistic and visual patterns, privileging predictably the voice of the elites; portraying migrants as groups of unfortunates or as menacing young men; and reporting on their rights through "our" activism, thereby legitimizing a discourse on migrants as undesirable "others" or as extraordinary strangers. Intermediation, at the same time, works more ambivalently. On the one hand, intermediation works as territorial border surveillance, when it links up global nodes of biometric data from the US to Australia and from Canada to Spain, sharing information and communications intelligence, even including voice and text messages of those considered as a threat (as the remit of the "5-Eyes Alliance"[1] and now "14-Eyes Alliance" allows states to do; Švenčionis 2020). On the other hand, it also connects narrative communities of solidarity, linking up subaltern voices of the city—and so humanizing migrants as competent professionals, vulnerable but agentive individuals, or catalysts of social change. Transmediation finally highlights the fact that the border is never only digital; it is also always situated and embodied. This means that, even though the boundary-drawing work of the border takes place through data profiling, platform connectivity, or broadcast narrativization, it is simultaneously always embedded in the contexts and bodies of those involved in it. We saw this, for instance, in the Registration Center, where the border consisted of infrastructural materials that went beyond datafication and included the derelict factory, and where police officers made their own cultural judgments on migrant posture and dress code as part of their monitoring process, but we also saw it in the Berlin and Athens neighborhoods where activists and migrants preferred to meet in person and spend time together in physical proximity, whether to play, learn a language, or eat and have fun outside online systems of surveillance.

The Mundanity of the Digital Border

Our response, then, to the question of what we actually do with those who "do not have a claim to earth" cannot be a singular one. While, as we argued in Chapter 2, migrants' civic status depends on whether they hold legal rights as residents or as successful asylum seekers, the question of rights and recognition is more complex than this. This is because the border assemblage is a multifarious structure routinely generating possibilities of exclusion and containment as much as minor acts of participation and recognition. Within this broader continuum of positions, migrants are encamped, deported, "othered," and marginalized or, when actively participating in established communities, often fitted within a specific template of success that privileges economic value over other kinds of social, cultural, and creative value. Yet, at the same time, as active narrators of their stories on social media and as participants on networked commons that make claims to the city and its resources, migrants regularly participate in urban infrastructures of welfare, contest their containment within stereotypical binaries, and open up their own space for individual creativity and political agency within and against security and the market.

This complexity of the digital assemblage, fragmented and discontinuous as its various operations are, highlights the diagnostic value of a granular analysis of the border: of how its technologies, narratives, and actors work to manage human mobility and how they navigate the border's hierarchies of human life in minor ways. What this focus on the marginal spaces, daily stories, liminal relationships, and lesser activities of the digital assemblage has helped us describe, then, is the mundane or under-the-radar nature of the digital border and its actors, its quotidian as opposed to its "crisis" experience (Amaya-Castro 2014 for the distinction). Assembled through field observations, interviews, and text analyses, what our analytical snapshots have, in other words, revealed is the *ordinariness* of the digital border. Whether it is routine debriefing process in the Chios Registration Center, the employment data updates at the job center, the migrants' Code Your Future sessions and Sunday meals or the Refugee Radio Network music and news programs, the digital border emerges through a set of mundane encounters, routines, stories, conversations and relations that are premised on yet somehow also subversive of the border assemblage (Anderson et al. 2009).

Even though this emphasis on the molecular practices of exclusion and "othering," as we saw in Chapters 1 and 2, has been theorized in critical research on border biopolitics, our own approach to the mundanity of the border has come to illuminate how this biopolitical matrix is also productive of subaltern identities and alternative subjectivities. Alongside infrastructures of control, mediations of resistance in the form of alternative digital networks and community media have indeed enabled migrants to speak out, make their experiences public, and demand to be heard.[2] Involving all the actors of the border, whether state bureaucracy, NGOs, community services, or activist groups, such mediations affirm, negotiate, or subvert the boundary-drawing work of the border in ways that highlight biopolitics as a versatile economy of power that entails both constraint and agency—what, after Wiertz, we could call a "biopolitics as multiple and becoming" (2020).

The Crisis Imaginary

From this analytical perspective, the vital function of the border and its networks of mediation lies not only in the way in which this assemblage controls migrant mobility, but also in the way it regulates our very ways of thinking about human mobility as well as our potential responses to it, in the first place. This bigger question came to the fore in the ways in which Europe and the rest of the global North responded to the 2015 arrivals as a "crisis" for the continent itself, not for vulnerable humanity. Why the vocabulary of "crisis"? we ask. What does "crisis" mean here, and, importantly, what political work does it perform in the context of human mobility and its mundane, everyday operations? It is these questions that shift our attention from the analytical puzzle of what we do with those who do not have a claim to the earth, to the normative one of what we should do with them—and it is this normative puzzle that we reflect on in the rest of our Conclusion.

Crisis as a Social Imaginary

We have already challenged the use of the term "crisis" in western public discourse, in our Introduction. We have there argued that the discourse of migration "crisis" decontextualized the 2015 moment from broader global developments, such as the long-term conflicts in Syria, Iraq, and Afghanistan, the rising scale of displacement as a result of destitution, war, economic inequality, and the environmental catastrophe caused primarily by and profiting the global North. As many of those predicaments have been consistently kept away from western public debates, the arrival of more than one million people at Europe's shores in 2015 appeared as unexpected, inexplicable, and in need of immediate security measures.

In our concluding argument, we now need to place this use of the term within a deeper understanding of "crisis," not just as a word that describes migrant arrivals on EU borders, but as a foundational linguistic act that regulates how we understand migration itself as an exclusively western concern centered around the mobility of non-western people towards the global North. Drawing on Taylor's use of the social imaginary as "those images, stories and legends" through which "people imagine their social existence, how they fit together with others . . . and the deeper normative notions and images that underlie these expectations" (2002: 106), we use the notion of the "crisis imaginary" to refer to the symbolic space of Eurocentric representations within which we are invited to imagine what migration means for "us," as western publics, and what emotions and actions "we" are expected to mobilize towards non-western subjects, in general. In setting up our horizon of expectations, we argue, the crisis imaginary establishes a hegemonic field of meanings wherein "we" are subsequently invited to engage with "our" public conversations of migration in ways that zoom into some of its dimensions as worthy of our attention while zooming out of others as irrelevant or inconsequential (Gutiérrez Rodríguez 2018).

Within this crisis imaginary, we contend, the meaning of the 2015 migrant arrivals, just as much as the 2018 American migrant caravan in the US, have been labeled as a sudden and troublesome change with dire implications for the future of the global North (Iannacone 2021). The imaginary thus defined the "crisis" around a dual temporality of emergency: as an *unmanageable event* in its real-time unfolding and as an *unpredictable menace* in the collective imagination of the continent's future (Krzyżanowski 2019 for the temporalities of crisis). The unmanageability of the "crisis," let us recall, referred primarily to the unprecedented scale of migrant arrivals in Europe. As the EU's 2015 Refugee Crisis Report put it, "the scale is immense": 1,011,700 by sea in 2015 and almost 34,900 by land compared to 280,000 total arrivals in 2014 (IOM 2015). Yet, the challenges such numbers ultimately created were not treated as *logistical*, that is, how the continent could agree on managing the distribution of migrant quotas amongst them, but as primarily *political*, that is, having to do with tensions inside the EU and its diverging asylum policies. While, as Metcalfe-Hough (2015) admits, "the practical challenge presented by the sheer scale of the crisis should not be underestimated," its administrative burden, she continues, was unevenly distributed, falling almost exclusively on the shoulders of certain countries. And it is this long-standing asymmetry in the treatment of migration among EU countries that turned the logistical into a political problem. As Garavoglia (2015), speaking of this asymmetry prior to the crisis, explains, "some countries are doing the heavy lifting in absolute terms: Germany's readiness to take over 40,000 migrants in 2014 being a case in point. Other member states are displaying exceptional generosity by accepting very significant intakes relative to the total number of applications received—witness Sweden's 74 percent recognition rate of refugee or subsidiary protection status in 2014. However, other EU countries show little solidarity both toward their fellow EU member states and toward asylum seekers worldwide."[3]

This skewed distributional pattern persisted in the 2015 "crisis" so that, with the exception of Sweden and Germany, where then-Chancellor Angela Merkel opened the borders to 890,000 people with her now famous pronouncement "We can do this" (Deutsche Welle 2020), the remaining EU nation-states swiftly moved to provisionally close their borders in an attempt to protect their sovereignty. Given that, in line with the Schengen agreement, such borders are normally open to free movement by European citizens, this closure introduced a significant anomaly to the political system of the Union—an anomaly that lasted until the 2016 stoppage of mobility from the countries of reception (Greece and Italy) and the further fortification of Europe's outer borders: "in the 2015–2016 European refugee crisis," as the EU Directorate General's for Internal Policies says in its own report, "the reintroduction of internal border controls was related to the arrival of asylum seekers" even though, "there has been no [. . .] assessment of the extent to which reintroducing border checks complies with the principles of proportionality and necessity" (Guild et al. 2016: 9).

Motivated not by any real risks but mostly by right-wing political agendas and their anti-migrant sentiment across a number of EU countries (Goździak and Márton 2018; Art 2011), what this anomaly of the Union's border closures revealed was not the threat of outsiders but the vulnerability inherent in the continent's own political process of integration and its constitutive mythology of Europe as united by shared interests and values. As Bojadžijev and Mezzadra put it, "it is clear [that] the future of this process [of integration—LC/MG] is precisely what is at stake in the current crisis," rendering the migration "crisis" in essence "a crisis of European migration policies" and of its dominant border regime,[4] and dictating that, to consolidate unity inside Europe, the EU eventually had to close off those outside.

We can here see how the crisis imaginary mobilizes a logistical discourse of unmanageability, where the European present appears overwhelmed by the sheer number of migrant arrivals, when, in fact, it is principally unsettled by its own unstable architecture. It is this vital but fragile architecture that the crisis imaginary was invoked to protect. Angela Merkel's "We can do this" moment can, in this context, be seen as the only public intervention that, as ephemeral as it was, sought to challenge this notion of "crisis" and open up what Zehfuss calls an "alternative imagination" where migrant arrivals are seen as an opportunity rather than a problem; in this sense, Zehfuss continues, "her [Merkel's] intervention can be read as departing from the political imaginary valorizing the appearance of control performed through bordering" (2020: 13).

Crisis and the Specter of Terrorism

If the crisis imaginary signals the present as extraordinary and uncontrollable, centered around rhetorical tropes of external threats to the global North, how does this imaginary manage to signal the future of migrant arrivals? Increasingly, it does so by mobilizing the specter of terror—a specter that, to echo Zehfuss's words above, had to "appear" to be "controlled" and eliminated. In the context of the migration "crisis" it was, as we showed in Chapter 4, the November 2015 Paris attacks (the third in France that year) that sharply shifted public discourse away from the "ecstatic humanitarianism" sentiment, following Alan Kurdi's death, towards the full-on securitization of the EU border that is now in place: "Paris changes everything," as German politician, Markus Söder, said at the time (Lyman and Smale 2015). And, indeed, even though as Roy reminds us, the "fear of Islam" had already been central in European migration policy for the past forty years (2012), this particular terrorist attack became a historic catalyst for prioritizing border protection over migration, even among those who had initially been open to receiving migrants. Since November 2015, "the refugee crisis in Europe can no longer be understood as separate from the crisis of terrorism" (Nail 2016: 158).

Despite the Paris attacks' real and long-term impact on border security, however, the links between migration and terrorism remain non-specific and tenuous. To begin with, the empirical fact is that, according to the 2017 Danish Institute for International Studies report on the migration "crisis," "the great majority of individuals involved in perpetrating terrorist attacks in Europe within the last decade have been EU citizens. Many have been foreign fighters, and most were already known to the European authorities" while "since January 2015, the terrorist threat related to refugee flows primarily stems from European foreign fighters who have travelled along migration routes to re-enter Europe undetected" (Manni et al. 2017: 4). This lack of substantial evidence of a link between migrants and terrorists (with the identities of the latter, mostly home-grown cases, already known to authorities; Hinkkainen 2013; Hafez and Mullins 2015) is further reflected in relevant EU documents. As one of the EU's own reports demonstrates, the security-related justifications that each country offered for closing its intra-Schengen (internal European) borders in 2015 were too elusive to provide solid grounds for their final decision: "there seems to be a noticeable shortage of detail on the reasons for the reintroduction of border controls" (EU 2016: 42), the report argues, further adding that "the justifications amount to no more than bare assertions without any evidence, explanation or other material that might substantiate the claim" (EU 2016: 43).

Notwithstanding the failure to establish a firm connection between migration and terrorism in reality, the link between the two is nevertheless routinely consolidated not only in policy documents but also in media discourse around the continent. Galantino's analysis of the Italian and German press during the "crisis," for instance, shows how the news conflated the two categories by use of a recurring argument, namely "that large flows of asylum seekers and migrants can be infiltrated by terrorists"—and so introduced a discursive "migration–terrorism nexus" that traversed the majority of news narratives in the two countries (2020; see also Sharma and Nijjar 2018; Sakellariou 2017; Boukala and Dimitrakopoulou 2018). In the absence of empirical evidence to substantiate the causal link between them, the premise of this nexus relies not on reality but on *potentiality*, that is on the possibility that migrant flows may be infiltrated by terrorists or that they may become radicalized in their new communities upon arrival: "the problem," as Zehfuss describes it, "is that 'we' do not know how people seeking refuge in Germany "will be at some point." Because "we" know the newcomers' possible development insufficiently, they pose a risk to "us" in the future" (2020: 12). Rather than acknowledging that the majority of migrant arrivals in 2015 (75%) consisted of people who were themselves fleeing war and terrorism in their own lands (UNHCR 2015), this speculative argument about terrorism became a basic premise of the crisis imaginary insofar as it instilled a sense of insecurity among western publics and so perpetuated a culture of fear for the "other" (Titley 2019).

The crisis imaginary emerges here not simply as a form of "othering" that constructs the migrant as a threat in the ways that we saw in Chapters 4 and 5, but as the condition that, in the first place, makes possible both the symbolic border of news storytelling and the territorial border with its own discourses and practices of migrant monitoring, surveillance, and classification. It is in this sense that the crisis imaginary cannot be thought of as simply a linguistic choice but as belonging to the broader western epistemology of national sovereignty and borders that we mentioned in Chapter 1: an order of discourse reproducing an orientalist imagination of migrants as racialized subjects that are always unknowable and dangerous—and so whose suffering or death is the unnoteworthy price to pay for "our" security. Seen from this perspective, de Genova claims, "the putative 'migrant crisis'" of Europe must be understood to be a historical moment of *racial crisis*, that is a crisis marked by "the appalling proliferation of almost exclusively non-European/non-white migrant and refugee deaths and other forms of structural violence and generalized suffering" (2018: 1768). Conceptions of non-whiteness as deviant or threatening among the populations that are marginalized, excluded, or left to die at the outer border of Europe are indeed central to the normative work that the crisis imaginary performs in western societies. But, as it zooms into the emergency, terror, and fear dimensions of the border, rendering those hyper-visible (and hyper-emotional), what exactly is it that the crisis imaginary keeps out of "our" view?

The Invisible Crises of the Digital Border

The crisis imaginary, we propose, renders invisible a series of truly extraordinary moments of emergency that, instead of identifying them as crises, it prefers to misconstrue or ignore. The first is the *crisis of the outer border*, which we discuss as a crisis of reception involving the entanglement of migration, and its administrative challenges, with the financial crisis of Greece—and the nation's concomitant difficulty to provide the infrastructures and resources of a first-destination country for migrants. The second is the *crisis of the inner border*, which we explain as a crisis of solidarity entailing the entanglement of migration and migrants' struggles for recognition with the neoliberal rollback of welfare and security crackdown in western cities. The third crisis, which we discuss in our concluding section, is the horrendous *crisis of the border's "deathworlds"*—spaces of in-between life and death (Mbembe 2019 in Bangstad and Nilsen 2019), neither the outer nor the inner border but of the elsewhere, most powerfully exemplified in the migrants' detention camp in Moria on the island of Lesbos.

The *crisis of the outer border* refers to the circumstances under which the official management of migrant reception was organized on the Greek islands in 2015. In Chapter 1, we examined how the dire circumstances of border security impacted not only migrants themselves but also the local authorities that had to construct the Registration Center from scratch and house its operations in a ramshackle former factory with borrowed infrastructures—from the e-generator to the heaters and the working desks. The contrast between the desolate conditions on-site and the data infrastructures online captures the discontinuous conditions of intermediation through which the global surveillance of migration occurs, and points to the ways in which the transnational circulation of data often relies on the invisibility of the material conditions that make this circulation possible, in the first place (Dijstelbloem 2020; Latonero and Kift 2018).

Behind this logistical crisis lies another crisis, the global economic crisis of 2008–2010 that had left Greece with meager human and financial resources to cope with a scale of human mobility unseen at its shores. The lack of infrastructures and human-power we witnessed there was due, to a large extent, to the country's financial bankruptcy and its continuing struggle with strict austerity measures put in place five years earlier to manage its national debt (Doxiadis and Placas 2018). Combined with longer-term institutional and administrative weaknesses that have plagued the country (Dalakoglou and Angelopoulos 2017), Greece was left with few resources to cope and, although by September 2015 it had already received €259.4 million in EU's AMIF (Asylum, Integration, and Migration Fund) budget (European Commission 2016a), the support was not enough to counter pressures that were disproportionately high for a nation under extreme strain. This meant that even if the Chios team, as we noted, worked hard to transport as many migrants as fast as possible, in Lesbos, which was the busiest arrival point, the asylum application process was so jammed that migrants had to wait in the thousands for days or weeks in the open air to be interviewed and registered.[5]

It was because of such dysfunctionalities at Europe's outer border that Greece was, at the time, "accused" by its EU partners "of having failed to register people, to prepare checkpoints for new arrivals at so-called hotspots on time, and to relocate as many refugees as it promised to" (Fotiadis 2015), and eventually, in March 2016, cited by EU countries as a reason for closing their own national borders to safeguard their security.[6] Entering a dramatic new phase in the outer border crisis by 2020, Greek islands have since seen themselves become "Europe's shields," turning into deterrence zones that seek to keep migrants outside the continent at all costs. Boats carrying thousands of people have been illegally pushed back to Turkey by the Greek Coast Guard with the support of Frontex, according to "mounting evidence" detailed by Stevis-Gridneff (2020) in a damning *New York Times* report, while drone technologies are used to spot and stop migrant entries to Europe before they can even voice their claims to asylum (Ahmed 2020). Those who make it as far as the islands remain trapped inside camps that prevent them from leaving the outer border—Greece here figuring more as the "dumping ground" (Kroet 2016a) of Europe than as its shield (Christopoulos and Spyropoulou 2019). The Greek islands, now island-camps, represent here the latest manifestation of the "hidden geographies of the enforcement archipelago," that Alison Mounzt records in her global study of the growing numbers of islands—including the Christmas Islands for Australia, Lampedusa for Italy, and the US territories of Guam and Saipan—that "thwart human mobility through confinement," leading to the "slow death of asylum itself" (2020: xv–xx).

The *crisis of the inner border* refers to the ever-expansive elasticity of the border, which multiplies systems of surveillance within cities and across urban neighborhoods and places of work and education, in what Marino calls the "technification of European security" (2021: 173). Technologies of unceasing control follow migrants in their cities of arrival as they go about their everyday lives, reminding them that they always and everywhere remain "on probation" and at risk of being expelled. These technologies mobilize systems of direct surveillance that require migrants to prove that they do not pose any security threat, and, alongside these systems, are demands that migrants transform themselves through the market. We saw in Chapter 2, for example, how the state and the market invest in digital training and "digital integration," creating opportunities for some to gain from online education and work through possible pathways of long-term recognition—on the condition that they perform as successful entrepreneurs. But we also saw that the hope of the few creates a crisis for the many, especially for those who are unable to benefit from such opportunities as they cannot meet the demands of swift digital integration into the market. Many migrants—for instance, women, persons with disabilities, and working-class migrants—are well aware of the fact that, at any time, they might be deemed as undeserving of welcome; the fear of being "ejected" from Europe is for them a real, everyday threat.

In dividing migrants into the deserving and the undeserving, those who can digitally integrate and those doomed to fail, this crisis of the inner border simultaneously also leads to a crisis of solidarity, as described in Chapter 3. The lack of sustained support for migrants as a result of the rollback of the welfare state and diminishing funding for migrant organizations comes with a huge emotional cost for both migrants and those supporting them—as the latter find themselves struggling to compensate for the lack of sustainable systems of care. Whereas, as our discussion revealed, resistance to the border does takes place on and through the city's networks of connectivity in everyday life, these same networks have nonetheless also experienced the harms, material and psychological, inflicted by the intersection of the migration "crisis" with the economic one and its austerity policies. This convergence of crises primarily affects migrants' systems of recognition, as it accentuates the already existing divisions between "good" and "bad" migrants, rewarding the former's entrepreneurial skills potentially eligible to long-term recognition and citizenship but "punishing" the latter for lagging behind.

The crisis of the camp of Moria "death-world," on the island of Lesbos, however, represents the darkest dimension of the invisible crises of the border. The largest of its kind in Europe, this "camp-city" with its steel gates and barbed wire fencing is, as Oberg puts it, "a surreal mix of an internment camp and shanty squatter encampment" (2018). Designed as a European Union "hotspot,"[7] a provisional site set up in 2015 to host a maximum of 3,000 people as they waited for their asylum applications to be processed, held until recently more than 13,000 people in an expanding sea of tents that was eventually burned down in September 2020.

Living under "horrendous conditions," as the 2019 MSF report puts it, the camp has become a "dead place[s] of non-connection" (Mountz 2020: 99), isolating those who had endured wars and perilous journeys, including an often life-threatening sea crossing to reach Europe, from the rest of the society (Médecins Sans Frontières 2019a). But the onset of the COVID-19 pandemic, another instance of a crisis-within-a-crisis, proved to be the last straw. The fire started when those encamped were worried that no measures had been taken to protect their health despite evidence of a rising number of infections among them; as Oxfam reported, the camp was put on lockdown to stop the spread of the virus yet "social distancing and good hygiene were all but impossible at the camp, given its squalid and cramped conditions" (Harlan and Labropoulou 2020). Following the fire, and as another piecemeal camp was swiftly set up on the island, migrants were left to survive on their own: "We don't have a place to sleep. We don't have anything to eat," Julia Bukasa, a young migrant, told Reuters, as she sat on the tarmac breastfeeding her eight-month-old infant (Papadimas and Kostantinidis 2020).

Like the island camps in Mounzt's study, the camps in Moria and other Greek islands, offer our final and most compelling response to Mbembe's question of what "we" in the global North do with those who can make no claim to the earth. Europe, following the lead of Australia's detention island policies it once condemned, has since 2016 confined migrants into legal but atrocious spaces of encampment, where law is used to suspend fundamental rights, enforcing life circumstances of "hell on earth" (Deutsche Welle 2020)—circumstances which fill them with despair and end up traumatizing them as much if not more than the experiences they fled from in the first place. "Moria has become a trigger for an acute expression of psychosis and post-traumatic stress disorder," MSF lead psychiatrist, Dr. Barberio, said in 2018, with his colleague, MSF Head of Mission in Greece, Louise Roland-Gosselin, adding that "I have been in some pretty horrendous camps and situations," including crisis zones in Congo and South Sudan, yet "I have to say that Moria is the camp in which I've seen the highest level of suffering" (Stevis-Gindeff and Lima 2020).

In this sense, the Moria camp belonged to a regime of border power that, we argue, is different both from the transitory, light-touch humanitarian security of the 2015 "crisis," that we described in Chapter 1, and from the entrepreneurial security of Chapter 2 in the post-"crisis" cities of Europe up to 2020. By extending security across time, and so keeping people "provisionally" within its confines for long periods, often years, but also by sustaining deeply precarious forms of life through minimal care—in overcrowded tents with insufficient toilets, showers, medical care, and food (Stevis-Gindeff and Lima 2020)[8]—Moria, like other regimes of island detention more broadly, sheds new light onto the corporeal, psychic, and political violence of the border. In so doing, it reveals that, despite their euphemistic name, the "hotspots" at the edges of Europe still operate within a 'state of exception,' to use Agamben's phrase again; borders before the border or liminal spaces removed from political and social life that reduce those encamped in them to "bare life."

Combined with the Mediterranean's leading positions among globally recorded migrant deaths (with 27,782 people recorded drowning between 2014-2021, IOM 2021), the necropolitical practices of the border come into stark relief (Mbembe 2003). Whether it is death "by indifference," as EU naval control turns a blind eye to sea-travelers in distress, by aggression, as it pushes them back and away from western shores[9] (Ahmed 2020; Basaran 2014; Stevis-Gridneff 2020), or "by exhaustion," in the shadow of suicidal ideation or violent death[10] (Welander and de Vries 2016), these spaces are literal "death worlds": "new and unique forms of social existence," as Mbembe describes them, "in which vast populations are subject to conditions of life conferring upon them the status of living dead" (2003: 21).

Set up specifically for migrant populations who move from the global South to the global North, these death-worlds are not simply markers of the crisis imaginary, where the protection of the west presupposes the exclusion and invisibility of its distant others (Squire 2017); they are simultaneously carriers of the colonial and racist legacies of oppression and violence that, as we have already argued, are largely responsible for the structural inequalities behind contemporary human mobility in the first place. Those seeking to reach safety in the global North, have, from this perspective, already been traumatized or impoverished in ways that highlight just how their destinies of precarity and abjection upon arrival rely, at least in part, on pre-existing structures and rationalities of western domination and violence. In this context, we can perhaps now more lucidly see how the crisis imaginary performs the work of concealing as much as that of revealing. For if, from the standpoint of the global North, the "crisis" refers to managerial emergencies caused by the large, or perceived as large, numbers of arriving populations, from the standpoint of "death-worlds," the crisis refers to the ontological emergency experienced by all those who struggle to survive against the odds in the death-worlds of Europe.

As we now come full circle, we return for a final time to our recurrent question as to the fate of those who do not have a claim to earth. It has become clearer by now how the "crisis" imaginary and its tactical in/visibilities raise the normative question that Mbembe asks of the postcolony: "in a context where everything is likely to come in contact with violence and death [. . .] in the quotidian technologies and practices of power as in the structures of imagination, what does it mean to say, 'I am a human being,' 'I am alive,' or still, 'I exist?' What does one mean when one affirms 'the desire to be free' and 'the capacity to decide for oneself?'" (2006: 154). Driving our own normative agenda, this question of the human highlights indeed the moral and political significance of an alternative response to the border that challenges the imaginary of migration as a "crisis." If, following Mbembe, we think of human dignity, recognition, and freedom as fundamental rights for migrants, then we need to push our understanding of migration beyond this imaginary's spectral fears of the other. Indeed, as we saw across the pages of this book, the digital border performs the paradoxical job of both containing and reproducing the same specter of fear that it itself creates, thereby amplifying suspicion of the other who must be pushed back yet cannot ever be fully repulsed.

The most important function of the imaginary is, in this sense, that it routinely acts as a pedagogy of crisis in western societies, that is, as a mundane practice of everyday learning that, through its tactical uses of visibility and invisibility, normalizes fear for migrants, legitimizes the state of exception at its borders, and silently accepts its death-worlds as "necessary" forms of violence in the name of "our" safety. The rise of alt-right politics in the global North (Main 2018) can be attributed, to a large extent, precisely to the security-migration nexus that lies at the heart of this pedagogy of crisis not only in the media, as we have already seen, but also in party-political communication—where, as Gattinara and Morales's cross-European study shows, "the more political parties stress the security aspects of immigration politics, the more public opinion perceives the issue as a security issue" (2017: 3). This pedagogy is further responsible for the broader cultural normalization of what Wodak (2019) calls "a post-shame era," where the boundaries of the sayable are shifting to incorporate migrant hate as a morally and politically legitimate claim in public discourse and policy-making: the proliferation of terms such as "clandestine" or "illegal" for migrants among broader dehumanizing vocabularies, but also the increasingly derogatory connotations of "humanitarians" for solidarity activists (in Greece and elsewhere), as well as the prolongation of migrants' inhumane encampments and the deliberate delays in processing their status are some of the consequences of this normalization. In so doing, the pedagogy of crisis ultimately parochializes transnational mobility as a right only of the global North, which recognizes its privileged citizens alone as legitimate cross-border travelers while treating all others as alien threats that need to be deterred.

A key ambition of ours in examining the digital border in this book has been, from this perspective, to interrogate the kinds of imaginaries the border articulates and the civic pedagogies of migration it makes possible. While this is not a book about migration policies, our analysis of the digital border points to two directions. First, the mediation networks of migration need to be re-organized so as to protect not only the populations of the global North but also the safety and the dignity of people on the move. This means that i) border intermediations that involve data extraction need to be scrutinized for their built-in biases and for the harms they inflict upon migrants; ii) networks of remediation should change the language and imagery they use to represent them away from reductive and damaging stereotypes, and should instead thematize migrant voice, showcasing migrants as historical agents with their own humanity—their own aspirations, opinions and desires; iii) social media intermediations need to encourage practices of migrant recognition, acknowledging that they are worthy individuals with diverse capabilities beyond the entrepreneurial skills favored by urban markets, and amplifying their voice without rendering invisible, irrelevant, and dispensable the most precarious of them.

Second, if Europe and the west at large, wishes to live up to its own self-description as a liberal continent supporting human rights and the protection of the vulnerable around the world, particularly those whose countries of origin are succumbing under the harsh realities of the planet (military, environmental, economic), then it should work to collectively take responsibility for the migrants reaching its shores. While this is clearly a complex matter that requires planetary collaboration and solution, the current state, where the continent either traps migrants in the death-worlds of the camps, or externalizes their management to third, unsafe countries, such as Libya, further intensifies the precarity of people on-the-move and so ends up running against Europe's own rule of law, "exposing," as Liguori puts it, "migrants and asylum seekers to serious human rights violations" (2019: 1).

This collective effort begins, we contend, with taking this immanent contradiction of the liberal west between human rights and border violence seriously. Rather than settling comfortably in the convenient invisibilities of the digital border and its "crisis" imaginary, we need to problematize its hierarchies and misrepresentations, denounce the inhumanities it conceals, and listen attentively to the migrant voices it seeks to silence. For, unless we see them precisely as human beings with the determination to make a difference in the societies they arrive at, rather than as threats to be kept out, Mbembe's question of how we treat those who do not have a claim to earth will remain one of the darkest, most disturbing moral conundrums of our world.

ACKNOWLEDGMENTS

We could have never written this book without the support, intellectual encounters, and collaborations with a number of colleagues and research participants. First, we would like to warmly thank the Department of Media and Communications, London School of Economics and Political Science, where we are both based, and especially its Head in 2015–17, Nick Couldry, for supporting and funding the departmental project *Migration and the Media*; our colleague Ellen Helsper for crucial support at the early stages of the project development; and our remarkable colleague Rafal Zaborowski who was a fellow co-traveler throughout the realization of this project. We would also like to thank the master's students and Ph.D. researchers who supported the project through coding and analysis. Specifically, behind the analysis of data in Chapter 4 and 5 lies the hard work of student coders Zuzana Brezinová, Leah Selig Chauhan, Antonios Dimitriadis, Joelle Eid, Lisa Elkhoury, Poliana Geha, Shreya Goenka, Safaa Halahla, Róbert Hegedűs, Gyorgyi Horvath, Seema Huneidi, Rosanna Hutchings, Leticia Ishibashi-Poppenwimmer, Götz Kadow, Kaylah Kleczka, Kristina Kolbe, Afroditi Koulaxi, Jan Krotký, Ana Lomtadze, Rita Nemeth, Sadichchha Pokharel, Corinne Schweizer, Karim Shukr, Ema Stastna, Sanja Vico, Pauline Vidal, and Felicity Ward, all working under the guidance, first and foremost, of Rafal Zaborowski and with support throughout the project's realization by Kristina Kolbe and, particularly, Tijana Stolic, who has been instrumental in the textual analysis process. Lilie would like to cordially thank, in particular, Rafal and Tijana, her two co-authors in journal publications from this project that have also informed the arguments of Chapters 4 and 5 of this book. Great appreciation goes also to Afroditi Koulaxi, who has not only supported the *Migration and the Media* project and research in Athens but also assisted us in the preparation of this manuscript. For the fieldwork in Chios, also conducted in the context of this Departmental project, we want to thank Daphne Milner for her valuable technical and emotional help and extend our appreciation to our friends and participants on the island of Chois for their warm welcome, invaluable support, but also life lessons of solidarity and perseverance. Special thanks go to Kostas Zafiris, without whose support fieldwork would have never realized in such richness, as well as Dimitris Frezoulis, Ermioni Frezouli, and Vicki Georgouli for their warm hospitality, insights, and willingness to share thoughts and experiences of solidarity and welcome.

For incredible editorial support and guidance, we would like to thank our academic editors, Aswin Punathambekar, Jonathan Gray, and Adrienne Shaw, especially Aswin for his sharp insight and advice, and Eric Zinner, NYU Press Editor-in-Chief for his commitment to this project. Also, the delivery of this book has substantially benefited from Judith Barrett's great professionalism and expertise as the copy editor.

Lilie Chouliaraki is grateful to the colleagues, collaborators, and friends who have engaged with the project and offered valuable insights in the writing of this book, particularly Bob Hariman at Northwestern University, Tristan Mattelart at Université Paris II—Panthéon-Assas, Pierluigi Musarò at the University of Bologna, Jonathan Ong at University of Massachusetts Amherst, Zizi Papacharissi at University of Illinois at Chicago, John Durham Peters at Yale University, Miriam Ticktin and Robin Wagner-Pacifici at the New School of Social Research and Barbie Zelizer at the University of Pennsylvania. The LSE-based reading group Humanitarian and Human Rights Communication was a wonderful hub of conversations and exchange of ideas in 2015–17, so special thanks go to its members Monika Krause, Mirca Madianou, Kate Nash, Shani Orgad, Ella McPherson, and Kate Wright. As always, the doctoral students at the Ph.D. program of LSE's Department of Media and Communications, which she has the privilege to be the Director of, have been a source of inspiration for her, particularly the contributions of Afroditi Koulaxi, Kat Higgins, and Tijana Stolic. Finally, she would like to acknowledge with appreciation the longer-term conversations with Christos Lazarides from the Greek Forum for Refugees for insightful observations on the realities and challenges of migrants and refugees in Athens and across Greece.

Myria Georgiou would like to express her deepest appreciation for collaboration, intellect, and critical devotion to the team of the *Resilient Communities, Resilient Cities: Digital Makings of the City of Refuge* (funded by LSE's Institute of Global Affairs as part of the Rockefeller Resilience Program), as well as for their generous agreement for us to share some of the project's findings in the context of this book. Specifically, warm thanks go to the project's core academic team—Deena Dajani, Suzanne Hall, and Kristina Kolbe—its assistants in Greece—Afroditi Koulaxi and Vivi Theodoropoulou, but also to the project's creative collaborators, Giles Lane and Marcia Chandra. Our collective work as a team has taken my engagement with the material and symbolic dimensions of transnational mobility, as well as the implications and responsibilities of our research conduct, in directions I could have never imagined. For inspiring conversations that advanced my understanding of migration in its particular and transnational manifestations, I would like to thank Giota Alevizou, Gareth Dale, Koen Leurs, Sandra Ponzanesi, Eugenia Siapera, Rob Sharp, Kevin Smets, Nicos Trimikliniotis, Vivi Theodoropoulou, Gavan Titley, and Natasa Vourna; and also these and many other colleagues and friends who provided invaluable feedback during events at Bologna University, Columbia University, Connecticut University, Loughborough University, Universidade Nova de Lisboa, USC, Utrecht University, and a number of welcoming events organized by ECREA's Diaspora, Migration, and Media Section. I would also like the warmly thank colleagues and friends who supported my research in Los Angeles, especially Tanita Enderes and Jessica Retis, but also Wendy Dembo and Amira Lopez. While not directly referenced in this book, research in Los Angeles has provided invaluable contextualization for the present analysis. Not least, I am indebted to all participants in research in Athens, Berlin, and London for their generosity and trust. I hope the spirit and delivery of this book reflects the great respect and admiration I have for them. Finally, I would like to thank my family, Elektra, Leon, and Kevin for endurance, support, and emotional boosting, especially at the most challenging moments of research conduct and write-up. You are part of my always-in-progress, bewildering life journey as a proud migrant. Elektra and Leon, I hope the world you'll grow to see and make will not be defined by walls but by cross-border solidarities.

NOTES

INTRODUCTION. THE DIGITAL BORDER

1 Our references to relevant literature here concern news narratives and do not extend to other media genres, such as non-fiction books, documentaries, or other art forms of visual storytelling such as film, where migrant voices are not only included but often constitute the thematic center of the work.

2 The vocabulary of reception is here not meant to unthinkingly reproduce the geography of border sovereignty, even if it inevitably carries nationalist connotations. Rather, throughout our narrative, the term performs two tasks depending on context: on the one hand, it reflects the self-description of border structures put in place to manage migrant arrivals—from Registration Center to migrant volunteers; on the other, it refers to the moral act of hospitality, of receiving-as-a-welcome, as defined by Silverstone: "welcoming the other in one's space, with or without any expectation of reciprocity" (2006: 139). While these are clearly distinct uses that do not always coincide, there are also interesting overlaps that we point to and comment on in the course of our analyses.

1. THE OUTER BORDER

1 Arrivals from Turkey to Greek islands between January and August 2015 increased by 886% compared to 2014. Chios is the second biggest entry point to Europe in the Eastern Mediterranean (personal communication with Chios border police officers, December 2015).

2 Our approach can be defined as "critical fieldwork" along the lines of Madison's definition, that is, as a knowledge-producing practice that ". . . takes us beneath surface appearances . . . bringing to light underlying and obscure operations of power," thereby also moving "from "what is" to "what could be" (Madison 2011: 5).

3 See European Commission document "Identification of Applicants (EURODAC)" (2016b), which defines the system as follows: "EURODAC makes it easier for EU States to determine responsibility for examining an asylum application by comparing fingerprint datasets."

4 Following 2015, digital connectivity through WhatsApp and Skype has been established between border authorities or NGOs and migrants, in ways that raise serious questions around the latter's privacy and safety (Aradau 2020; Madianou 2019; 2021).

2. THE INNER BORDER

1. According to the EU's Migration Data Portal, "2.4 million refugees and people in refugee-like situations and 860 thousand asylum-seekers (pending cases) were hosted in EU-27 Member States at the end of 2018." Accessible at https://migrationdataportal.org/.
2. "Berlin received around 5% of all refugees coming to Germany: in 2015 well over 50,000 asylum seekers were registered in the city. This number sharply decreased to 16,889 asylum seekers in 2016 and 6,770 asylum seekers in 2017 and 720 in January 2018 (Landesamt für Flüchtlingsangelegenheiten 2017)" (OECD 2018b: 27; see also OECD 2020, *Working Together for Local Integration of Migrants and Refugees in Berlin OECD Report*. Available at www.oecd-ilibrary.org/.)
3. Despite their differences, all three cities share two important commonalities: they have been under pressure from rising xenophobic forces and, over the five years of our timeline, they have been variously subjected to government decisions to intensify surveillance over migrants; at the same time, with important variations, they all had some networks of reception in place, including advanced digital infrastructures provided both by state actors and grassroots activists in response to the needs presented by arriving migrants. All three cities represent, in this sense, politically ambiguous environments where progressive politics for the right to the city co-existed with securitized practices of policing and surveillance and the market values of urban entrepreneurship.
4. Led by Myria Georgiou, this study took place across the three cities from 2017 to 2019 (M. Georgiou—Principle Investigator; S. Hall—Co-Investigator; D. Dajani—Research Fellow; K. Kolbe—Research Assistant; the project also benefited from fieldwork support by A. Koulaxi and P. Theorodopoulou in Athens; and it was supported by the Rockefeller Foundation in collaboration with the Institute of Global Affairs, London School of Economics). The data were collected during creative workshops with migrant newcomers and civil society actors in each city (a collaboration with the creative studio Proboscis, where participants identified and discussed digital and material needs, resources, and obstacles that make/constrain the city of refuge); and during individual storytelling walks in the city with migrants and civic actors. Participants were invited to narrate their experiences with migration through the city by taking us to the places that mattered to them and by driving the narrative in their storytelling; our role was primarily to listen rather than to frame the conversation (the walk–storytelling methodology developed in collaboration with Counterpoints Arts, and specifically the photographer Marcia Chandra, and its creative outputs are available at www.digitalcityofrefuge.com).
5. For instance, overall unemployment in Athens has been consistently high in the past half-decade, "a staggering 51%" in November 2017 (OECD 2018a: 13). London and Berlin offered better, albeit varying, employment prospects for migrants.

London has not received a large number of post-2015 migration yet hosts large numbers of established migrant communities from across the world (Georgiou 2019). Finally, Berlin, with only 8% urban unemployment (EURES 2020) and with the 2016 Integration Act in place, it has been best positioned to absorb migrant labor force into its markets, yet, according to Germany's Commissioner for Immigration, Refugees, and Integration (Chazan 2017), "only a quarter to a third of refugees will be in work in five years' time," that is, up to 2022.

3. THE INNER BORDER AS NETWORKED COMMONS

1. See earlier reference to the project *Resilient Communities, Resilient Cities? Digital Makings of the City of Refuge*.
2. See also earlier reference to the project *Resilient Communities, Resilient Cities? Digital Makings of the City of Refuge*.
3. www.refugio.berlin.
4. www.refugio.berlin/veranstaltungen/regelmaessiges-angebot.
5. www.refugio.berlin/veranstaltungen/regelmaessiges-angebot.
6. Migrants need to connect on Skype to get pre-registration status. The process involves them being held in a virtual queue for days and subsequently have to wait for appointments for many months, sometimes more than a year.
7. https://baynatna.de.
8. For instance, according to the Migration Observatory report, entitled "Migration in the UK: Overview" (Walsh 2020), "most non-EU citizens who are not yet permanently settled residents are ineligible for income-based jobseekers' allowance and universal credit."
9. See, for instance, the *Politico EU* online publication, entitled "Thousands of Refugees Exploited as Illegal Workers in Germany," which states that "in some German states up to 50 percent of refugees work illegally" (Kroet 2016b). See also the Migration Observatory report "Irregular Immigration in the UK" (Walsh 2020), which provides an estimate of between 800,000 and 1.2 million irregular migrants in 2019, though the Observatory calls for caution in reading these numbers as they are no more than estimates.
10. See Aegean Solidarity Network UK, 2020.
11. An analysis made by RSA and PRO ASYL showed that by the end of June 2020, a total of 2,484 status holders had accessed rental subsidies through the program. This is far below the 11,000 beneficiaries requested to leave their accommodation that month, while more people continue to be granted international protection. For more information, see Refugee Support Aegean 2020.

4. NARRATIVE AND VOICE IN NEWS STORIES

1. The analysis of this chapter draws on and reformulates the argument in Chouliaraki and Zaborowski, "Voice and Community in the 2015 Refugee Crisis: A Content Analysis of News Coverage in Eight European Countries," *International Communication Gazette* 79, no. 6–7 (2017).

2   The analysis of this chapter draws on and reformulates the argument in Chouliaraki and Stolic, "Rethinking Media Responsibility in the Refugee 'Crisis': A Visual Typology of European News," *Media, Culture & Society* 39, no. 8 (2017).
3   The *Migration and the Media* project was funded by the Department of Media and Communications at the London School of Economics and Political Science (2015–2018). The authors worked closely with Dr. Rafal Zaborowski in conducting the study and analyzing the data; this project would not have been possible without him. Furthermore, fundamental to the development of the project was the support and guidance of our colleague, Ellen Helsper, the analytical work of Tijana Stolic, and the tireless commitment of the coders: Zuzana Brezinová, Leah Selig Chauhan, Antonios Dimitriadis, Joelle Eid, Lisa Elkhoury, Poliana Geha, Shreya Goenka, Safaa Halahla, Róbert Hegedűs, Gyorgyi Horvath, Seema Huneidi, Rosanna Hutchings, Leticia Ishibashi-Poppenwimmer, Götz Kadow, Kaylah Kleczka, Kristina Kolbe, Afroditi Koulaxi, Jan Krotký, Ana Lomtadze, Rita Nemeth, Sadichchha Pokharel, Corinne Schweizer, Karim Shukr, Ema Stastna, Sanja Vico, Pauline Vidal, and Felicity Ward.
4   See, for instance, van Dijk 1991, Wright 2002, Triandafyllidou 2013, and for the recent crisis see Musarò 2017, Berry et al. 2016, Gillespie et al. 2016, Georgiou and Zaborowski 2017, Chouliaraki 2017, Chouliaraki and Stolic 2017. It is worth mentioning that even literature discussing the 2015 "crisis" does so with different geographical foci and different methodological tools. The research on media, migrants, and refugees remains thus internally diverse, as the *news focus* in question may include, for example, publicity stories published by the Italian Navy on their website (Musarò 2017), UK press stories (Ibrahim and Howarth 2016) and European press articles (Berry et al. 2016), refugee selfies (Chouliaraki 2017), or refugees' mobile media and social networks (Gillespie et al. 2016).
5   Specifically, we focus on the broadsheet newspaper websites as a crucial and authoritative resource of remediation of the "crisis" for both European audiences and policymakers; firstly, because of its scale, pace, and duration, the 2015 migration event could only be reported extensively and in detail by established news organizations in the countries under study; and secondly, because, due to their reputation and reach, these news sites functioned as primary sources of knowledge about migrants not only among European publics but also among migration experts and decision-makers (Georgiou and Zaborowski 2017).
6   Separated roughly by two-month intervals, each of these 2015 periods serves to capture the dynamically changing narrative frames surrounding the "crisis" in the sense that each marks a distinctive shift in the representation of migrants. Specifically, each represents the following moments: (i.) *Careful tolerance* (July) was inaugurated by Hungary's refusal to admit migrants, erecting a physical barrier along its borders with Serbia (July 13, 2015) and is generally marked by dramatic daily stories about humanitarian efforts on the Mediterranean mixed with anxieties fueled by stories of migrant violence. (ii.) *Ecstatic humanitarianism* (September) was marked by the photographs of three-year-old Alan Kurdi on a Turkish

shore (September 3, 2015), which shifted the focus of media narratives towards humanitarian concern and the need to help migrants. (iii.) *Fear and securitization* (November) was initiated by the terror attacks in Paris (November 13, 2015), when the previous trend was reversed and security discourse dominated over humanitarian assistance; Europe was in shock, and migrants were blamed.

7   The newspapers we analyzed are: *Pravo, Lidove Noviny* (Czech Republic); *Le Monde, Le Figaro* (France); *Süddeutsche Zeitung, Frankfurter Allgemeine Zeitung* (Germany); *EFSYN, Kathimerini* (Greece); *Magyar Nemzet, Népszabadság* (Hungary); *Irish Independent, The Irish Times* (Ireland); *Vecernje Novosti, Blic* (Serbia); *The Guardian, The Times, The Independent, The Daily Telegraph* (UK). We have included in our sample the two main Arabic language European newspapers— *Al-Hayat* and *Al-Araby Al-Jadeed*. The decision to include the Arab European press was an attempt to incorporate into our analysis Arabic media narratives and priorities in covering a primary Arab migration at the time. Within this decision, we recognize the Arab European press as important element of European mediascapes (for more details on these choices see Georgiou and Zaborowski 2017).

8   While the two Lampedusa shipwrecks and the drowning of Alan Kurdi had an immediate but transitory impact on news reporting and public debate on the crisis, the Paris terrorist attacks had a lasting impact. Following a period of intense deliberation among European nation-states, the attacks led to the EU's decision to close national borders in March 2016, blocking approximately 58,000 migrants in Greece—a decision that is still operative.

9   Each of these three periods of time (July, September, November 2015) constitutes an important turning point in the European media narrative of the crisis. See endnote 6 of this chapter.

10   We observed each key moment in the press across ten working days following the event. The two largest stories concerning migrant arrivals to Europe in each of the ten daily editions were sampled. The remaining gaps in sampling were, when necessary, systematically filled by stories from different days in the period up to two weeks outside of our time frame (for as long as relevant articles were available for the constitution of the sample). The articles were subsequently coded and then analyzed using quantitative content analysis, driven by coding categories informed by our conceptual framework. In a pilot study, the reliability was assessed through intercoder reliability test conducted by two independent researchers. The codebook was subsequently revised and items which did not meet the criteria were removed from the study. The revised codebook was then used to code the 1,200 articles on the sample. While our conceptual focus here is built around voice and patterns of speech attribution, nonetheless our broader study addressed a number of further questions that have informed our analysis. These included: What are the specific frames of positive and negative actions relating to the management of "the crisis"? What are the emotional frames of migrant representation? And how do these differ across three distinct time periods in 2015?

11   These percentages are rounded to the closest numerical unit.

5. VISIBILITY AND RESPONSIBILITY IN NEWS IMAGERY

1. According to the United Nations High Commissioner for Refugees, the "top three nationalities of entrants of the over one million Mediterranean Sea arrivals between January 2015 and March 2016 were Syrian (46.7%), Afghan (20.9%) and Iraqi (9.4%)." See "Monthly Arrivals by Nationality to Greece, Italy and Spain. January 2015–March 2016," United Nations High Commissioner for Refugees, 2016, 2. Available at http://data2.unhcr.org/.

2. Examples of these positive representations can be found in genres beyond the news report, either in journalistic testimonies that take up migrant voices and amplify them in their own terms, as in the Pulitzer Prize-winning narrative *Enrique's Journey: The Story of a Boy's Dangerous Odyssey to Reunite With His Mother*, by Sonia Nazario, which has been published in eight languages: www.un.org/. They may also be found in long-form current affairs programs, in the press or television, such as the UK's Channel 4 documentary on Lampedusa that includes voices of migrants who have experienced the deadly crossing explaining their plight and the reasons for risking their lives to cross the Mediterranean: www.channel4.com/news/lampedusa-mediterranean-deadliest-migration-routes-libya. Further representations can be found in artistic projects, such as Bouchra Khalili's video installation *The Mapping Journey Project* (2008–11), on exhibition at MoMA (New York) and the Barbican (London), where eight men and women used markers to trace their itinerary on a map while describing their journey of hope in three languages, Arabic, Italian, and English: www.ansamed.info/. Finally, there is the *Selfie: Je Suis Refugee* visual art project consisting of refugee selfies and curated by Patricia Fransceschetti: www.patriciafranceschetti.com/.

6. SUBALTERN VOICE AND DIGITAL RESISTANCE

1. Find the Refugee Radio Network at www.refugeeradionetwork.net.
2. *Migrant Voice* can be found at migrantvoice.org.
3. *Are You Syrious?* can found at https://medium.com/are-you-syrious.
4. William Barrowcliffe, "Syed's Story: 'I Came to the UK to Study and Lost My Future,'" www.migrantvoice.org/.

CONCLUSION. THE CRISIS IMAGINARY

1. The 5-Eyes alliance consists of five countries collaborating to exchange communications and electronic intelligence—US, USA, Canada, Australia, New Zealand—and added to that are the 9-Eyes alliance (+Denmark, France, Netherlands, Norway) and the 14-Eyes alliance (+Belgium, Germany, Italy, Spain, Sweden), which also have agreements for intelligence exchanges and collaborations.
2. Such networks are, at this moment, enhanced by newer forms of participatory media, such as VR productions on the lived experience of what it means to flee violence and war (as in Alejandro Iñaritu's VR immersive tour into refugee's personal journeys in *Carne y Arena*, https://carne-y-arena.com/), or games (like

the smartphone application *Bury Me, My Love*, which invites the gamer to act as a named migrant and make difficult choices along the precarious journey).

3   See also media analysis in the article "Migrant Crisis: Migration to Europe Explained in Seven Charts," *BBC News,* March 2016, www.bbc.co.uk. "Tensions in the EU," according to the BBC, "have been rising because of the disproportionate burden faced by some countries, particularly the countries where the majority of migrants have been arriving: Greece, Italy and Hungary." And see UNHCR for a timeline of the conflicting positions and trajectories of European countries to the "crisis," titled "2015: The Year of Europe's Refugee Crisis," www.unhcr.org/.

4   This regime is based on the EU Dublin Agreement on Asylum (1990), which, in principle, "operates on the assumption that, as the asylum laws and practices of the EU States are based on the same common standards, they allow asylum seekers to enjoy similar levels of protection in all EU Member States." In practice, however, the Agreement leaves the responsibility of the asylum process to first destination countries (such as Greece and Italy). In so doing, it disadvantages migrants by keeping them in limbo for the long periods of time their applications are under review. See UNHCR document on "The Dublin Regulation," www.unhcr.org/.

5   In Lesbos, for instance, July 2015 saw the arrival of 15,254 migrants and refugees, compared with 921 the same month the previous year, so that "there were times" during July–August, "where on the island of Lesbos 9,000 people were estimated to wait for a place on a boat to leave for Athens or Thessaloniki." See Dimitriadi and Sarantaki (2019: 14) in European Union-funded (H2020) Project CEASEVAL Report Number 28: "Borders and the Mobility of Migrants in Greece" (Evaluation of the Common European Asylum System): http://ceaseval.eu/publications/28_WP4_Greece.pdf.

6   Greece has benefited from 2.64 billion euros from the EU between 2015 and 2020 "to better manage migration and borders" (European Commission 2020). This funding has largely supported policies that have turned the country into one of "Europe's shields" (alongside Italy and Spain).

7   The "hotspot approach" seeks to "provide a platform for the agencies to intervene, rapidly and in an integrated manner, in frontline Member States when there is a crisis due to specific and disproportionate migratory pressure at their external borders." See "Explanatory Note on the 'Hotspot' Approach," Statewatch, 2015, www.statewatch.org/. There are currently five hotspots in Greece (one in each of the migrant arrival islands: Samos, Lesbos, Chios, Leros, and Kos) and five in Italy (Taranto, Messina, Lampedusa, Trapani, and Pezzalo).

8   Since September 2021, a new EU-funded facility has been in operation on the island of Samos. This is a €38m asylum-seeker Center with much-needed new facilities (restaurants, air-conditioning, playgrounds), but also one constructed as a prison surrounded by high fences with barbed wire and strict gate controls to keep people inside. Migrants and NGOs have complained about this prison-like design, but, as Manos Logothetis, a Greek official overseeing the project, said, "the

EU itself had questioned the multi-layered fencing surrounding the Samos facility" but had "to follow the law." See Helena Smith, "Why Greece's Expensive New Migration Camps Are Outraging NGOs," *Guardian,* 19 September 2021, www.theguardian.com.

9. There have been increasing reports, investigations, and migrant testimonies on illegal pushbacks of migrants on small boats from Greek waters to Turkish waters since 2019, see for example the human rights' sea monitoring organization *Mare Liberum* (https://mare-liberum.org/) and *The Guardian* report of migrant testimonies, titled "Greece Accused of Refugee 'Pushbacks' After Family Avoid Being Forced Off Island," June 29, 2021, and also its investigative report on the story titled "Revealed: 2,000 Refugee Deaths Linked to Illegal EU Pushbacks," May 5, 2021, www.theguardian.com.

10. For the high percentages of psychotic episodes, self-harm, suicidal ideation, and depression in Moria and other hotspots, see the International Rescue Committee (IRC) Report "Unsupported, Unprotected, Uncertain: Recommendations to Improve the Mental Health of Asylum Seekers on Lesvos," September 2018, www.rescue.org/.

BIBLIOGRAPHY

Accenture. "Shaping the New Digital Border Agency: The Border as an Asset." 2017. www.accenture.com.
Aegean Solidarity Network Team UK. "Athens/Chios—The Unmentionables." *Aegean Solidarity Network*. Accessed 30 November 2020. http://asnteamuk.org.
Affichard, Joëlle, Jean-Baptiste de Foucauld, and Étienne Balibar, eds. "Inégalités, Fractionnement Social, Exclusion." In *Justice Sociale et Inégalités / Sous la dir. de Joëlle Affichard et Jean-Baptiste de Foucauld*, 149–61. Société. Ed. du Seuil, 1992.
Agamben, Giorgio. *Homo Sacer: Sovereign Power and Bare Life*. Translated by Daniel Heller-Roazen. Redwood City, CA: Stanford University Press, 1998.
Agnew, John. "Borders on the Mind: Re-Framing Border Thinking." *Ethics & Global Politics* 1, no. 4 (2008): 175–91. https://doi.org/10.3402/egp.v1i4.1892.
Ahmed, Kaamil. "EU Accused of Abandoning Migrants to the Sea with Shift to Drone Surveillance." *Guardian*, 28 October 2020. www.theguardian.com/.
Accenture. "AI Technology for Border Services." *Accenture*. Accessed 28 November 2020. www.accenture.com.
AIDA. "Asylum Information Database | IALS." 2019. Accessed 17 December 2020. https://ials.sas.ac.uk/.
———. "Statistics—Greece | Asylum Information Database." Accessed 17 December 2020. www.asylumineurope.org/.
Ajana, Btihaj. "Augmented Borders: Big Data and the Ethics of Immigration Control." *Journal of Information, Communication and Ethics in Society* 13 (9 March 2015): 58–78. https://doi.org/10.1108/JICES-01-2014-0005.
Al-Ghazzi, Omar. "An Archetypal Digital Witness: The Child Figure and the Media Conflict over Syria." *International Journal of Communication* 13 (2019): 3225–3243.
Albahari, Maurizio. "The Birth of a Border: Policing by Charity on the Italian Maritime Edge." In *Border Encounters: Asymmetry and Proximity at Europe's Frontiers*, edited by Jutta Lauth Bacas and William Kavanagh. Berghahn Books, 2013.
———. "Europe's Refugee Crisis." *Anthropology Today* 31, no. 5 (2015): 1–2. https://doi.org/10.1111/1467-8322.12196.
Alevizou, Giota. "Civic Media & Placemaking: (Re)Claiming Urban & Migrant Rights across Digital and Physical Spaces." In *The SAGE Handbook of Media and Migration*, edited by Kevin Smets, Koen Leurs, Myria Georgiou, and Saskia Witteborn. London: SAGE, 2020. https://doi.org/10.4135/9781526476982.

Ålund, Aleksandra, and Carl-Ulrik Schierup. "Making or Unmaking a Movement? Challenges for Civic Activism in the Global Governance of Migration." *Globalizations* 15, no. 6 (2019): 79–93. https://doi.org/10.1080/14747731.2018.1446599.

Amaya-Castro, Juan, M. "International Refugees and Irregular Migrants: Caught in the Mundane Shadow of Crisis." *Netherlands Yearbook of International Law* (2014): 65–88. The Hague: TMC Asser Press.

Amnesty International. "The Global Refugee Crisis: A Conspiracy of Neglect." Amnesty International. 2015. www.amnesty.org.

Amoore, Louise, and Rita Raley. "Securing with Algorithms: Knowledge, Decision, Sovereignty." *Security Dialogue* 48, no. 1 (1 February 2017): 3–10. https://doi.org/10.1177/0967010616680753.

Amoore, Louise, Stephen Marmura, and Mark Salter. "Editorial: Smart Borders and Mobilities: Spaces, Zones, Enclosures." *Surveillance and Society* 5 (1 April 2008). https://doi.org/10.24908/ss.v5i2.3429.

Anderson, Bridget, Nandita Sharma, and Cynthia Wright. "Why No Borders?" *Refuge: Canada's Journal on Refugees* 26, no. 2 (2009): 5–18.

Andersson, Ruben. "Video, Algorithms and Security: How Digital Video Platforms Produce Post-Sovereign Security Articulations." *Security Dialogue* 48, no. 4 (2017): 354–372. https://doi.org/10.1177/0967010617709875.

———. *No Go World: How Fear Is Redrawing Our Maps and Infecting Our Politics.* Oakland: University of California Press, 2019.

Andreas, Peter. "Redrawing the Line: Borders and Security in the Twenty-First Century." *International Security* 28 (2003): 78–111. https://doi.org/10.1162/016228803322761973.

Anthias, Floya. *Translocational Belongings: Intersectional Dilemmas and Social Inequalities.* New York: Routledge, 2021.

Aradau, Claudia. "Experimentality, Surplus Data and the Politics of Debilitation in Borderzones." *Geopolitics* (2020): 1–21. https://doi.org/10.1080/14650045.2020.1853103.

Archakis, Argiris, Sofia Lampropoulou, and Villy Tsakona. "'I'm not Racist but I Expect Linguistic Assimilation': The Concealing Power of Humor in an Anti-Racist Campaign." *Discourse, Context, and Media* 23 (June 2018): 53–61.

Arendt, Hannah. *The Origins of Totalitarianism.* First edition. New York: Harcourt, Brace, Jovanovich, 1976.

———. *The Human Condition.* Second edition. Chicago: University of Chicago Press, 1998.

Art, David. *Inside the Radical Right: The Development of Anti-Immigrant Parties in Western Europe.* Cambridge University Press, 2011.

Awad, Isabel, and Jonathan Tossell. "Is the Smartphone Always a Smart Choice? Against the Utilitarian View of the "Connected Migrant." *Information, Communication & Society* (26 September 2019): 1–16. https://doi.org/10.1080/1369118X.2019.1668456.

Awumbila, Mariama. "Drivers of Migration and Urbanization in Africa: Key Trends and Issues." *International Migration* 7, no. 8 (2017).
Ayoub, Joey. "Why Fortress Europe and the European Union Can't Coexist." *Byline Times*, 2 April 2020. https://bylinetimes.com/.
Azoulay, Ariella. "Getting Rid of the Distinction between the Aesthetic and the Political." *Theory, Culture & Society* 27 (1 December 2010): 239–62. https://doi.org/10.1177/0263276410384750.
———. *The Civil Contract of Photography*. New York: Zone Books, [2008] 2012.
Bacas, Jutta Lauth, and William Kavanagh, eds. *Border Encounters: Asymmetry and Proximity at Europe's Frontiers*. First edition. Berghahn Books, 2013.
Back, Les, and Shamser Sinha. *Migrant City*. London: Routledge, 2018.
Balabanova, Ekaterina, and Alex Balch. "Norm Destruction, Norm Resilience: The Media and Refugee Protection in the UK and Hungary during Europe's 'Migrant Crisis.'" *Journal of Language and Politics* 19, no. 3 (1 May 2020): 413–35. https://doi.org/10.1075/jlp.19055.bal.
Balibar, Étienne. "The Borders of Europe." In *Cosmopolitics: Thinking and Feeling beyond the Nation*, edited by Pheng Cheah, Bruce Robbins, and Social Text Collective. Minneapolis: University of Minnesota Press, 1998.
Bakewell, Oliver. "Research Beyond the Categories: The Importance of Policy Irrelevant Research into Forced Migration." *Journal of Refugee Studies* 21, no. 4 (2008): 432–453.
Bangstad, Sindre, and Torbjørn Tumyr Nilsen. "Thoughts on the Planetary: An Interview with Achille Mbembe." *New Frame*, 5 September 2019. www.newframe.com/.
Banks, James. "Unmasking Deviance: The Visual Construction of Asylum Seekers and Refugees in English National Newspapers." *Critical Criminology* 20, no. 3 (1 September 2012): 293–310. https://doi.org/10.1007/s10612-011-9144-x.
Bansak, Kirk, Jens Hainmueller, and Dominik Hangartner. "Europeans Support a Proportional Allocation of Asylum Seekers." *Nature Human Behaviour* 1, no. 7 (2017): 1–6.
Barenboim, Deanna. "The Specter of Surveillance: Navigating 'Illegality' and Indigeneity among Maya Migrants in the San Francisco Bay Area." *PoLAR: Political and Legal Anthropology Review* 39, no. 1 (May 2016): 79–94. https://doi.org/10.1111/plar.12132.
Barlow, John Perry. "A Declaration of the Independence of Cyberspace." Electronic Frontier Foundation, 1996. www.eff.org.
Barnett, Clive. "On the Milieu of Security: Situating the Emergence of New Spaces of Public Action." *Dialogues in Human Geography* 5, no. 3 (1 November 2015): 257–70. https://doi.org/10.1177/2043820615607758.
Barthes, Roland. *Image, Music, Text*. New York: Hill and Wang, 1977.
Basaran, Tugba. "Saving Lives at Sea: Security, Law and Adverse Effects." *European Journal of Migration and Law* 16, no. 3 (16 October 2014): 365–87. https://doi.org/10.1163/15718166-12342061.

———. "The Saved and the Drowned: Governing Indifference in the Name of Security." *Security Dialogue* 46, no. 3 (1 June 2015): 205–20. https://doi.org/10.1177 /0967010614557512.

Bauman, Zygmunt. *Europe of Strangers*. University of Oxford. Transnational Communities Programme, 1998.

Baycan-Levent, Tüzin, and Peter Nijkamp. "Characteristics of Migrant Entrepreneurship in Europe." *Entrepreneurship & Regional Development* 21, no. 4 (1 July 2009): 375–97. https://doi.org/10.1080/08985620903020060.

Baynatna. "The Arabic Library." Accessed 30 November 2020. https://baynatna.de.

BBC. "Migration to Europe in Charts." *BBC News*, 11 September 2018. www.bbc.com/.

———. "Child Migrants: What Is Happening at the US Border?" *BBC News*. Accessed 17 April 2021. https://www.bbc.co.uk/.

Beduschi, Ana. "International Migration Management in the Age of Artificial Intelligence." Rochester, NY: Social Science Research Network, 10 February 2020. https://papers.ssrn.com/.

Benjamin, Ruha. *Race after Technology*. Cambridge: Polity, 2019.

Benkler, Yochai. *The Wealth of Networks: How Social Production Transforms Markets and Freedom*. New Haven, CT: Yale University Press, 2006.

Benson, Rodney. *Shaping Immigration News*. Cambridge: Cambridge University Press, 2013.

Benson, Rodney and Tim Wood. "Who Says What or Nothing at All? Speakers, Frames, and Frameless Quotes in Unauthorized Immigration News in the United States, Norway, and France." *American Behavioral Scientist* 59, no. 7 (2015): 802–821. https://doi.org/10.1177%2F0002764215573257.

Berger, John. *Ways of Seeing*. New York: Penguin Books, 1973/1990.

Berry, Mike, Inaki Garcia-Blanco, and Kerry Moore. "Press Coverage of the Refugee and Migrant Crisis in the EU: A Content Analysis of Five European Countries." Geneva: United Nations High Commissioner for Refugees, 11 February 2016. www.unhcr.org.

Bibri, Simon. "The Anatomy of the Data-Driven Smart Sustainable City: Instrumentation, Datafication, Computerization and Related Applications." *Journal of Big Data* 6 (4 July 2019). https://doi.org/10.1186/s40537-019-0221-4.

Bigo, Didier. "The (In)securitization Practices of the Three Universes of EU Border Control: Military/Navy–Border Guards/Police–Database Analysts." *Security Dialogue* 45, no. 3 (2014): 209–225.

Bigo, Didier, Engin Isin, and Evelyn Ruppert, eds. *Data Politics: Worlds, Subjects, Rights*. Routledge, 2019. https://doi.org/10.4324/9781315167305.

Birla, Ritu. "Postcolonial Studies: Now That's History." In *Can the Subaltern Speak?: Reflections on the History of an Idea*, edited by Rosalind Morris. New York: Columbia University Press, 2010.

Birnbaum, Emily. "Trump, Dem Talk of 'Smart Wall' Thrills Tech Companies." *The Hill*, 31 January 2019. https://thehill.com.

Bleiker, Roland. "Writing Visual Global Politics: In Defence of a Pluralist Approach—a Response to Gabi Schlag, 'Thinking and Writing Visual Global Politics.'" *International Journal of Politics, Culture, and Society* 32, no. 1 (1 March 2019): 115–23. https://doi.org/10.1007/s10767-018-9299-5.

Bleiker, Roland, David Campbell, Emma Hutchison, and Xzarina Nicholson. "The Visual Dehumanisation of Refugees." *Australian Journal of Political Science* 48, no. 4 (1 December 2013): 398–416. https://doi.org/10.1080/10361146.2013.840769.

Boffey, Daniel. "EU Border 'Lie Detector' System Criticised as Pseudoscience." *Guardian*, 2 November 2018. www.theguardian.com/.

Bojadžijev, Manuela, and Sandro Mezzadra. "'Refugee Crisis' or Crisis of European Migration Policies?" *FocaalBlog*, 12 November 2012, 5.

Boltanski, Luc. *Distant Suffering: Morality, Media and Politics*. Translated by Graham D. Burchell. Cambridge: Cambridge University Press, 1999. https://doi.org/10.1017/CBO9780511489402.

Bolter, David Jay and Richard Grusin. *Remediation: Understanding New Media*. Cambridge, MA: MIT Press, 2000.

Booker, Cara L., Yvonne J. Kelly, and Amanda Sacker. "Gender Differences in the Associations between Age Trends of Social Media Interaction and Well-Being among 10–15 Year Olds in the UK." *BMC Public Health* 18, no. 1 (20 March 2018): 321. https://doi.org/10.1186/s12889-018-5220-4.

Boukala, Salomi and Dimitra Dimitrakopoulou. "Absurdity and the 'Blame Game' within the Schengen Area: Analyzing Greek (Social) Media Discourses on the Refugee Crisis." *Journal of Immigrant & Refugee Studies* 16, no. 1–2 (2018): 179–197.

Bowker, Geoffrey C., Wiebe E. Bijker, W. Bernard Carlson, and Trevor Pinch. *Sorting Things Out: Classification and Its Consequences*. New edition. Cambridge, MA: MIT Press, 2000.

Bozdağ, Çiğdem. "Bottom-up Nationalism and Discrimination on Social Media: An Analysis of the Citizenship Debate about Refugees in Turkey." *European Journal of Cultural Studies* 23, no. 5 (2020): 712–730.

Bozdağ, Çiğdem, and Kevin Smets. "Understanding the Images of Alan Kurdi with "Small Data": A Qualitative, Comparative Analysis of Tweets about Refugees in Turkey and Flanders (Belgium)." *International Journal of Communication* 11 (2017): 24.

Bradley, Karin. "Open-Source Urbanism: Creating, Multiplying and Managing Urban Commons." *FOOTPRINT* (11 June 2015), 91–107. https://doi.org/10.7480/footprint.9.1.901.

Brink, Bert van den, and David Owen, eds. *Recognition and Power: Axel Honneth and the Tradition of Critical Social Theory*. Cambridge: Cambridge University Press, 2007. https://doi.org/10.1017/CBO9780511498732.

Broeders, Dennis. "The New Digital Borders of Europe: EU Databases and the Surveillance of Irregular Migrants." *International Sociology—INT SOCIOL* 22 (1 January 2007): 71–92. https://doi.org/10.1177/0268580907070126.

Buchanan, Sara, Bethan Grillo, Terry Threadgold, Tom Wengraf, and Article 19. *What's the Story?: Results from Research into Media Coverage of Refugees and Asylum Seekers in the UK*. London: Article 19, 2003.

Burman, Erica. "Innocents Abroad: Western Fantasies of Childhood and the Iconography of Emergencies." *Disasters* 18, no. 3 (1994): 238–53. https://doi.org/10.1111/j.1467-7717.1994.tb00310.x.

Butler, Judith. *Frames of War: When Is Life Grievable?* London: Verso, 2009.

Buzan, Barry, and Ole Wæver. *Regions and Powers: The Structure of International Security*. Cambridge: Cambridge University Press, 2003.

Caffentzis, George, and Silvia Federici. "Commons against and beyond Capitalism." *Community Development Journal* 49, no.1 (1 January 2014): 92–105. https://doi.org/10.1093/cdj/bsu006.

Calhoun, Craig. "A World of Emergencies: Fear, Intervention, and the Limits of Cosmopolitan Order." *Canadian Review of Sociology/Revue Canadienne de Sociologie* 41 (1 November 2004): 373–95. https://doi.org/10.1111/j.1755-618X.2004.tb00783.x.

Cammaerts, Bart. "Disruptive Sharing in a Digital Age: Rejecting Neoliberalism?" *Continuum* 25, no. 1 (2011): 47–62.

Cantat, Celine, Eda Sevinin, Ewa Maczynska, and Tegiye Birey. *Challenging the Political Across Borders: Migrants' and Solidarity Struggles*. Budapest: Central European University, 2019.

Carling, Jørgen. "The End of Migrants As We Know Them?" *Jørgen Carling* (blog), 20 September 2016. https://jorgencarling.org/.

Carter, Donald, and Heather Merrill. "Bordering Humanism: Life and Death on the Margins of Europe." *Geopolitics* 12, no. 2 (1 May 2007): 248–64. https://doi.org/10.1080/14650040601168867.

Carville, Justin. "Intolerable Gaze: The Social Contract of Photography." *Photography and Culture* 3, no. 3 (2010): 353–58.

Cavarero, Adriana. *Relating Narratives: Storytelling and Selfhood*. London: Routledge, 1997.

Chandler, D. C. "Review Article: Risk and the Biopolitics of Global Insecurity." *Conflict, Security & Development* 10, no. 2 (May 2010): 287–97. https://doi.org/10.1080/14678801003666024.

Chandler, Nahum Dimitri. *X—the Problem of the Negro as a Problem for Thought*. New York: Fordham University Press, 2014.

Chatterton, Paul. "Seeking the Urban Common: Furthering the Debate on Spatial Justice." *City* 14 (1 December 2010): 625–28. https://doi.org/10.1080/13604813.2010.525304.

Chazan, Guy. "Most Refugees to Be Jobless for Years." *Financial Times*, 22 June 2017. www.ft.com.

Cheah, Pheng, Bruce Robbins, and Social Text Collective, eds. *Cosmopolitics: Thinking and Feeling beyond the Nation*. Minneapolis: University of Minnesota Press, 1998.

Cheney-Lippold, John. *We Are Data: Algorithms and the Making of Our Digital Selves.* New York: New York University Press, 2017.

Chouliaraki, Lilie. *The Spectatorship of Suffering.* First edition. London: SAGE, 2006.

———. "The Mediation of Suffering and the Vision of a Cosmopolitan Public." *Television & New Media* 9, no. 5 (September 2008): 371–91. https://doi.org/10.1177/1527476408315496.

———. *The Ironic Spectator: Solidarity in the Age of Post-Humanitarianism.* First edition. Cambridge, MA: Polity, 2012.

———. "Re-Mediation, Inter-Mediation, Trans-Mediation." *Journalism Studies* 14, no. 2 (1 April 2013): 267–83. https://doi.org/10.1080/1461670X.2012.718559.

———. "Symbolic Bordering: The Self-Representation of Migrants and Refugees in Digital News." *Popular Communication* 15, no. 2 (3 April 2017): 78–94. https://doi.org/10.1080/15405702.2017.1281415.

Chouliaraki, Lilie, and Norman Fairclough. *Discourse in Late Modernity: Rethinking Critical Discourse Analysis.* Edinburgh: Edinburgh University Press, 1999.

Chouliaraki, Lilie, and Myria Georgiou. "Hospitality: The Communicative Architecture of Humanitarian Securitization at Europe's Borders." *Journal of Communication* 67, no. 2 (2017): 159–80. https://doi.org/10.1111/jcom.12291.

Chouliaraki, Lilie, Myria Georgiou, Rafal Zaborowski, and W. A. Oomen. *The European "Migration Crisis" and the Media: A Cross-European Press Content Analysis.* London School of Economics and Political Science, 14 June 2017.

Chouliaraki, Lilie, and Tijana Stolic. "Rethinking Media Responsibility in the Refugee 'Crisis': A Visual Typology of European News." *Media, Culture & Society* 39, no. 8 (November 2017): 1162–77. https://doi.org/10.1177/0163443717726163.

Chouliaraki, Lilie, and Rafal Zaborowski. "Voice and Community in the 2015 Refugee Crisis: A Content Analysis of News Coverage in Eight European Countries." *International Communication Gazette* 79, no. 6–7 (November 2017): 613–35. https://doi.org/10.1177/1748048517727173.

Christensen, Miyase, and André Jansson. "Complicit Surveillance, Interveillance, and the Question of Cosmopolitanism: Toward a Phenomenological Understanding of Mediatization." *New Media & Society* 17, no. 9 (1 October 2015): 1473–91. https://doi.org/10.1177/1461444814528678.

Christopoulos, Dimitris, and Georgia Spyropoulou. "Buffer States: Greek–Turkish Framing on the EU Externalisation Policy of Refugee Management." In *Conflict and Cooperation: From Europeanization to De-Europeanization,* edited by Alexis Heraclides and Gizem A. Çakmac, 271–286. London: Routledge, 2019.

Clarke, Jennifer. "Transnational Actors in National Contexts: Migrant Organizations in Greece in Comparative Perspective." *Southeast European and Black Sea Studies* 13, no. 2 (2013): 281–301.

Clarke, Jennifer, Asteris Huliaras, and Dimitri A. Sotiropoulos. *Austerity and the Third Sector in Greece: Civil Society at the European Frontline.* Routledge, 2016.

Clayton, Jonathan, and Hereward Holland. "Over One Million Sea Arrivals Reach Europe in 2015." UNHCR, 2015. https://www.unhcr.org/.

Coleman, Mathew, and Kevin Grove. "Biopolitics, Biopower, and the Return of Sovereignty." *Environment and Planning D: Society and Space* 27, no 3 (2009): 489–507. https://doi.org/10.1068%2Fd3508.

Cossé, Eva. "From Chaos in Moria to Despair in Athens, Greece: Refugees Live Rough on the Streets of Central Athens." Human Rights Watch, 20 August 2020. www.hrw.org.

Côté-Boucher, Karine. *Border Frictions: Gender, Generation and Technology on the Frontline*. Abingdon, Oxon; New York, NY: Routledge, 2020.

Couldry, Nick. *Why Voice Matters: Culture and Politics After Neoliberalism*. First edition. Los Angeles: SAGE, 2010.

Couldry, Nick, and Ulises A. Mejias. "Data Colonialism: Rethinking Big Data's Relation to the Contemporary Subject." *Television & New Media*, 20, no. 4 (2 September 2018): 336–349. https://doi.org/10.1177/1527476418796632.

Cox, Ruth. "Recognition and Immigration." In *Recognition Theory as Social Research: Investigating the Dynamics of Social Conflict*, edited by Shane O'Neil and Nicholas H. Smith, 192–212. London: Palgrave Macmillan UK, 2012. https://doi.org/10.1057/9781137262929_10.

Crawley, Heaven, Simon McMahon, and Katharine Jones. "Victims and Villains: Migrant Voices in the British Media." Centre for Trust, Peace, and Social Relations, Coventry University, 2 February 2016. https://pureportal.coventry.ac.uk.

Crawley, Heaven, and Dimitris Skleparis. "Refugees, Migrants, Neither, Both: Categorical Fetishism and the Politics of Bounding in Europe's 'Migration Crisis.'" *Journal of Ethnic and Migration Studies* 44, no. 1 (2018): 48–64.

Crone, Manni, Maja Felicia Falkentoft, Teemu Tammikko, and Danish Institute for International Studies. *An Extraordinary Threat?: Europe's Refugee Crisis and the Threat of Terrorism*. Copenhagen: DIIS, 2017.

Crul, Maurice. "Super-Diversity vs. Assimilation: How Complex Diversity in Majority-Minority Cities Challenges the Assumptions of Assimilation." *Journal of Ethnic and Migration Studies* 42, no. 1 (2 January 2016): 54–68. https://doi.org/10.1080/1369183X.2015.1061425.

Dalakoglou, Dimitris, and Georgios Agelopoulos, eds. *Critical Times in Greece: Anthropological Engagements with the Crisis*. First edition. London: Routledge, 2017.

Darling, Jonathan. "Becoming Bare Life: Asylum, Hospitality, and the Politics of Encampment." *Environment and Planning D: Society and Space* 27, no. 4 (1 August 2009): 649–65. https://doi.org/10.1068/d10307.

Datta, Ayona. "A 100 Smart Cities, a 100 Utopias." *Dialogues in Human Geography* 5, no. 1 (1 March 2015): 49–53. https://doi.org/10.1177/2043820614565750.

———. "The Digital Turn in Postcolonial Urbanism: Smart Citizenship in the Making of India's 100 Smart Cities." *Transactions of the Institute of British Geographers* 43, no. 3 (2 March 2018): 405–19. https://doi.org/10.1111/tran.12225.

Davies, William. "Neoliberalism: A Bibliographic Review." *Theory, Culture & Society* 31, no. 7-8 (1 December 2014): 309–17. https://doi.org/10.1177/0263276414546383.

Dayan, Daniel. "On Morality, Distance and the Other: Roger Silverstone's Media and Morality." *International Journal of Communication* 1 (2007): 113–122.

De Genova, Nicholas. "Spectacles of Migrant 'Illegality': The Scene of Exclusion, the Obscene of Inclusion." *Ethnic and Racial Studies* 36, no. 7 (1 July 2013): 1180–98. https://doi.org/10.1080/01419870.2013.783710.

———. "Border Struggles in the Migrant Metropolis." *Nordic Journal of Migration Research* 5 (1 March 2015). https://doi.org/10.1515/njmr-2015-0005.

———, ed. *The Borders of "Europe": Autonomy of Migration, Tactics of Bordering*. Durham, NC: Duke University Press, 2017.

———. "The 'Migrant Crisis' as Racial Crisis: Do Black Lives Matter in Europe?" *Ethnic and Racial Studies* 41, no. 10 (9 August 2018): 1765–82. https://doi.org/10.1080/01419 870.2017.1361543.

Dekker, Rianne, Godfried Engbersen, Jeanine Klaver, and Hanna Vonk. "Smart Refugees: How Syrian Asylum Migrants Use Social Media Information in Migration Decision-Making." *Social Media + Society* 4, no. 1 (1 March 2018): 1–11. https://doi.org/10.1177/2056305118764439.

Deutsche Welle. "Hell on Earth—Greece's Moria Refugee Camp and Its Tortured History." *Deutsche Welle*. Accessed 24 December 2020. www.dw.com/.

Deutsche Welle. "'We Can Do This!'—Merkel's Famous Words Five Years on after Refugee Influx to Germany." *Deutsche Welle*. Accessed 2 July 2021. www.dw.com/.

Deuze, Mark. "Participation, Remediation, Bricolage: Considering Principal Components of a Digital Culture." *Information Society* 22, no. 2 (2006): 63–75.

"Digital City of Refuge." Accessed 24 December 2020. www.digitalcityofrefuge.com/.

Dijstelbloem, Huub. "Europe's New Technological Gatekeepers. Debating the Deployment of Technology in Migration Policy." *Amsterdam Law Forum* 1 (2009). https://dare.uva.nl/.

———. "Bordering a Hybrid World: Infrastructural Isolation and the Governance of Human and Nonhuman Mobility." *Global Perspectives* 1, no. 1 (11 May 2020). https://doi.org/10.1525/gp.2020.12789.

Dijstelbloem, Huub, and Dennis Broeders. "Border Surveillance, Mobility Management and the Shaping of Non-Publics in Europe." *European Journal of Social Theory* 18 (20 February 2014): 21–38. https://doi.org/10.1177/1368431014534353.

Dillon, Michael. "Underwriting Security." *Security Dialogue* 39, no. 2–3 (1 April 2008): 309–32. https://doi.org/10.1177/0967010608088780.

Diminescu, Dana. "The Connected Migrant: An Epistemological Manifesto." *Social Science Information* 47, no. 4 (1 December 2008): 565–79. https://doi.org/10.1177/0539018408096447.

Dimitriadi, Angeliki, and Antonia-Maria Sarantaki. "Borders and the Mobility of Migrants in Greece." 2019. Accessed 24 December 2020. http://ceaseval.eu/.

Dines, Nick, Nicola Montagna, and Elena Vacchelli. "Beyond Crisis Talk: Interrogating Migration and Crises in Europe." *Sociology* 52 (2018): 439–47. https://doi.org/10.1177/0038038518767372.

Doherty, Ben. "A Short History of Nauru, Australia's Dumping Ground for Refugees." *Guardian*, 9 August 2016. Accessed 17 April 2021. www.theguardian.com/.

Downing, John, and Charles Husband. *Representing Race: Racisms, Ethnicity and the Media*. First edition. London: SAGE, 2005.

Doxiadis, Evdoxios, and Aimee Placas, eds. *Living Under Austerity: Greek Society in Crisis*. First edition. Berghahn Books, 2018. https://doi.org/10.2307/j.ctvw04g5j.

Dreher, Tanja. "Speaking up or Being Heard? Community Media Interventions and the Politics of Listening." *Media, Culture & Society* 32, no. 1 (2010): 85–103.

Duffield, Mark. "Total War as Environmental Terror: Linking Liberalism, Resilience, and the Bunker." *South Atlantic Quarterly* 110, no. 3 (1 July 2011): 757–69. https://doi.org/10.1215/00382876-1275779.

Edkins, Jenny. "Sovereign Power, Zones of Indistinction, and the Camp." *Alternatives: Global, Local, Political* 25, no. 1 (2000): 3–25.

———. *Trauma and the Memory of Politics*. Cambridge: Cambridge University Press, 2003.

El-Enany, Nadine. "Aylan Kurdi: The Human Refugee." *Law and Critique* 27, no. 1 (1 April 2016): 13–15. https://doi.org/10.1007/s10978-015-9175-7.

Ellis, John. "Television as Working Through." In *Television and Common Knowledge*, edited by Jostein Gripsrud, 55–70. London: Routledge, 1999.

Ellis-Petersen, Hanna. "Rohingya Crisis: Bangladesh Says It Will Not Accept Any More Myanmar Refugees." *Guardian*, 1 March 2019. www.theguardian.com/.

Eubanks, Virginia. *Automatic Inequality: How High-tech Tools Profile, Police, and Punish the Poor*. New York: Picador, 2018.

EURES. "Labour Market Information—Berlin—European Commission." Accessed 18 December 2020. https://ec.europa.eu/.

European Commission. "EU Funding for Migration and Security: How It Works." *Migration and Home Affairs*. 6 December 2016a. https://ec.europa.eu/.

———. "Identification of Applicants (EURODAC)." *Migration and Home Affairs*, 6 December 2016b. https://ec.europa.eu.

———. "Annual Report on Migration and Asylum 2017." *Migration and Home Affairs*. 24 May 2018. https://ec.europa.eu.

———. "What's New on the EC's Research & Innovation Web Site." 26 October 2018. https://ec.europa.eu/.

———. "Managing Migration: EU Financial Support to Greece." European Commission, 2020. https://ec.europa.eu/.

European Parliament. "Asylum and Migration in the EU." 30 June 2017. www.europarl.europa.eu.

Faist, Thomas. "The Migration-Security Nexus: International Migration and Security Before and After 9/11." In *Migration, Citizenship, Ethnos*, edited by Y. M. Bodemann and G. Yurdakul. New York: Palgrave Macmillan, 2006.

Fassin, Didier. "Policing Borders, Producing Boundaries. The Governmentality of Immigration in Dark Times." *Annual Review of Anthropology* 40, no. 1 (21 October 2011): 213–26. https://doi.org/10.1146/annurev-anthro-081309-145847.

Feldman, Ilana, and Miriam Ticktin. "Introduction: Government and Humanity." In *In the Name of Humanity: The Government of Threat and Care*, edited by Ilana Feldman and Miriam Ticktin. Durham, NC: Duke University Press, 2010.

Finn, Donovan. "DIY Urbanism: Implications for Cities." *Journal of Urbanism: International Research on Placemaking and Urban Sustainability* 7, no. 4 (2 October 2014): 381–98. https://doi.org/10.1080/17549175.2014.891149.

Flyvbjerg, Bent. "Bringing Power to Planning Research: One Researcher's Praxis Story." *Journal of Planning Education and Research* 21 (1 June 2002): 353–66. https://doi.org/10.1177/0739456X0202100401.

———. "Phronetic Planning Research: Theoretical and Methodological Reflections." Rochester, NY: Social Science Research Network, 1 September 2004. https://papers.ssrn.com/.

———. "Case Study." In *The SAGE Handbook of Qualitative Research*, edited by Norman K. Denzin and Yvonna S. Lincoln, fourth edition, 301–16. Thousand Oaks, CA: SAGE, 2005.

Fotiadis, Apostolis. "Kicking Greece out of Schengen Won't Stop the Refugee Crisis." *Guardian*, 2 December 2015. www.theguardian.com/.

Foucault, Michel. *Abnormal: Lectures at the Collège de France 1974—1975*. Edited by Valerio Marchetti and Graham Burchell. London: Verso, 2003.

Fraser, Nancy. "Foucault on Modern Power: Empirical Insights and Normative Confusions." In *Unruly Practices: Power, Discourse and Gender in Contemporary Social Theory*, edited by Nancy Fraser. Cambridge: Polity, 1989.

———. *Scales of Justice: Reimagining Political Space in a Globalizing World*. New York: Columbia University Press, 2010.

Frontex. "Migratory Map." Accessed 28 November 2020. https://frontex.europa.eu.

Gajjala, Radhika. "Introduction." In *Cyberculture and the Subaltern: Weavings of the Virtual and Real*, edited by Radhika Gajjala. Lanham, MD: Lexington Books, 2013.

Galantino, Maria Grazia. "The Migration-Terrorism Nexus: An Analysis of German and Italian Press Coverage of the 'Refugee Crisis.'" *European Journal of Criminology* (10 January 2020). https://doi.org/10.1177/1477370819896213.

Gale, Peter. "The Refugee Crisis and Fear: Populist Politics and Media Discourse." *Journal of Sociology* 40, no. 4 (1 December 2004): 321–40. https://doi.org/10.1177/1440783304048378.

Garavoglia, Matteo. "Why Europe Can't Handle the Migration Crisis." *Brookings Institution*, 2015. https://webcache.googleusercontent.com/.

Gardner, C. *Passing By: Gender and Public Harassment*. Berkeley: University of California Press, 1995.

Garrelts, Nantke, Bruce Katz, Luise Noring. "Cities and Refugees: The German Experience." *Brookings Institution* (blog), 18 September 2016. www.brookings.edu.

Garrett, Bradley. "The Privatisation of Cities' Public Spaces Is Escalating. It Is Time to Take a Stand." *Guardian*, 4 August 2015.

Gattinara, Pietro Castelli and Laura Morales. "The Politicization and Securitization of Migration in Western Europe: Public Opinion, Political Parties and the

Immigration Issue." *Handbook on Migration and Security*, edited by Phillippe Bourbeau. Edgar Elgar Publishing, 2017.

Georgiou, Myria. *Diaspora, Identity and the Media: Diasporic Transnationalism and Mediated Spatialities*. Cresskill, NJ: Hampton Press, 2006.

———. *Media and the City: Cosmopolitanism and Difference*. Cambridge, UK: Polity Press, 2013.

———. "Does the Subaltern Speak? Migrant Voices in Digital Europe." *Popular Communication* 16, no. 1 (2 January 2018): 45–57. https://doi.org/10.1080/15405702.2017.1412440.

———. "City of Refuge or Digital Order? Refugee Recognition and the Digital Governmentality of Migration in the City." *Television & New Media* 20, no. 6 (1 September 2019): 600–616.

Georgiou, Myria, Wallis Motta, and Sonia Livingstone. "Community through Digital Connectivity? Communication Infrastructure in Multicultural London Final Report." The London School of Economics and Political Science, 2016.

Georgiou, Myria, Suzanne Hall, and Deena Dajani. "Suspension: Disabling the City of Refuge?" *Journal of Ethnic and Migration Studies* (7 July 2020): 1–17. https://doi.org/10.1080/1369183X.2020.1788379.

Georgiou, Myria, and Rafal Zaborowski. "Refugee 'Crisis'? Try 'Crisis in the European Press.'" *OpenDemocracy: Free Thinking for the World*, 17 November 2016. www.opendemocracy.net.

———. "Media Coverage of the 'Refugee Crisis': A Cross-European Perspective." Monograph. *Council of Europe*, 18 April 2017. https://edoc.coe.int/.

Gillespie, Marie, Lawrence Ampofo, Margaret Cheesman, Becky Faith, Evgenia Iliadou, Ali Issa, Souad Osseiran, and Dimitris Skleparis. "Mapping Refugee Media Journeys: Smartphones and Social Media Networks." *The Open University*. 2016. https://doi.org/10.13140/RG.2.2.15633.22888.

Gillespie, Marie, Souad Osseiran, and Margie Cheesman. "Syrian Refugees and the Digital Passage to Europe: Smartphone Infrastructures and Affordances." *Social Media + Society* 4, no. 1 (2018). https://doi.org/10.1177/2056305118764440.

Ghosh, Amitav. *Gun Island*. London: John Murray Publishers, 2019.

Give Something Back to Berlin. "About." 2019. Accessed 24 December 2020. https://gsbtb.org/about/.

Goldring, Luin, and Patricia Landolt, eds. *Producing and Negotiating Non-Citizenship: Precarious Legal Status in Canada*. Toronto: University of Toronto Press, 2013.

Gottlob, Anita, and Hajo Boomgaarden. "The 2015 Refugee Crisis, Uncertainty and the Media: Representations of Refugees, Asylum Seekers and Immigrants in Austrian and French Media." *Communications* 45, no. 1 (18 December 2019). https://doi.org/10.1515/commun-2019-2077.

Goździak, Elżbieta M., and Péter Márton. "Where the Wild Things Are: Fear of Islam and the Anti-Refugee Rhetoric in Hungary and in Poland." *Central and Eastern European Migration Review* 7, no. 2 (2018): 125–51.

Gray, Harriet, and Anja K. Franck. "Refugees as/at Risk: The Gendered and Racialized Underpinnings of Securitization in British Media Narratives." *Security Dialogue* 50, no. 3 (1 June 2019): 275–91. https://doi.org/10.1177/0967010619830590.

Greene, Alexandra. "Mobiles and 'Making Do': Exploring the Affective, Digital Practices of Refugee Women Waiting in Greece." *European Journal of Cultural Studies* (20 August 2019). https://doi.org/10.1177/1367549419869346.

Griegson, Fay. "Rohingya Dying at Sea as Countries Refuse Entry." *Times*, 26 April 2020. Accessed 23 April 2021. www.thetimes.co.uk/.

Guild, Elspeth, Sergio Carrera, Lina Vosyliūtė, Kees Groenendijk, Evelien Brouwer, Didier Bigo, Julien Jeandesboz, and Médéric Martin-Mazé. "Internal Border Controls in the Schengen Area: Is Schengen Crisis-Proof?: Study for the LIBE Committee." Brussels: Directorate-General for Internal Policies, 2016. www.europarl.europa.eu/.

Günay, Cengiz, and Nina Witjes. *Border Politics: Defining Spaces of Governance and Forms of Transgressions*. Springer, 2016.

Gürsel, Duygu. "The Emergence of the Enterprising Refugee Discourse and Differential Inclusion in Turkey's Changing Migration Politics." *Movements: Journal for Critical Migration and Border Regime Studies* 3, no. 2 (2017): 133–146.

Gutiérrez Rodríguez, Encarnación. "The Coloniality of Migration and the 'RefugeeCrisis': On the Asylum-Migration Nexus, the Transatlantic White European Settler Colonialism-Migration and Racial Capitalism." *Refuge: Canada's Journal on Refugees/Refuge: revue canadienne sur les réfugiés* 34, no. 1 (2018).

Guzman-Garcia, Melissa. "Mobile Sanctuary: Latina/o Evangelicals Redefining Sanctuary and Contesting Immobility in Fresno, CA." *Journal of Ethnic and Migration Studies* (13 May 2020): 1–19. https://doi.org/10.1080/1369183X.2020.1761780.

Gynnild, Astrid. "The Visual Power of News Agencies." *Nordicom Review* 38, Special Issue 2 (2017): 25–39.

Haas, Hein de, Stephen Castles, and Mark Miller. *The Age of Migration: International Population Movements in the Modern World*. Sixth edition. Guilford Press, 2019.

Hafez, Mohammed, and Creighton Mullins. "The Radicalization Puzzle: A Theoretical Synthesis of Empirical Approaches to Homegrown Extremism." *Studies in Conflict & Terrorism* 38, no 11 (2015): 958-975.

Haggerty, Kevin D., and Richard V. Ericson. "The Surveillant Assemblage." *British Journal of Sociology* 51, no. 4 (December 2000): 605–22. https://doi.org/10.1080/00071310020015280.

Hall, Stuart, ed. *Representation: Cultural Representations and Signifying Practices*. Maidenhead, BRK, England: Open University Press, 1997.

Hall, Stuart, Brian Roberts, John Clarke, Tony Jefferson, and Chas Critcher. *Policing the Crisis: Mugging, the State, and Law and Order*. London: Macmillan, 1978.

Hall, Suzanne. "Migrant Urbanisms: Ordinary Cities and Everyday Resistance." *Sociology* 49, no. 5 (October 2015): 853–69. https://doi.org/10.1177/0038038515586680.

———. "Migrant Margins: The Streetlife of Discrimination." *Sociological Review* 66, no. 5 (1 September 2018): 968–83. https://doi.org/10.1177/0038026118771282.

Hall, Suzanne, Julia King, and Robin Finlay. "Migrant Infrastructure: Transaction Economies in Birmingham and Leicester, UK." *Urban Studies* 54, no. 6 (2016): 1311–27. https://doi.org/10.1177/0042098016634586.

Han, Byung-Chul. *Expulsion of the Other: Society, Perception and Communication Today*. Translated by Wieland Hoban. Cambridge, UK: Polity Press, 2018.

Hansen, Lene. "Theorizing the Image for Security Studies: Visual Securitization and the Muhammad Cartoon Crisis." *European Journal of International Relations* 17, no. 1 (1 March 2011): 51–74. https://doi.org/10.1177/1354066110388593.

Hariman, Robert, and John Louis Lucaites. *The Public Image: Photography and Civic Spectatorship*. Chicago: University of Chicago Press, 2016.

Harlan, Chico, and Elinda Labropoulou. "Fire Destroys Europe's Largest Migrant Camp, Which Had Been under Coronavirus Lockdown." *Washington Post*, 9 September 2020. Accessed 24 December 2020. www.washingtonpost.com/.

Harney, Nicholas. "The Ritualisation of Hospitality: Comparative Notes at the Frontiers of Migration." ResearchGate, 2017. www.researchgate.net/.

Harvey, David. *Rebel Cities: From the Right to the City to the Urban Revolution*. New York: Verso, 2012.

Heath-Kelly, Charlotte, and Erzsébet Strausz. "The Banality of Counterterrorism 'after, after 9/11'? Perspectives on the Prevent Duty from the UK Health Care Sector." *Critical Studies on Terrorism* 12, no. 1 (17 July 2018): 89–109. https://doi.org/10.1080/17539153.2018.1494123.

Heck, Axel. "Visuality and Security." In *Oxford Research Encyclopedia of Communication*, edited by Axel Heck. Oxford University Press, 2018. https://doi.org/10.1093/acrefore/9780190228613.013.624.

Heeks, Richard, and Satyarupa Shekhar. "Datafication, Development and Marginalised Urban Communities: An Applied Data Justice Framework." *Information, Communication & Society* 22, no. 7 (7 June 2019): 992–1011. https://doi.org/10.1080/1369118X.2019.1599039.

Hegde, Radha Sarma. *Mediating Migration*. Polity Press, 2016.

Hersh, Arielle. "Migrant- and Refugee-Squatting and the Right to the City: The Case of Refugee Strike House. *Compass*, 2018. https://wp.nyu.edu.

Heyman, Josiah, and John Symons. "Borders." In *A Companion to Moral Anthropology*, edited by Didier Fassin, 540–57. West Sussex: John Wiley, 2012.

Hill, Dave. "Haringey to Welcome Syrian Refugees as London Struggles to Take Its Share." *Guardian*, 16 November 2016. www.theguardian.com/.

Hinkkainen, Kaisa. "Homegrown Terrorism: The Known Unknown." *Peace Economics, Peace Science and Public Policy* 19, no. 2 (2013): 157–182.

Hintz, Arne, Lina Dencik, and Karin Wahl-Jorgensen. *Digital Citizenship in a Datafied Society*. Cambridge, UK: Polity, 2018.

Hobson, Barbara, ed. *Recognition Struggles and Social Movements: Contested Identities, Agency and Power*. Cambridge: Cambridge University Press, 2003.

Holmwood, John, K. Bhambra Gurminder, and Sue Scott. "Integrated Communities: A Response to The Government's Strategy Green Paper," November 2017. http://discoversociety.org.
Honneth, Axel. *The Struggle for Recognition: The Moral Grammar of Social Conflicts.* Polity, 1995.
———. *Disrespect: The Normative Foundations of Critical Theory.* First edition. Cambridge: Polity Press, 2007.
Horsti, Karina. "Visibility without Voice: Media Witnessing Irregular Migrants in BBC Online News Journalism." *African Journalism Studies* 37, no. 1 (2 January 2016): 1–20. https://doi.org/10.1080/23743670.2015.1084585.
Howarth, Anita, and Yasmin Ibrahim. "Review of Humanitarian Refuge in the United Kingdom: Sanctuary, Asylum, and the Refugee Crisis." *Politics & Policy* 46, no. 3 (2018): 348–91. https://doi.org/10.1111/polp.12254.
Howden, Daniel, Apostolis Fotiadis, Ludek Stavinoha, and Ben Holst. "Seeing Stones: Pandemic Reveals Palantir's Troubling Reach in Europe." *Guardian.* 2 April 2021. Accessed 18 April 2021. www.theguardian.com.
Huliaras, Asteris, Dimitri A. Sotiropoulos, and Jennifer Clarke. *Austerity and the Third Sector in Greece: Civil Society at the European Frontline.* Ashgate Publishing, 2015.
Hussein, Faheem, Abdullah Hasan Safir, Dina Sabie, Zulkarin Jahangir, and Syed Ishtiaque Ahmed. "Infrastructuring Hope: Solidarity, Leadership, Negotiation, and ICT among the Rohingya Refugees in Bangladesh." *ICTD2020: Proceedings of the 2020 International Conference on Information and Communication Technologies and Development,* Article 12 (June 2020): 1–12. https://doi.org/10.1145/3392561.3394640.
Hyndman, Jennifer. *Managing Displacement: Refugees and the Politics of Humanitarianism.* First edition. Minneapolis: University of Minnesota Press, 2000.
I Am a Migrant. "About," 1 September 2020. https://iamamigrant.org/.
Iannacone, Jeannette I. "Crisis Interpretation: The Global Rhetorical Arena of the 2018 Migrant Caravan 'Crisis.'" *Public Relations Review* 47, no. 2 (2021). https://doi.org/10.1016/j.pubrev.2021.102034.
iBorderCtrl. Homepage. Accessed 2 July 2021. www.iborderctrl.eu.
iBorderCtrl? No!. Homepage. Accessed 28 November 2020. https://iborderctrl.no/.
Ibrahim, Maggie. "The Securitization of Migration: A Racial Discourse1." *International Migration* 43, no. 5 (2005): 163–87. https://doi.org/10.1111/j.1468-2435.2005.00345.x.
Ibrahim, Yasmin. *Politics of Gaze: The Image Economy Online.* Routledge, 2019.
Ibrahim, Yasmin, and Anita Howarth. "Imaging the Jungles of Calais: Media Visuality and the Refugee Camp." *Networking Knowledge: Journal of the MeCCSA Postgraduate Network* 9, no. 4 (24 May 2016). https://doi.org/10.31165/nk.2016.94.446.
Ilan, Jonathan. *The International Photojournalism Industry: Cultural Production and the Making and Selling of News Pictures.* New York: Routledge, 2018.
IOM. "Irregular Migrant, Refugee Arrivals in Europe Top One Million in 2015: IOM." International Organization for Migration, 22 December 2015. www.iom.int/.

IOM. "Chapter 1. Migration and Migrants: A Global Overview." *World Migration Report*, 2020. https://publications.iom.int/.

IRC. "Unprotected, Unsupported, Uncertain." International Rescue Committee, 25 September 2018. www.rescue.org/.

Isin, Engin F. *Being Political: Genealogies of Citizenship*. Minneapolis: University of Minnesota Press, 2002.

Isin, Engin F., and Evelyn Ruppert. *Being Digital Citizens*. London: Rowman & Littlefield International, 2015.

Jessop, Bob, and Ngai-Ling Sum. "An Entrepreneurial City in Action: Hong Kong's Emerging Strategies in and for (Inter)Urban Competition." *Urban Studies* 37, no. 12 (1 November 2000): 2287–2313. https://doi.org/10.1080/00420980020002814.

Jonas, Hans. "The Imperative of Responsibility." In *The Imperative of Responsibility: In Search of an Ethics for the Technological Age*, edited by Hans Jonas. University of Chicago Press, 1984.

Jong, Sara de, and Petra Dannecker. "Managing Migration with Stories? The IOM 'i am a migrant' Campaign." *Journal Für Entwicklungspolitik* 33, no. 1 (2017): 75–101.

Kanchanavally, S., R. Ordonez, and J. Layne. "Mobile Target Tracking by Networked Uninhabited Autonomous Vehicles via Hospitability Maps." In *Proceedings of the 2004 American Control Conference* 6 (2004): 5570–75 https://doi.org/10.23919/ACC.2004.1384741.

Keane, John. *Global Civil Society?* Cambridge University Press, 2003.

Kingsley, Patrick. "'Better to Drown': A Greek Refugee Camp's Epidemic of Misery." *New York Times*, 3 October 2018. www.nytimes.com/.

Kitchin, Rob. "Big Data, New Epistemologies and Paradigm Shifts." *Big Data & Society* 1, no. 1 (1 April 2014): 2053951714528481. https://doi.org/10.1177/2053951714528481.

———. *The Data Revolution: Big Data, Open Data, Data Infrastructures and Their Consequences*. Los Angeles: SAGE, 2014.

———. "Making Sense of Smart Cities: Addressing Present Shortcomings." *Cambridge Journal of Regions, Economy and Society* 8, no. 1 (1 March 2015): 131–36. https://doi.org/10.1093/cjres/rsu027.

Knight, Daniel M. "The Desire for Disinheritance in Austerity Greece." *Focaal* 80 (1 March 2018): 30–42. https://doi.org/10.3167/fcl.2018.800103.

Krause, Monika *The Good Project: Humanitarian Relief NGOs and the Fragmentation of Reason*. Chicago: University of Chicago Press, 2014.

Kroet, Cynthia. "Greece Refuses to Be EU's Migrant Dumping Ground." *Politico*, 9 September 2016a. www.politico.eu/.

———. "Thousands of Refugees Exploited as Illegal Workers in Germany." *Politico*, 30 August 2016b. www.politico.eu.

Krzyżanowski, Michał. "Brexit and the Imaginary of 'Crisis': A Discourse-Conceptual Analysis of European News Media." *Critical Discourse Studies* 16, no. 4 (8 August 2019): 465–90. https://doi.org/10.1080/17405904.2019.1592001.

Krzyżanowski, Michał, Anna Triandafyllidou, and Ruth Wodak. "The Mediatization and the Politicization of the 'Refugee Crisis' in Europe." *Journal of Immigrant &*

Refugee Studies 16, no. 1–2 (3 April 2018): 1–14. https://doi.org/10.1080/15562948.2017.1353189.

Kundnani, Arun, and Ben Hayes. "The Globalisation of Countering Violent Extremism Policies." *Undermining Human Rights, Instrumentalising Civil Society*. Amsterdam: Transnational Institute, 2018.

Labrianidis, Lois. "Investing in Leaving: The Greek Case of International Migration of Professionals." *Mobilities* 9, no 2 (2013): 314–335.

Lafleur, Jean-Michel, and Elsa Mescoli. "Creating Undocumented EU Migrants through Welfare: A Conceptualization of Undeserving and Precarious Citizenship." *Sociology* 52, no. 3 (2018): 480–496.

"Landesamt für Flüchtlingsangelegenheiten wird ein Jahr alt." City of Berlin. 26 July 2017. www.berlin.de/.

Lane, Jeffrey. *The Digital Street*. Oxford: Oxford University Press, 2019.

Larin, Stephen J. "Is It Really about Values? Civic Nationalism and Migrant Integration." *Journal of Ethnic and Migration Studies* 46, no. 1 (2 January 2020): 127–41. https://doi.org/10.1080/1369183X.2019.1591943.

Latonero, Mark, and Paula Kift. "On Digital Passages and Borders: Refugees and the New Infrastructure for Movement and Control." *Social Media + Society* 4, no.1 (20 March 2018): 1–11. https://doi.org/10.1177/2056305118764432.

Latonero, Mark, Keith Hiatt, Antonella Napolitano, Giulia Clericetti, and Melanie Penagos. "Digital Identity in the Migration & Refugee Context: Italy Case Study." Data & Society, 2019.

Lawrence, Regina G. *The Politics of Force: Media and the Construction of Police Brutality*. Berkeley: University of California Press, 2000.

Leese, Matthias. "Exploring the Security/Facilitation Nexus: Foucault at the "Smart" Border." *Global Society* 30, no. 3 (2 July 2016): 412–29. https://doi.org/10.1080/13600826.2016.1173016.

Lefebvre, Henri. *Writings on Cities*. Translated by Eleonore Koffman and Elizabeth Lebas. Cambridge, MA: Wiley-Blackwell, 2010.

Lemke, Thomas. *Biopolitics: An Advanced Introduction*. New York: New York University Press, 2011.

Leurs, Koen. "Communication Rights from the Margins: Politicising Young Refugees' Smartphone Pocket Archives." *International Communication Gazette* 79, no. 6–7 (1 November 2017): 674–98. https://doi.org/10.1177/1748048517727182.

Leurs, Koen, and Sandra Ponzanesi. "Connected Migrants: Encapsulation and Cosmopolitanization." *Popular Communication* 16, no. 1 (2 January 2018): 4–20. https://doi.org/10.1080/15405702.2017.1418359.

Leurs, Koen, and Tamara Shepherd. "Datafication & Discrimination." In *The Datafied Society: Studying Culture through Data*, edited by Mirko Tobias Schafer and Karin van Es. Amsterdam: Amsterdam University Press, 2017.

Leurs, Koen, and Kevin Smets. "Five Questions for Digital Migration Studies: Learning from Digital Connectivity and Forced Migration In(to) Europe." *Social Media + Society* 4, no. 1 (1 January 2018). https://doi.org/10.1177/2056305118764425.

Liguori, Anna. *Migration Law and the Externalization of Border Controls: European State Responsibility*. Routledge, 2019.

Lim, Merlyna. "Clicks, Cabs, and Coffee Houses: Social Media and Oppositional Movements in Egypt, 2004–2011." *Journal of Communication* 62 (1 April 2012). https://doi.org/10.1111/j.1460-2466.2012.01628.x.

Lemberg-Pedersen, Martin, Johanne Rübner Hansen, and Oliver Joel Halpern. "The political economy of entry governance." Working Paper 1.3, Advancing Alternative Migration Governance. Copenhagen: Aalborg University, 2020. https://vbn.aau.dk/.

Lyman, Rick, and Alison Smale. "Paris Attacks Shift Europe's Migrant Focus to Security." *New York Times*, 15 November 2015. www.nytimes.com/.

Lyon, David. "Digital Citizenship and Surveillance| Surveillance Culture: Engagement, Exposure, and Ethics in Digital Modernity." *International Journal of Communication* 11 (14 February 2017): 824–42.

MacPhee, Graham. "Escape from Responsibility: Ideology and Storytelling in Arendt's *The Origins of Totalitarianism* and Ishiguro's *The Remains of the Day*." *College Literature* 38 (1 December 2011): 176–201. http://dx.doi.org/10.1353/lit.2011.0010.

Madianou, Mirca. "The Biometric Assemblage. Surveillance, Experimentation, Profit, and the Measuring of Refugee Bodies." *New Media and Society* 20, no. 6 (2019): 581–599.

———. "Nonhuman Humanitarianism: When 'AI for Good' Can Be Harmful." *Information, Communication & Society* 24, no. 6 (2021): 850–868.

Madianou, Mirca, Jonathan Corpus Ong, Liezel Longboan, and Jayeel S. Cornelio. "The Appearance of Accountability: Communication Technologies and Power Asymmetries in Humanitarian Aid and Disaster Recovery." *Journal of Communication* 66, no. 6 (2016): 960–81. https://doi.org/10.1111/jcom.12258.

Madison, D. Soyini. *Critical Ethnography: Method, Ethics, and Performance*. Second edition. Thousand Oaks, CA: SAGE, 2011.

Main, Thomas J. *The Rise of the Alt-Right*. Brookings Institution Press, 2018.

Malafouri, Eleni Ioanna. "'Who Are They & Why Are They Here?': A Media Analysis of the Negative Portrayal of Immigrants in the Mainstream Greek Press." 2015. http://muep.mau.se.

Malkki, Liisa H. "Speechless Emissaries: Refugees, Humanitarianism, and Dehistoricization." *Cultural Anthropology* 11, no. 3 (1996): 377–404. https://doi.org/10.1525/can.1996.11.3.02a00050.

Mancini, Paolo, Marco Mazzoni, Giovanni Barbieri, Marco Damiani, and Matteo Gerli. "What Shapes the Coverage of Immigration." *Journalism* 22, no. 5 (May 2019).

Mansell, Robin. *Communication by Design: The Politics of Information and Communication Technologies*. Edited by Roger Silverstone. New edition. Oxford: Oxford University Press, 1998.

Marino, Sara. *Mediating the Refugee Crisis: Digital Solidarity, Humanitarian Technologies and Border Regimes*. Palgrave Macmillan, 2021. https://doi.org/10.1007/978-3-030-53563-6.

Massey, Doreen. *For Space*. London: SAGE, 2005.
Mattelart, Tristan. "Media, Communication Technologies and Forced Migration: Promises and Pitfalls of an Emerging Research Field." *European Journal of Communication* 34, no 6 (2019): 582–593.
Mattern, Shannon. "All Eyes on the Border." *Places Journal*, 25 September 2018. https://doi.org/10.22269/180925.
Mayer, Margit. "Cities as Sites of Refuge and Resistance." *European Urban and Regional Studies* (8 September 2017). https://doi.org/10.1177/0969776417729963.
Mbembe, Achille. "Necropolitics." *Public Culture* 15, no. 1 (1 January 2003): 11–40. https://doi.org/10.1215/08992363-15-1-11.
———. "On the Postcolony: A Brief Response to Critics." *African Identities* 4, no. 2 (1 October 2006): 143–78. https://doi.org/10.1080/14725840600761096.
———. "Bodies as Borders." *From European South* 4 (2019): 5–18.
———. "Presidential Lecture." Stanford Humanities Center, October 22, 2020. Accessed July 2 2021. www.youtube.com/.
McAuliffe, Marie, Binod Khadria, and Céline Bauloz. "Report Overview: Providing Perspective on Migration and Mobility in Increasingly Uncertain Times." In *World Migration Report 2020*. Geneva: IOM, 2019.
Médecins Sans Frontières (MSF) International. "Moria Camp," September 2019a. www.msf.org/.
———. "Greek and EU Authorities Deliberately Neglecting People Trapped on Islands," 5 September 2019b. www.msf.org/.
Mehta, Uday S. "Liberal Strategies of Exclusion." *Politics & Society* 18, no. 4 (1 December 1990): 427–54. https://doi.org/10.1177/003232929001800402.
Mekdjian, Sarah. "Urban Artivism and Migrations: Disrupting Spatial and Political Segregation of Migrants in European Cities." *Cities* 77 (1 July 2018): 39–48. https://doi.org/10.1016/j.cities.2017.05.008.
Memou, Antigoni. "Spectacular Images of the 'Refugee Crisis.'" *Photographies* 12 (2 January 2019): 81–97. https://doi.org/10.1080/17540763.2018.1501728.
Metcalfe-Hough, Victoria. "A Migration Crisis? Facts, Challenges and Possible Solutions." ODI, 2015. www.odi.org/.
Mezzadra, Sandro. "The Right to Escape." *Ephemera* 4, no. 3 (2004): 267–75. www.semanticscholar.org/.
———. "The Gaze of Autonomy: Capitalism, Migration, and Social Struggles." In *The Contested Politics of Mobility: Borderzones and Irregularity*, edited by Vicki Squire, 121–42. London: Routledge, 2011.
———. "Forces and Forms: Governmentality and Bios in the Time of Global Capital." *Positions: Asia Critique* 27, no. 1 (1 February 2019): 145–58. https://doi.org/10.1215/10679847-7251858.
Migration Data Portal. "Migration Data in Europe." *Migration Data Portal*. Accessed 24 December 2020. http://migrationdataportal.org/.
Miller, Susan. "Monitoring Migrants in the Digital Age: Using Twitter to Analyze Social Media Surveillance." *Colorado Technical University* 17 (2018): 395–420.

Millner, Naomi. "From 'Refugee' to 'Migrant' in Calais Solidarity Activism: Re-Staging Undocumented Migration for a Future Politics of Asylum." *Political Geography* 30, no. 6 (2011): 320–28. https://doi.org/10.1016/j.polgeo.2011.07.005.

Mirzoeff, Nicholas. "On Visuality." *Journal of Visual Culture* 5 (1 April 2006): 53–79. https://doi.org/10.1177/1470412906062285.

Missing Migrants. "Missing Migrants: Tracking Deaths Along Migratory Routes." Accessed 2 July 2021. https://missingmigrants.iom.int/.

Misra, Tanvi. "Where Refugees and Locals Connect in a Divided Berlin." *Bloomberg*, 11 January 2018. www.bloomberg.com/.

Moeller, Susan D. "A Hierarchy of Innocence: The Media's Use of Children in the Telling of International News." *International Journal of Press/Politics* 7, no. 1 (1 January 2002): 36–56. https://doi.org/10.1177/1081180X0200700104.

Moffette, David, and Shaira Vadasaria. "Uninhibited Violence: Race and the Securitization of Immigration." *Critical Studies on Security* 4, no. 3 (1 September 2016): 291–305. https://doi.org/10.1080/21624887.2016.1256365.

Molnar, Petra. "Technology on the Margins: AI and Global Migration Management from a Human Rights Perspective." *Cambridge International Law Journal* 8, no. 2 (2019): 305–330. https://doi.org/10.4337/cilj.2019.02.07.

Moore, Jack. "Alan Kurdi's Father Was One of Three Men Tried by a Turkish Court for Alleged People-Smuggling." *Newsweek*, 12 February 2016. www.newsweek.com.

Moore, Kerry, Bernhard Gross, and Terry Threadgold, eds. *Migrations and the Media*. New edition. New York: Peter Lang, 2012.

Mountz, Alison. *The Death of Asylum: Hidden Geographies of the Enforcement Archipelago*. Minneapolis: University of Minnesota, 2020.

Mortensen, Mette, and Hans-Jörg Trenz. "Media Morality and Visual Icons in the Age of Social Media: Alan Kurdi and the Emergence of an Impromptu Public of Moral Spectatorship." *Javnost—The Public* 23, no. 4 (1 October 2016): 343–62. https://doi.org/10.1080/13183222.2016.1247331.

Mostafanezhad, Mary. "Angelina Jolie and the Everyday Geopolitics of Celebrity Humanitarianism in a Thailand-Burma Border Town." In *Celebrity Humanitarianism and North-South Relations: Politics, Place and Power*, edited by Lisa Ann Richey, 27–47. London; New York: Routledge, 2016.

Moulin, Carolina. "Ungrateful Subjects? Refugee Protests and the Logic of Gratitude." In *Citizenship, Migrant Activism and the Politics of Movement*, edited by Peter Nyers and Kim Rygiel, 66–84. London: Routledge, 2012.

Müller, Birgit. "The Skeleton versus the Little Grey Men: Conflicting Cultures of Anti-Nuclear Protest at the Czech-Austrian Border." In *Border Encounters: Asymmetry and Proximity at Europe's Frontiers*, 68–89. Berghahn Books, 2013. https://www.jstor.org.

Munkejord, Mai Camilla. "His or Her Work–Life Balance? Experiences of Self-employed Immigrant Parents." *Work, Employment and Society* 31, no. 4 (2017): 624–639.

Mountz, Alison. *The Death of Asylum: Hidden Geographies of the Enforcement Archipelago*. Minneapolis: University of Minnesota, 2020.

Musarò, Pierluigi. "Mare Nostrum: The Visual Politics of a Military-Humanitarian Operation in the Mediterranean Sea." *Media, Culture & Society* 39, no. 1 (2016): 11–28. https://doi.org/10.1177/0163443716672296.

———. "A Humanitarian Battlefield: Redefining Border Control as Saving Victims." In *The Routledge Companion to Media and Humanitarian Action*, edited by Purnaka L. de Silva and Robin Andersen. Routledge, 2017. https://doi.org/10.4324/9781315538129.

———. "Performing Metaphors into a Physical Space. The Role of Participatory Theater in Promoting Social Coexistence between Citizens and Newcomers." *LSE Media and Communications* (2018): 1–27.

———. "Aware Migrants: The Role of Information Campaigns in the Management of Migration." *European Journal of Communication* 34 (11 November 2019): 026732311988616. https://doi.org/10.1177/0267323119886164.

Nail, Thomas. *Theory of the Border*. Oxford: Oxford University Press, 2016.

Naranjo, Diego and Petra Molnar. "The Privatization of Migration Control." *Centre for International Governance Innovation*, 2020. Accessed 17 April 2021. www.cigionline.org/articles/privatization-migration-control.

Natale, Simone, and Emiliano Treré. "Vinyl Won't Save Us: Reframing Disconnection as Engagement." *Media, Culture & Society* 42, no. 4 (May 2020): 626–33. https://doi.org/10.1177/0163443720914027.

Nedelcu, Mihaela, and Ibrahim Soysüren. "Precarious Migrants, Migration Regimes and Digital Technologies: The Empowerment-Control Nexus." *Journal of Ethnic and Migration Studies* (29 August 2020): 1–17. https://doi.org/10.1080/1369183X.2020.1796263.

Nianias, Helen. "Refugees in Lesbos: Are There Too Many NGOs on the Island?" *Guardian*, 5 January 2016. www.theguardian.com.

Nienaber, Michael. "Germany Spends Record 23 Billion Euros on Refugees." *Reuters*, 20 May 2019. www.reuters.com.

Noble, Greg. "The Discomfort of Strangers: Racism, Incivility and Ontological Security in a Relaxed and Comfortable Nation." *Journal of Intercultural Studies* 26, no. 1–2 (February 2005): 107–20. https://doi.org/10.1080/07256860500074128.

de Norohna L. "Unpacking the Figure of the 'Foreign Criminal': Race, Gender and the Victim-Villain Binary." *Criminal Justice, Borders and Citizenship Research Paper* No. 2600568, (2015). https://ssrn.com/.

Nyers, Peter. "Emergency or Emerging Identities? Refugees and Transformations in World Order." *Millennium* 28, no. 1 (1 March 1999): 1–26. https://doi.org/10.1177/03058298990280010501.

———. *Rethinking Refugees: Beyond State of Emergency*. First edition. New York: Routledge, 2006.

Oberg, Charles N. "A Child's Playground: A Syrian Boy at the Moria Refugee Camp, Lesbos, Greece." *Pediatrics* 142, no. 1 Meeting Abstract (1 May 2018): 536–536.

O'Connell, Alice R. "The Paris Agreement, Forced Migration, and America's Changing Refugee Policy." *Loyola University Chicago International Law Review* 16 (2020): 265.

OECD. "Key Data on Migrant Presence and Integration in Athens." 26 July 2018a, 17–22. https://doi.org/10.1787/9789264304116-4-en.

———. "Migration Snapshot of the City of Berlin." 6 September 2018b, 25–30. https://doi.org/10.1787/9789264305236-6-en.

———. "Working Together for Local Integration of Migrants and Refugees in Athens." Accessed 24 December 2020. www.oecd-ilibrary.org/.

Oeppen, Ceri. "'Leaving Afghanistan! Are You Sure?' European Efforts to Deter Potential Migrants through Information Campaigns." *Human Geography* 9, no. 2 (30 June 2016): 57–68.

Oliver, Kelly, Lisa M. Madura, and Sabeen Ahmed, eds. *Refugees Now: Rethinking Borders, Hospitality and Citizenship*. London: Rowman & Littlefield Publishers, 2019.

Ostrom, Elinor. *Governing the Commons: The Evolution of Institutions for Collective Action*. Cambridge: Cambridge University Press, 1990.

Owens, Patricia. "Reclaiming 'Bare Life'?: Against Agamben on Refugees." *International Relations* 23 (1 December 2009): 567–82. https://doi.org/10.1177/0047117809350545.

Paasi, Anssi. "Border Studies Reanimated: Going Beyond the Territorial/Relational Divide." *Environment and Planning A* 44, no. 10 (2012): 2303–2309.

Paik, A. Naomi. *Rightlessness: Testimony and Redress in U.S. Prison Camps since World War II*. Illustrated edition. Chapel Hill: University of North Carolina Press, 2016.

Pallister-Wilkins, Polly. "Humanitarian borderwork." In *Border Politics, Defining Spaces of Governance and Forms of Transgressions*, edited by Cengiz Günay and Nina Witjes, 85–103. Cham: Springer, 2017.

———. "Hotspots and the Geographies of Humanitarianism." *Environment and Planning D: Society and Space* 38, no. 6 (2020): 991–1008.

Pantti, Mervi, and Markus Ojala. "Caught between Sympathy and Suspicion: Journalistic Perceptions and Practices of Telling Asylum Seekers' Personal Stories." *Media, Culture & Society* 41 (9 February 2018): 016344371875617. https://doi.org/10.1177/0163443718756177.

Papadimas, Alkis and Konstantinidis, Lefteris. "Thousands Homeless after Fire Guts Migrant Camp on Greek Island." *Reuters*, 9 September 2020. www.reuters.com/article/.

Papadopoulos, Dimitris, and Vassilis Tsianos. "After Citizenship: Autonomy of Migration, Organisational Ontology and Mobile Commons." *Citizenship Studies* 17 (1 April 2013). https://doi.org/10.1080/13621025.2013.780736.

Parker, Noel, and Nick Vaughan-Williams et al. "Lines in the Sand? Towards an Agenda for Critical Border Studies." *Geopolitics* 14, no. 3 (21 August 2009): 582–87. https://doi.org/10.1080/14650040903081297.

Parks, Malcolm R. "Big Data in Communication Research: Its Contents and Discontents." *Journal of Communication* 64, no. 2 (1 April 2014): 355–60. https://doi.org/10.1111/jcom.12090.

Perkowski, Nina. "Deaths, Interventions, Humanitarianism and Human Rights in the Mediterranean 'Migration Crisis.'" *Mediterranean Politics* 21, no. 2 (3 May 2016): 331–35. https://doi.org/10.1080/13629395.2016.1145827.

Perng, Sung-Yueh, Rob Kitchin, and Darach Mac Donncha. "Hackathons, Entrepreneurial Life and the Making of Smart Cities." *Geoforum* 97 (2018): 189–197.

Peuter, Greig de, and Nick Dyer-Witheford. "Commons and Cooperatives." *Communication Studies Faculty Publications*, 1 July 2010. https://scholars.wlu.ca/.

Phillips, Anna. "Recognition and the Struggle for Political Voice." In *Recognition Struggles and Social Movements: Contested Identities, Agency and Power*, edited by Barbara Hobson, 263–73. Cambridge: Cambridge University Press, 2003.

Pickering, Michael. *Stereotyping: The Politics of Representation*. New York: Palgrave, 2001.

Plantin, Jean-Christophe, and Aswin Punathambekar. "Digital Media Infrastructures: Pipes, Platforms, and Politics." *Media, Culture & Society* 41, no. 2 (2018): 163–74. https://doi.org/10.1177/0163443718818376.

Polletta, Francesca. *It Was Like a Fever: Storytelling in Protest and Politics*. Chicago: University of Chicago Press, 2006.

Ponzanesi, Sandra, and Koen Leurs. "On Digital Crossings in Europe." *Crossings: Journal of Migration & Culture* 5, no. 1 (1 March 2014): 3–22. https://doi.org/10.1386/cjmc.5.1.3_1.

Pötzsch, Holger. "The Emergence of iBorder: Bordering Bodies, Networks, and Machines": *Environment and Planning D: Society and Space*, 1 January 2015. https://doi.org/10.1068/d14050p.

Privacy International. "Communities at Risk: How Governments Are Using Tech to Target Migrants." 2019. Accessed 28 November 2020. http://privacy international.org.

Purkayastha, Bandana. "Migration, Migrants, and Human Security." *Current Sociology* 66, no 2 (2018): 167–191.

Ragazzi, Francesco. "Countering Terrorism and Radicalisation: Securitising Social Policy?" *Critical Social Policy* 37, no. 2 (1 May 2017): 163–79. https://doi.org/10.1177/0261018316683472.

Raimondi, Valeria. "For 'Common Struggles of Migrants and Locals': Migrant Activism and Squatting in Athens." *Citizenship Studies* 23, no. 6 (18 August 2019): 559–76. https://doi.org/10.1080/13621025.2019.1634373.

Rajaram, Prem Kumar. "Humanitarianism and Representations of the Refugee." *Journal of Refugee Studies* 15, no. 3 (1 September 2002): 247–64. https://doi.org/10.1093/jrs/15.3.247.

Ram, Monder, Trevor Jones, and María Villares-Varela. "Migrant Entrepreneurship: Reflections on Research and Practice." *International Small Business Journal* 35, no. 1 (2017): 3–18.

Rath, Jan, and Veronique Schutjens. "Advancing the Frontiers in Ethnic Entrepreneurship Studies." *Tijdschrift voor Economische en Sociale Geografe* 110, no. 5 (2019): 579–587. https://doi.org/10.1111/tesg.12398.

Ravelin, Mateo. "Anti-Migrant Propaganda in the United Kingdom in the Wake of the 'Refugee Crisis' (2015–2016): Othering of Refugees and Migrants in the British Press," ResearchGate, 29 April 2020. www.researchgate.net/.

Refugee Support Aegean (RSA) & Stiftung PRO ASYL. "Kurdestan Darwesh and Others v. Greece and the Netherlands Application No. 52334/19 before the European Court of Human Rights." 4 June 2020. https://rsaegean.org.

———. "Recognised but Unprotected: The Situation of Refugees in Victoria Square." 3 August 2020. https://rsaegean.org.

Refugio. "REFUGIO Home." Accessed 30 November 2020. www.refugio.berlin.

———. "Regelmäßiges Angebot." Accessed 30 November 2020. www.refugio.berlin/.

Reuters. "Fire Breaks Out at Greece's Overcrowded Moria Refugee Camp." *Reuters*, 9 September 2020. www.reuters.com/.

Rietig, Victoria. "Moving Beyond Crisis: Germany's New Approaches to Integrating Refugees into the Labor Market." *Migration Policy Institute*. 2016.

Rishbeth, Clare. *The Collective Outdoors: Memories, Desires and Becoming Local in an Era of Mobility. Companion to Public Space*. Routledge, 2020. https://doi.org/10.4324/9781351002189-3.

Rosamond, Annika Bergman. "The Digital Politics of Celebrity Activism Against Sexual Violence: Angelina Jolie as Global Mother." In *Understanding Popular Culture and World Politics in the Digital Age*, edited by Laura J. Shepherd and Caitlin Hamilton. New York: Routledge, 2016.

Rose, Nikolas. *Inventing Our Selves: Psychology, Power, and Personhood*. Revised edition. Cambridge: Cambridge University Press, 1998.

———. *The Politics of Life Itself: Biomedicine, Power, and Subjectivity in the Twenty-First Century*. Princeton: Princeton University Press, 2007.

Ross, Karen. "The Journalist, the Housewife, the Citizen and the Press Women and Men as Sources in Local News Narratives." *Journalism* 8 (1 August 2007): 449–73. https://doi.org/10.1177/1464884907078659.

Roy, Ananya, and Aihwa Ong, eds. *Worlding Cities: Asian Experiments and the Art of Being Global*. Malden, MA: Wiley-Blackwell, 2011.

Roy, Olivier. "Europe and the Mediterranean: When Obsession for Security Misses the Real World." EUI Working Paper. *RSCAS 2012/20 Robert Schuman Centre For Advanced Studies Global Governance Programme* 16 (2012): 1–10.

RRN. "RRN." Accessed 18 December 2020. www.refugeeradionetwork.net/.

Russo, Katherine. "Floating Signifiers, Transnational Affect Flows: Climate-Induced Migrants in Australian News Discourse." In *Life Adrift: Climate Change, Migration, Critique*, edited by Andrew Baldwin and Giovanni Bettini. London: Rowman & Littlefield, 2017.

Sakellariou, Alexandros. "Fear of Islam in Greece: Migration, Terrorism, and "Ghosts" from the Past." *Nationalities Papers* 45, no. 4 (4 July 2017): 511–23. https://doi.org/10.1080/00905992.2017.1294561.

Sánchez-Monedero, Javier, and Lina Dencik. "The Politics of Deceptive Borders: 'Biomarkers of Deceit' and the Case of iBorderCtrl." *Information, Communication & Society* (3 August 2020): 1–18. https://doi.org/10.1080/1369118X.2020.1792530.

Sandel, Michael J. *The Tyranny of Merit: What's Become of the Common Good*. New York: Farrar, Strauss and Giroux, 2020.

Sandvik, Kristin. "Unpacking World Refugee Day: Humanitarian Governance and Human Rights Practice?" *Journal of Human Rights Practice* 2 (23 June 2010): 287–98. https://doi.org/10.1093/jhuman/huq003.

Scharff, Christina. "The Psychic Life of Neoliberalism: Mapping the Contours of Entrepreneurial Subjectivity." *Theory, Culture & Society* 33, no. 6 (1 November 2016): 107–22. https://doi.org/10.1177/0263276415590164.

Schuster, Liza. "A Sledgehammer to Crack a Nut: Deportation, Detention and Dispersal in Europe." *Social Policy & Administration* 39, no. 6 (2005): 606–21. https://doi.org/10.1111/j.1467-9515.2005.00459.x.

Schwiertz, Helge, and Helen Schwenken. "Introduction: Inclusive Solidarity and Citizenship along Migratory Routes in Europe and the Americas." *Citizenship Studies* 24 (30 April 2020): 405–23. https://doi.org/10.1080/13621025.2020.1755155.

Sennett, Richard. *The Conscience of the Eye: The Design and Social Life of Cities*. New York: W. W. Norton & Company, 1992.

Sharma, Sanjay, and Jasbinder Nijjar. "The Racialized Surveillant Assemblage: Islam and the Fear of Terrorism." *Popular Communication* 16 (2 January 2018): 72–85. https://doi.org/10.1080/15405702.2017.1412441.

Shome, Raka, and Radha S. Hegde. "Postcolonial Approaches to Communication: Charting the Terrain, Engaging the Intersections." *Communication Theory* 12, no. 3 (2002): 249–270.

Siefkes, Christian. *From Exchange to Contributions: Generalizing Peer Production into the Physical World*. Berlin: Ed. Siefkes, 2007.

Sigona, Nando. "The Politics of Refugee Voices: Representations, Narratives, and Memories." In *The Oxford Handbook of Refugee and Forced Migration Studies*, edited by Elena Fiddian-Qasmiyeh, Gil Loescher, Katy Long, and Nando Sigona, 369–82. Oxford University Press, 2014. https://doi.org/10.1093/oxfordhb/9780199652433.001.0001.

Silverstone, Roger. *Television and Everyday Life*. Routledge, 1994.

———. "Complicity and Collusion in the Mediation of Everyday Life." *New Literary History* 33, no. 4 (2002): 761–80.

———. *Media and Morality: On the Rise of the Mediapolis*. First edition. Cambridge, UK: Polity, 2006.

Silverstone, Roger, and Robin Mansell. "The Politics of Information and Communication Rechnologies." In Communication by Design: The Politics of Information and Communication Technologies, edited by Roger Silverstone and Robin Mansell, 213–228. Oxford: Oxford University Press, 1996.

Sky News. "Texas: 'Dangerous' US Migrant Detention Centres on Mexico Border a 'Ticking Time Bomb.'" *Sky News*, 3 July 2019. https://news.sky.com/.

Smets, Kevin, and Çiğdem Bozdağ. "Editorial Introduction. Representations of Immigrants and Refugees: News Coverage, Public Opinion and Media Literacy." *Communications* 43, no. 3 (28 August 2018): 293–99. https://doi.org/10.1515/commun-2018-0011.

Sohn, Christophe. "Navigating Borders' Multiplicity: The Critical Potential of Assemblage." *Area*, 7 December 2015. https://doi.org/10.1111/area.12248.

Sontag, Susan. *On Photography*. New edition. London: Penguin, 1979.

———. *Regarding the Pain of Others*. New edition. London: Penguin, 2004.

Soysal, Yasemin Nuhoglu. *Limits of Citizenship: Migrants and Postnational Membership in Europe*. Illustrated edition. Chicago: University of Chicago Press, 1994.

Spivak, Gayatri Chakravorty. "Can the Subaltern Speak?" In *Can the Subaltern Speak? Reflections on the History of an Idea*, edited by R. C. Morris, 21–78. New York: Columbia University Press, 2010.

———. *The Spivak Reader: Selected Works of Gayatri Chakravorty Spivak*. Psychology Press, 1996.

Squire, Vicki. *The Contested Politics of Mobility: Borderzones and Irregularity*. Edited by Vicki Squire. London: Routledge, 2011.

———. "Governing Migration through Death in Europe and the US: Identification, Burial and the Crisis of Modern Humanism." *European Journal of International Relations* 23, no. 3 (1 September 2017): 513–32. https://doi.org/10.1177/1354066116668662.

Squire, Vicki, and Jennifer Bagelman. "Taking Not Waiting: Space, Temporality and Politics in the City of Sanctuary Movement." In *Migration and Citizenship: Migrant Activism and the Politics of Movement*, edited by Peter Nyers and Kim Rygiel. Routledge, 2012. www.routledge.com/.

Stanton, Jenny. "Second Passenger Claims Aylan Kurdi's Father Was Driving Boat on Which His Son Died." *Daily Mail*, 14 September 2015. www.dailymail.co.uk.

Stevis-Gridneff, Matina. "E.U. Border Agency Accused of Covering Up Migrant Pushback in Greece." *New York Times*, 26 November 2020. www.nytimes.com/.

Stevis-Gridneff, Matina, and Mauricio Lima. "After Fire Razes Squalid Greek Camp, Homeless Migrants Fear What's Next." *New York Times*, 13 September 2020. www.nytimes.com/.

Sturken, Marita, and Lisa Cartwright. *Practices of Looking: An Introduction to Visual Culture*. Oxford University Press, 2009.

Švenčionis, Tadas. "5-Eyes, 9-Eyes, and 14-Eyes Agreement Explained." *Cybernews*, 18 December 2020. https://cybernews.com/.

Tacchi, Jo. "Digital Engagement: Voice and Participation in Development." In *Digital Anthropology*, edited by Heather A. Horst and Daniel Miller, 225–41. London: Berg, 2012.

Tagaris, Karolina. "EU Must Stop 'Racist Criteria' in Refugee Relocation—Greece." *Reuters*, 11 October 2015. https://uk.reuters.com.

Tardis, Matthieu. "US Immigration Policy: The Making of a Crisis." *Center for Migrations and Citizenship*. www.ifri.org/.

Taylor, Charles. "Modern Social Imaginaries." *Public Culture* 14, no. 1 (2002): 91–124.

Tazzioli, Martina. "The Temporal Borders of Asylum: Temporality of Control in the EU Border Regime." *Political Geography* 64 (26 February 2018): 13–22.

——. "Extract, Datafy and Disrupt: Refugees' Subjectivities between Data Abundance and Data Disregard." *Geopolitics*, 4 October 2020. https://doi.org/10.1080/14650045.2020.1822332.

Tazzioli, Martina, and William Walters. "Migration, Solidarity and the Limits of Europe." *Global Discourse* 9, no. 1 (29 January 2019): 175–90. https://doi.org/10.1332/204378918X15453934506030.

Techfugees. "About Us." *Techfugees*. Accessed 24 December 2020. https://techfugees.com/.

Tervonen, Miika, and Anca Enache. "Coping with Everyday Bordering: Roma Migrants and Gatekeepers in Helsinki." *Ethnic and Racial Studies* 40, no. 7 (28 May 2017): 1114–31. https://doi.org/10.1080/01419870.2017.1267378.

Tesch, Renata. *Qualitative Research: Analysis, Types, and Software Tools*. Bristol, PA: Falmer Press, 1990.

Thorbjørnsrud, Kjersti, and Tine Figenschou. "Consensus and Dissent after Terror: Editorial Policies in Times of Crisis." *Journalism* 19 (12 July 2016). https://doi.org/10.1177/1464884916657519.

Ticktin, Miriam. "Where Ethics and Politics Meet." *American Ethnologist* 33, no. 1 (2006): 33–49. https://doi.org/10.1525/ae.2006.33.1.33.

——. *Casualties of Care: Immigration and the Politics of Humanitarianism in France*. University of California Press, 2011a.

——. "How Biology Travels: A Humanitarian Trip." *Body & Society* (2 June 2011b). https://doi.org/10.1177/1357034X11400764.

——. "A World without Innocence." *American Ethnologist* 44, no. 4 (2017): 577–90. https://doi.org/10.1111/amet.12558.

Titley, Gavan. *Racism and Media*. First edition. Thousand Oaks, CA: SAGE, 2019.

Tomlinson, John. "Beyond Connection: Cultural Cosmopolitan and Ubiquitous Media." *International Journal of Cultural Studies* 14, no. 4 (1 July 2011): 347–61. https://doi.org/10.1177/1367877911403246.

Topak, Özgün E. "The Authoritarian Surveillant Assemblage: Authoritarian State Surveillance in Turkey." *Security Dialogue* 50, no. 5 (1 October 2019): 454–72. https://doi.org/10.1177/0967010619850336.

Triandafyllidou, Anna. *Circular Migration between Europe and Its Neighbourhood: Choice or Necessity?* Oxford: Oxford University Press, 2013.

Trilling, Daniel. "How the Media Contributed to the Migrant Crisis." *Guardian*, 1 August 2019. www.theguardian.com.

Trimikliniotis, Nicos. *Migration and the Refugee Dissensus in Europe: Borders, Security and Austerity*. New York: Routledge, 2019.

Trimikliniotis, Nicos, Dimitris Parsanoglou, and Vassilis S. Tsianos. *Mobile Commons, Migrant Digitalities and the Right to the City*. Palgrave Macmillan UK, 2015. https://doi.org/10.1057/9781137406910.

Turner, Bryan S. "T. H. Marshall, Social Rights and English National Identity." *Citizenship Studies* 13, no. 1 (1 February 2009): 65–73. https://doi.org/10.1080/13621020802586750.

Tyyskä, Vappu, Jenna Blower, Samantha Deboer, Shunya Kawai, and Ashley Walcott. "Canadian Media Coverage of the Syrian Refugee Crisis: Representation, Response, and Resettlement." *Geopolitics, History, and International Relations* 10 (1 January 2018): 148–66. https://doi.org/10.22381/GHIR10120187.

United Nations. "Migration." Accessed July 2 2021. www.un.org/.

United Nations High Commissioner for Refugees. "Europe Refugees & Migrants Emergency Response. Nationality of Arrivals to Greece, Italy and Spain: January 2015–March 2016," 2016. http://data2.unhcr.org.

———. "Connecting Refugees." UNHCR. Accessed 28 November 2020. www.unhcr.org.

———. "Syrian Students' Library Helps Arabic Culture Blossom in Berlin." Accessed 30 November 2020. www.unhcr.org.

———. "The Dublin Regulation." Accessed 24 December 2020. www.unhcr.org/.

———. "UNHCR Warns Asylum under Attack at Europe's Borders, Urges End to Pushbacks and Violence Against Refugees." 2021. Accessed 23 April 2021. www.unhcr.org/.

van Delft, Hadewijch, Cees Gorter, and Peter Nijkamp. "Ethnic Entrepreneurship Opportunities in the European City: A Comparative Policy Study." *International Journal of Economic Development* 5, no. 3 (2003).

van Dijck, José. *The Culture of Connectivity: A Critical History of Social Media.* Oxford: Oxford University Press, 2013.

van Dijk, Teun A. *Racism and the Press.* London: Routledge, 1991.

Van Doorn, Niels, Fabian Ferrari, and Mark Graham. "Migration and Migrant Labour in the Gig Economy: An Intervention." Available at SSRN. 2020. https://admin.platformlabor.net/.

van Houtum, Henk, Olivier Thomas Kramsch, and Wolfgang Zierhofer, eds. *Bordering Space.* Burlington, VT: Ashgate, 2005.

Vargas-Silva, Carlos, and Cinzia Rienzo. "Migrants in the UK: An Overview." Migration Observatory. Accessed 30 November 2020. https://migrationobservatory.ox.ac.uk.

Vaughan-Williams, Nick. "'We Are Not Animals!' Humanitarian Border Security and Zoopolitical Spaces in Europe." *Political Geography* 45 (1 March 2015a): 1–10. https://doi.org/10.1016/j.polgeo.2014.09.009.

———. *Europe's Border Crisis: Biopolitical Security and Beyond.* Oxford: Oxford University Press, 2015b.

Vidal, Marta. "'We Lost Our Homes and Country, but We Also Lost Our Books.'" *Al Jazeera*, 12 October 2018. www.aljazeera.com.

Villa, Dana. *Politics, Philosophy, Terror: Essays on the Thought of Hannah Arendt.* Princeton, NJ: Princeton University Press, 1999.

Vukov, Tamara. "Target Practice: The Algorithmics and Biopolitics of Race in Emerging Smart Border Practices and Technologies." *Transfers* 6, no. 1 (2016): 80–97.

Vukov, Tamara, and Mimi Sheller. "Border Work: Surveillant Assemblages, Virtual Fences, and Tactical Counter-Media." *Social Semiotics* 23, no. 2 (1 April 2013): 225–41. https://doi.org/10.1080/10350330.2013.777592.

Vuori, Juha, and Rune Saugmann. *Visual Security Studies: Sights and Spectacles of Insecurity and War*. Routledge, 2018.
Wall, Melissa, Madeline Otis Campbell, and Dana Janbek. "Syrian Refugees and Information Precarity." *New Media & Society* 19, no. 2 (2015): 240–54. https://doi.org/10.1177/1461444815591967.
Walsh, James. "Remapping the Border: Geospatial Technologies and Border Activism." *Environment and Planning D: Society and Space* 31, no. 6 (1 December 2013): 969.
Walsh, Peter William. "Irregular Migration in the UK." Migration Observatory. Accessed 30 November 2020. https://migrationobservatory.ox.ac.uk.
Walters, William. "The Frontiers of the European Union: A Geostrategic Perspective." *Geopolitics* 9, no 3 (2004): 674–698. https://doi.org/10.1080/14650040490478738.
Walters, William. "Foucault and Frontiers: Notes on the Birth of the Humanitarian Border." In *Governmentality: Current Issues and Future Challenges*, edited by Susanne Krasmann, Ulrich Bröckling, and Thomas Lemke, 138–64. New York: Routledge, 2011.
Ward, Robin, and Richard Jenkins. *Ethnic Communities in Business: Strategies for Economic Survival*. Cambridge University Press, 1984.
Warrell, Helen. "Inside Prevent, the UK's Controversial Anti-Terrorism Programme." *Financial Times*, 23 January 2019. www.ft.com/.
Watson, Scott D. *The Securitization of Humanitarian Migration: Digging Moats and Sinking Boats*. First edition. Routledge, 2009.
Welander, Marta, and Leonie Ansems De Vries. "Refugees, Displacement, and the European 'Politics of Exhaustion.'" OpenDemocracy. Accessed 24 December 2020. www.opendemocracy.net/.
Wiertz, Thilo. "Biopolitics of Migration: An Assemblage Approach." *Environment and Planning C: Politics and Space*, 22 July 2020. https://doi.org/10.1177/2399654420941854.
Willoughby-Herard, Tiffany. *Waste of a White Skin: The Carnegie Corporation and the Racial Logic of White Vulnerability*. Illustrated edition. Oakland: University of California Press, 2015.
Wilmott, Annabelle Cathryn. "The Politics of Photography: Visual Depictions of Syrian Refugees in U.K. Online Media." *Visual Communication Quarterly* 24, no. 2 (3 April 2017): 67–82. https://doi.org/10.1080/15551393.2017.1307113.
Wodak, Ruth. *The Politics of Fear: What Right-Wing Populist Discourses Mean*. London: Sage Publications, 2015/2020.
———. "Entering the "Post-shame Era": The Rise of Illiberal Democracy, Populism and Neo-authoritarianism in Europe." *Global Discourse* 9, no. 1 (2019): 195–213.
Wright, Terence. "Moving Images: The Media Representation of Refugees." *Visual Studies* 17, no. 1 (1 January 2002): 53–66. https://doi.org/10.1080/1472586022000005053.
———. "Collateral Coverage: Media Images of Afghan Refugees, 2001." *Visual Studies* 19, no. 1 (1 April 2004): 97–112. https://doi.org/10.1080/1472586042000204870.

Wyss, Anna. "Stuck in Mobility? Interrupted Journeys of Migrants with Precarious Legal Status in Europe." *Journal of Immigrant & Refugee Studies* 17, no. 1 (2 January 2019): 77–93. https://doi.org/10.1080/15562948.2018.1514091.

Yamamura, Sakura, and Paul Lassalle. "Proximities and the Emergence of Regional Industry: Evidence of the Liability of Smallness in Malta." *European Planning Studies* 28, no. 2 (2020): 380–99.

Yuval-Davis, Nira, Georgie Wemyss, and Kathryn Cassidy. *Bordering*. Cambridge, UK: Polity, 2019.

Zaborowski, Rafal, and Myria Georgiou. "Gamers versus Zombies? Visual Mediation of the Citizen/Non-Citizen Encounter in Europe's 'Refugee Crisis.'" *Popular Communication* 17, no. 2 (3 April 2019): 92–108. https://doi.org/10.1080/15405702.20 19.1572150.

Zaman, Tahir. "What's So Radical about Refugee Squats? An Exploration of Urban Community-Based Responses to Mass Displacement in Athens." In *Challenging the Political Across Borders: Migrants' and Solidarity Struggles*, edited by Tegiye Birey, Celine Cantat, Ewa Maczynska, and Eda Sevinin, 129–62. CPS Books. Budapest: Central European University, 2019.

Zehfuss, Maja. "'We Can Do This': Merkel, Migration and the Fantasy of Control." *International Political Sociology* 15, no. 2 (13 November 2020): 172–189. https://doi .org/10.1093/ips/olaa026.

Zeit Online. "Asylpolitik: Handys von einreisenden Asylbewerbern sollen überprüft werden." *Die Zeit*, 19 February 2017. www.zeit.de.

Zia-Ebrahimi, Reza. "Self-Orientalization and Dislocation: The Uses and Abuses of the 'Aryan' Discourse in Iran." *Iranian Studies* 44, no. 4 (1 July 2011): 445–72. https://doi .org/10.1080/00210862.2011.569326.

Zijlstra, Judith, and Ilse van Liempt. "Smart(Phone) Travelling: Understanding the Use and Impact of Mobile Technology on Irregular Migration Journeys." *International Journal of Migration and Border Studies* 3 (1 January 2017): 174. https://doi.org/10 .1504/IJMBS.2017.083245.

Zivi, Karen. *Making Rights Claims: A Practice of Democratic Citizenship*. Oxford University Press, 2012.

INDEX

activist commons, 93–96, 99–100, 170
activist groups, 50
activists: agency of, 140; compassionate solidarity of, 55–56; digital border with, 21, 24, 26; on media, 50; S27 as, 93, 100; staff of, 36; Unmentionables as, 94–95, 98, 100
Afghanistan, 42, 66, 200n1 (chapt. 5)
Agamben, Giorgio, 33–35, 107–8, 187
agency: of activists, 140; digital border and, 20; entrepreneurial securitization and, 81; of migrants, 21, 108, 150, 156; migrants without, 159; outer borders for, 13, 35; of public, 130–31; resistance as, 19; of subaltern, 20, 161
Ahmed, Kaamil, 35–36, 100
AI. *See* artificial intelligence
AI border security, 3–4
Amnesty International, 128
Andreas, Peter, 15
anti-migrant rhetoric, 5
Aplotaria (online newspaper), 50
Arabic language, 91–92, 111–12, 199n7
Arabic Library (Baynatna, Berlin), 91–92, 98–100
Arab Spring, 83, 94–95
Arendt, Hannah, 116, 119, 124–25, 139–40, 146, 167; on storytelling, 110
Are You Syrious? (migrant network), 162, 200n3
artificial intelligence (AI), 3–4, 34, 171–72
assemblages: as border, 6–7, 171–72; Chios Island definition of, 36; digital border as, 8–13, 18, 20, 36; of humanitarian securitization, 31; outer borders as mediation, 13; resistance and digital border, 8, 22
asylum, 3, 61, 96–97
Athens, 59; downtown of, 66–67; employment prospects in, 196n5; Farzant Karmangar center in, 90; housing in, 95, 197n11; migrant numbers and, 66, 196n3; Mobile Library of, 88–91, 100; public resources in, 86; squat networks in, 24, 95–96, 100, 186
Australia, 3, 131–32, 175, 184, 186
Aware Migrants (digital project), 152, 158–61
Ayia Ermioni village, 38–39
Azoulay, Ariella, 132, 143

Bangladesh, 66
Barnett, Clive, 39
Beduschi, Ana, 34
Benson, Rodney, 17, 107, 113
Berlin, 59; Baynatna in, 91–92; employment prospects in, 196n5; with Give Something Back to Berlin, 76–77; migrant numbers and, 66, 196nn2–3; Neukölln neighborhood of, 66, 68, 88, 93, 100; public resources in, 86; Refugio in, 88; squat networks in, 24, 95–96, 100, 186
Bigo, Didier, 14–15
biometric data: as assessment, 11–12, 22, 178; into legal or illegal, 4, 14, 34, 42–43, 54

biopolitical power relations, 31–32; for alternatives, 176–77; entrepreneurial securitization by, 12; fingerprint identification system in, 41–42; as human micro-monitoring, 14; for identification and management, 8–9; on migrants, 33; online sources legitimizing, 5; as risk assessment, 9
Bleiker, Roland, 131–32
Boltanski, Luc, 136–37, 139
borders: Accenture security for, 4; AI on, 3–4, 34, 171–72; alternative response to, 188–89; assemblages as, 6–7, 171–72; citizenship space and security for, 22–23; as digital, 6, 10, 21; elasticity of, 148; EU closing, 66, 196n3; as impalpable, 14–15; industrial complex at, 4; media at, 9, 174–75; migration crisis and, 11; as ordinary, 175–77; as process, 7, 171, 173; for reception, 21, 183, 195n2 (chapt. 1); study of digital, 18–19; as symbolic, 3, 171–72; technology and exclusion at, 7, 21. *See also* symbolic border; territorial border
boundary-drawing process, 7, 171, 173
Bozdağ, Çiğdem, 109
Buchanan, Sara, 139
#buildthewall, 5
Bukasa, Julia, 186
Burman, Erica, 138
Butler, Judith, 109

camp identification bracelets, 33
careful tolerance, 112, 198n6, 199n10
Cavarero, Adriana, 110, 126
CBS. *See* Critical Border Studies
celebrity benevolence, 141–43
Chatterton, Paul, 83
Chechen Republic, 42–43
Cheney-Lippold, John, 34
Chios Island: assemblage definition at, 36; compassionate solidarity at, 32; DoW, ICRD, and NRC at, 44; as Europe entry point, 31; mediation network of, 36–37; migrant debriefing at, 9, 36, 40, 176; military securitization at, 32; scholar fieldwork at, 37–39; securitized care at, 32; territorial border and, 23–24, 31, 195n1 (chapt. 2); UNHCR running, 31. *See also* Registration Center
cities: CVE policies in, 86; datafication and, 63–64; entrepreneurial migrants in, 60; entrepreneurial securitization in, 12; migrant belonging and, 87; migrant collaboration in, 67; migrant controls in, 58; migrants to, 60; scholars and migrants of, 196n4; as territorial border, 58–59, 185; thrown-togetherness and, 82, 85, 89, 92, 97; as unfamiliar, 81–82
citizenship: borders and expressions of, 22–23; employment for, 60–62; inner territorial border, 59; media excluding, 114–15; power over rights and, 7; Western norms of, 12, 22
civic participation, 64, 74, 76–77, 132–33, 145
classification, 4, 7, 13
Code Your Future, 89–90, 176
co-existence, 21, 26, 81
Collective Kitchen, 37, 39, 49, 52
colonialism, 9, 13–14, 188
commons. *See* networked commons
compassionate solidarity, 32, 38, 49–53, 55–56
conditional conviviality, 65, 67, 73–80
connected migrant, 47, 91, 150, 185, 197n6
consequences: of migrant arrivals, 120–23, *121*, *122*; for migrants, 19, 72, 106, 189
"A Conspiracy of Neglect" (Amnesty International), 128
Couldry, Nick, 110–11, 149, 166
counter-violent extremism (CVE) policies, 86
crisis: digital border with invisible, 183–90; as global economics, 183–84, 201n5; media on migration, 5, 11–12,

16; migration as racial, 34; perception on, 26–27, 177–78; as social imaginary, 11, 177–80; of territorial border, 183; terrorism and, 180–82; 2016–2020 as post-, 23, 67, 81
Critical Border Studies (CBS), 13, 15, 21, 31–35
Critical Data Studies, 31–35
Critical Migration Studies, 59–60
cross-examinations, as face-to-face, 42
cultural commons, 82–84, 90–93, 97
CVE. See counter-violent extremism policies

Danish Institute for International Studies report, 181
databases, 3, 9; entrepreneurial information in, 68–70; entrepreneurial securitization and, 174; EU Migration Data Portal as, 196n1; Eurodac and transnational, 53–54; on migrants, 14–15; terrorism and, 34
datafication: at Chios Registration Center, 175; of civic life, 64; harm of, 72, 189–90; job center profiling as, 10, 12, 68, 98; of migrants, 9–10, 173, 175; on smart cities, 63–64; of territorial border, 32–35
dehumanization: as feature, 34; imagery as, 133; as interrupted, 35; of migrants, 107–9, 128–30, 133–34, 189; thesis of, 32–33; voice lack for, 150
Deleuze, 6
detention, 1, 3, 40, 42, 166; colonial racism and, 9, 188; Moria camp as, 96, 183, 186–87, 201nn7–8
digital border. See specific subjects
digital identification, 4, 7
digital intermediation and transmediation, 24
digital monitoring, 3
digital networks, 63, 92
Digital Urban Studies, 59, 63

Diminescu, Dana, 47, 150
disinformation, 16–18
Doctors of the World (DoW), 44
double articulation, 6–7
DoW. See Doctors of the World
drones, 4
Drop in the Ocean, 44
Dublin Agreement on Asylum (EU), 201n4

economy of visibility, 128–33, 143–47
economy of voice, 109–11, 116, 123–28
ecstatic humanitarianism, 112, 199n10; Kurdi moment of, 117–18, 138; Paris attacks reducing, 17, 42, 113–14, 117, 120–21, 138, 180–81, 198n6 (chapt. 4); rhetoric of, 122, *122*
Edkins, Jenny, 33
education. See pedagogic commons
Egypt, 84
emergency care, 44–45, 51, 173
empathic responsibility, 137–38
employment: for citizenship, 60–62; conditional conviviality for, 74; as illegal, 93, 197n9; neoliberal economics and migrant, 62, 78–80, 100; NRPF or, 93, 197n8; prospects of, 196n5; securitized self-responsibility and, 67–71; self-responsibilization and, 70; work training and, 67
enforcement, 14, 166, 184–85
entrepreneurial migrants: in cities, 60; databases and, 68–70; EU attracting, 90; hackathons for refugees and, 74; mediation networks and, 62–63; or parasitical, 5, 12, 16–17
entrepreneurial securitization, 175; agency and, 81; by biopolitical power relations, 12; cities and, 12; as data and social networks, 174; digital training for, 86; in Europe, 24; humanitarian securitization replaced by, 58–59; #Iamamigrant and, 155–56; inner border and, 63–65, 78–81; power and, 20, 22, 93; shift to, 20

Eritrea, 66
EU. *See* European Union
Eurodac, 4, 11–12, 20, 40, 172, 195n3 (chapt. 1); fingerprint identification system of, 41–42; transnational data and, 53–54
Europe: Chios Island as entry point and, 31; entrepreneurial securitization in, 24; Frontex of, 31, 40–41, 184; inner territorial border of, 78; migration crisis and 2015 in, 2–3, 10–11; #refugeesnotwelcome of, 5; on responsibility, 128–29; scholar migration in, 18–19; security for, 44, 189; terrorism from, 181
European Union (EU): boat pushbacks by, 187, 202n9; colonial conquest and borders of, 13–14; on Greece, 184, 201n6; hotspot approach of, 186–87, 201n7; on iBorderCtrl, 3–4; on migrant entrepreneurs, 90; on migration, 179–80, 201n4; neoliberal economics of, 86; Schengen agreement in, 179, 181; staff of, 36; 2016 border closures by, 66, 196n3
Eurosur, 11–12

Facebook, 5, 21, 50–51, 56, 81, 84
Farzant Karmangar cultural center, 90
Fassin, Didier, 7
fear and securitization, 112, 198n6, 199n10
fingerprint identification system, 41–42, 195n3 (chapt. 1)
5-Eyes alliance, 175, 200n1 (conclusion)
Foucault, Michel, 7–8, 10
14-Eyes alliance, 175, 200n1 (conclusion)
Frontex, 31, 40–41, 184

Gajjala, Radhika, 150
Galantino, Maria Grazia, 181
Gattinara, Pietro Castelli, 189
generalization, 107–8, 117–18, 123
de Genova, Nicholas, 34, 60, 182
Germany: Merkel of, 179–80; migrant numbers and, 66, 179, 196n2; RRN from, 152, 161–64, 176, 200n1 (chapt. 6). *See also* Berlin
al-Ghazzi, Omar, 138
Ghosh, Amitav, 10
Gillespie, Marie, 16
Give Something Back to Berlin, 76–77
Glasgow Girls (UK), 165
global economic crisis, 183–84, 201n5
grassroots agencies, 152–53; conditional conviviality and, 74; intermediation and, 161–68; networked commons and, 98; by NGOs and grassroots, 148; pedagogic commons as, 83, 88–90; squat networks by, 24, 95–96, 100, 186; on symbolic border, 161; voice and social media by, 148
Greece: boat pushbacks by, 187, 202n9; EU on, 184, 201n6; Frontex of, 31, 40–41, 184; global economic crisis on, 183–84, 201n5
Greek islands: debriefing interviews at, 9, 19; global economic crisis on, 183–84, 201nn5–6; as migrant "dumping ground," 184; Moria camp in, 96, 183, 186–87, 201nn7–8; "Nobel Prize to Greek Islanders" for, 50–52
Gun Island (Ghosh), 10

Haas, Hein de, 1–2
hackathons for refugees, 74–77
Hall, Suzanne, 60
Hariman, Robert, 131
Haringey neighborhood, 66
Harney, Nicholas, 141
Heath-Kelly, Charlotte, 86
Heck, Axel, 131
hierarchical structures: of digital intermediation and transmediation, 24; with migrant-entrepreneur, 16–17; of migrant voices, 37, 49, 55, 116, 174; of

NGOs, 47; of power, 20; racism and, 12, 14; social media in, 55; of voice, 116, 124; of West, 19
historicity, 19–20, 22
Horsti, Karina, 149–50
hotspot approach, 186–87, 201n7
housing, 24, 95–96, 100, 186, 197n11
humanitarian care: digital border with, 21, 26, 173; empathic responsibility and, 137–38; Eurodac speed as, 42, 195n3 (chapt. 1); media on, *123*; for migrant children and families, 17; responsibility and post-, 141–43; securitized care and, 44–49; sovereignty subordinating, 33–34; in victim/threat binary, 17; violence or border, 189–90
humanitarian securitization, 24; assemblages of, 31; entrepreneurial securitization replacing, 58–59; at entry points and practices, 105; #Iamamigrant and, 155; outer borders and, 53–57; power and, 11, 22

#Iamamigrant, 149, 152–58, 161, 165, 169
#Iamarefugee, 152, 155
iBorderCtrl technology, 3–4, 8
Ibrahim, Yasmin, 131
ICRD. *See* Red Cross
images: border cameras for, 4; as dehumanization, 133; on migrant need, 136; by migrants, 200n2 (chapt. 5); on migrants, 25–26; news and, 128–29, 143; news imagery as, 128; photographic theory and, 130–31; of race and terrorism, 144–45; symbolic border as news, 129–30
information and communication technologies, 6
inner border, 7; cities as, 58–59, 185; entrepreneurial securitization and, 63–65, 78–81; entrepreneurship, and digital citizenship of, 59; of Europe, 78; networked commons and, 81, 85, 100–101; as site of contestation, 82; surveillance and, 185
institutional initiatives, 169. *See also Aware Migrants*; #Iamamigrant
intermediations, 20, 23–24, 82, 148; on authentic or non-authentic migrants, 42; of Chios Island, 32, 36; definition of, 172; digital communications for, 50; grassroots activism and, 161–68; infrastructure for, 85; neoliberal labor markets and digital, 63; NGOs and, 153–58; pre-electronic means for, 47–48, 56; of securitized care, 46–48; surveillance through online, 63, 99
International Organization for Migration (IOM), 60, 62, 152–54, 157–58
International Relations (IR), 13, 15
interveillance, 74, 77
IOM. *See* International Organization for Migration
IR. *See* International Relations
Iran, 66
Iraq, 200n1 (chapt. 5)
Iwabuchi, Koichi, 156

Jessop, Bob, 64
job centers: data profiling at, 10, 12, 68, 98; London and interviews at, 9; resistance and, 68; for surveillance, 63, 68; training and judgment at, 71–72
journalism. *See* media

Kaur, Gurmit, 166
Kurdi, Alan, 17, 74; ecstatic humanitarian moment and, 117–18, 138; media on, 113, 117, 128, 138, 142, 180, 198n6, 199n8; politicians on, 117–18; Twitter graphics on, 141–43

Lampedusa shipwrecks, 184, 199n8, 200n2
languages: Arabic source as, 91–92, 111–12, 199n7; racialized sorting on, 9

legality and illegality: asylum registries for, 61; biometric data for, 4, 14, 34, 42–43, 54; as deserving or undeserving, 185–86; digital connectivity for, 91, 185, 197n6; employment in, 93, 197n9; Eurodac for, 42; intermediations and, 42; for migrants, 175–77, 189, 200n2 (conclusion); Pakistanis and Chechens in, 43

Lesbos Island, 31, 41, 184; Moria camp on, 96, 183, 186–87, 201nn7–8

Leurs, Koen, 34, 126–27, 170

lie detectors, 4

life seekers, 5

Liguori, Anna, 190

Lim, Merlyna, 84, 94–95

local actors, 39

London, 59, 196n3; Code Your Future in, 89–90, 176; employment prospects in, 196n5; Haringey neighborhood of, 66; job center interviews in, 9; public resources in, 86

London School of Economics (LSE), 105

Lucaites, John Louis, 131

Macaulay, Larry, 162

machine code, 9

Madianou, Mirca, 4, 15, 48

Malkki, Liisa H., 108

Marino, Sara, 185

Massey, Doreen, 82

Mbembe, Achille, 1, 3, 26, 171, 186–88, 190

media: activists on, 50; at border, 9, 174–75; citizens excluded by, 114–15; on compassionate groups, 50; on digital control and surveillance, 3; economy of visibility and, 130–33; economy of voice and, 109–11; on humanitarian vs. defensive actions, *123*; on Kurdi, 113, 117, 128, 138, 142, 180, 198n6, 199n8; as left wing, 113; on migrant arrival consequences, 120–23, *121*, *122*; migrant portrayals by, 117, *118*; on migrants, 21, *118*, 120, 174–75; migrant storytelling by, 16, 195n1 (chapt. 1); on migration crisis, 5, 11–12, 16; newspaper websites as, 111, 174, 198n5; news photography of, 128–29, 143; politicians on crisis and, 113, 117–18, 124–25; remediations and, 20; scholars on sources and, 111–13; with silencing, collectivization, and decontextualization, 112; silencing by, 107, 112, 125; Silverstone on ethics and, 133–34; symbolic border, 17–18; symbolic border by, 105, 124; symbolic border stereotypes by, 7, 190; on 2015 migration crisis, 111–12, 198nn5–6, 199n9; on victim/threat, 16–17, 107, 134; West protected by, 134

mediation: Chios Island network of, 36–37; digital border assemblages and networks of, 8, 18, 20; double articulation of, 6–7; dynamics of, 20; entrepreneurial migrants and networks of, 62–63; outer border as, 13; techno-symbolic assemblages and, 8, 18–20, 58

Merkel, Angela, 179–80

Metcalfe-Hough, Victoria, 178–79

migrant camps, 31, 37, 39, 49, 52. *See also* Chios Island; Lesbos Island

migrant connectivity, 63

migrant-entrepreneur, 16–17

#migrantlivesmatter, 5

migrants: experience diversity of, 109; as infantilized, 138; numbers of international, 1, 11; as "people like us," 52; reasons for, 120; trauma for, 77. *See also specific subjects*

Migrant Voice (UK) (migrant network), 161–62, 165–68, 200n2 (chapt. 6)

migrantvoice.org, 152

migration: causes of, 1–2; data, AI, drones on, 3; enforcement and control of, 166; EU on, 179–80, 201n4; locations for, 2; narratives, 5; power over, 7; as racial crisis, 34; terrorism links with, 181–82;

voice and news on, 107, 198n4; as zero-sum game, 139–40
Migration and the Media (LSE project), 105
Migration Data Portal (EU), 196n1
military securitization: at Chios Island, 32; digital border with, 21, 24, 26; "others" classified by, 40–44; Registration Center for, 31, 36, 38, 39–41; for security, 43
Miller, Susan, 87
Mirzoeff, Nicholas, 135
Mobile Library, 88–91, 93, 100
Moeller, Susan D., 137–38
monitorial responsibility, 136–37
Morales, Laura, 189
Moria camp, 96, 183, 186–87, 201nn7–8
Mostafanezhad, Mary, 142–43
Mounzt, Alison, 184–86

Natale, Simone, 93–94, 98
neoliberal economics: austerity of, 100, 183; education and, 88, 90; of EU, 86; on hackathons, 77; for migrants, 12, 24, 59, 70, 73; migrants and employment in, 62, 78–80, 100; as norm, 22, 63–65, 77, 79, 173; self-responsibilization and, 70; West capitalism and, 16–17
Nethope, 47
networked commons, 174; for cultural encounters, 82–84, 90–93; culture in, 82–84, 90–93; grassroots agencies and, 98; inner border and, 81, 85, 100–101; pedagogy in, 82–84; political activism and, 82–84, 93–97, 99–100; politics in, 82–84; power and limits of, 97–101; for resistance, 85–86, 97, 185; as struggle space, 83–85; surveillance and, 84, 98; urban networks for, 81
Neukölln neighborhood (Berlin), 66, 68, 88, 93, 100
NGO. *See* nonprofit organizations
9-Eyes alliance, 175, 200n1 (conclusion)
"Nobel Prize to Greek islanders," 50–52

Noble, Greg, 87
nonprofit organizations (NGO), 36, 44, 46–48, 93, 148, 152–58
no recourse to public funds (NRPF), 93, 197n8
Norwegian Refugee Council (NRC), 44
NRPF. *See* no recourse to public funds

O'Connell, Alice R., 109
Oeppen, Ceri, 159–60
online media: *Aware Migrants* with, 158–61; Facebook and WhatsApp as, 56; migrant websites and, 151–52; for power or resistance, 24; remediations and migrant meanings by, 106; for surveillance, 63, 65; on symbolic border, 6; on 2015 migration crisis, 105; voice in storytelling and, 25, 124
orientalism: migrant governance as, 87, 127, 150, 157; migrant narratives as, 16, 56, 112–13, 124, 129, 160–61, 183
"others," 144, 146; migrants as, 59, 107, 114, 125–26, 131–32, 134, 182; military securitization classifying, 40–44
outer border, 1, 4–7, 13–15, 32–36, 183; Chios Island and, 23–24, 31, 195n1 (chapt. 2); humanitarian security or, 53–57. *See also* territorial border
Owens, Patricia, 107–8

Paik, A. Naomi, 141
Pakistan, 43, 66
Pallister-Wilkins, Polly, 5
Paris attacks: migrants and, 17, 120–21, 138, 180; reporting on, 113–14, 117; terrorism and, 42, 117, 181, 198n6, 199n8
Parker, Noel, 14
passivity, 107–10
pedagogic commons, 82–84, 86, 88–90, 176; as digital and pre-digital, 94, 97; squat networks in, 24, 95–96, 100, 186
Phillips, Anna, 111
photographic theory, 130–31

240 | INDEX

platformed narratives, 6, 106
politics: activist commons with, 93; of digital border, 173–75; image meanings in, 131; on Kurdi, 117–18; media and left-wing politics, 113; of migrant crisis, 178–79, 189; networked commons and activism in, 82–84, 93–97, 99–100; photography and civic duty, 132–33; as right-wing politics, 113, 179–80; on 2015 migration crisis, 113, 117–18, 124–25; of voice and storytelling, 110, 124–25
Ponzanesi, Sandra, 170
power, 6; on activist commons, 93; biopower as sovereign, 14; boundary-drawing process and, 7, 171, 173; digital border assemblages and trajectories of, 8–13, 18, 20, 36; entrepreneurial securitization and, 20, 22, 93; humanitarian securitization and, 11, 22; iBorderCtrl technology and, 8; on migrants, 20, 58; Moria camp as, 96, 183, 186–87, 201nn7–8; of networked commons, 97–101; online media for, 24; techno-symbolic assemblages and, 8, 18, 20, 58
precarity, 82
Prevent Strategy (UK), 86–87
Purkayastha, Bandana, 2

racialized profiles, 9, 34, 188
racism, 9, 139, 188; *Aware Migrants* and, 158–61; exclusion as, 58, 182; hierarchical structures and, 12, 14; #Iamamigrant and, 156–58; sousveillance and, 64, 98; terrorism images and, 144–45
Raimondi, Valeria, 96
Rath, Jan, 60
reception, 21, 183, 195n2 (chapt. 1)
Red Cross (ICRD), 44
refugeemigrants.org, 152
refugee numbers, 1, 196n1

Refugee Radio Network (RRN) (migrant network), 152, 161–64, 176, 200n1 (chapt. 6)
refugeeradionetwork.net, 200n1 (chapt. 6)
#refugeesnotwelcome, 5
#refugeeswelcome, 5
Refugio, 88
Registration Center (Chios Island), 31, 38, 39, 41, 183; care provisions at, 45, 51, 173; datafication at, 175; Eurodac data identification tech at, 172; migrant debriefing at Chios, 9, 36, 40, 176; as reception, 195n1 (chapt. 1)
remediations, 20, 23–24, 172; activist groups and, 50; of Chios Island, 32, 36; as platform-driven storytelling, 6, 106; of securitized care, 45–46; symbolic border and, 128
Resilient Communities, Resilient Cities? (study), 67
resistance, 19, 24, 56–57, 149–50; digital border assemblages and dialectics of, 8, 22; job centers and, 68; migrants and digital, 148; *Migrant Voice* as, 165; networked commons for, 85–86, 97, 185; outer borders for, 35
responsibility, 128–43, 145–46
Rohingya refugee crisis, 2
Roland-Gosselin, Louise, 187
Ross, Karen, 125
Roy, Ananya, 180–81
RRN. *See* Refugee Radio Network

S27 (activist group), 93, 100
Salih, Roza, 165
Samos island, 201n8
Saugmann, Rune, 131
Schengen agreement, 179, 181
Schudson, Michael, 137
Schutjens, Veronique, 60
securitized care, 21, 24, 32, 44–49
securitized precarity, 65, 67, 71–73, 78–79, 81

securitized self-responsibility, 9, 65, 67–71, 78
security, 42–45, 138–40, 189; agent experiences in, 54; enforcement of national, 14
self-responsibilization, 70
silencing: economy of voice and, 123–26; by media, 107, 112, 125; of migrants, 25, 110, 113–14, *114*, 116–18, 123, 150–51, 172; of public, 116, 125; in voice hierarchy, 116, 124
Silverstone, Roger, 6, 145–46, 172, 195n2 (introduction); on ethics and media, 133–34; on hospitality, 140; on responsibility, 130
smartphones, 16, 24, 34, 48–49, 195n4
Smets, Kevin, 109, 126–27
social categorizations, 7
social justice, 84–85, 94–95
social media, 51, 55, 148; graphics of, 141–42; hashtags of, 5; NGOs on, 48; for surveillance, 63, 65, 87
Söder, Markus, 180
Sohn, Christophe, 6
Sontag, Susan, 131
sorting, 9
sousveillance, 64, 98
sovereignty, 13, 33–34
spatiotemporal trajectories, 22
Spivak, Gayatri, 110, 149–52, 168–69
squat networks, 24, 95–96, 100, 186
Squire, Vicki, 21
Stevis-Gridneff, Matina, 184
storytelling: #Iamamigrant as, 149, 152–58, 161, 165, 169; media for migrant, 16, 195n1 (chapt. 1); online media and voice in, 25, 124; politics of, 110, 124–25; remediation as, 106
Strausz, Erzsébet, 86
subaltern: agency of, 20, 161; as disadvantaged, 62, 64, 129–30, 134–36, 174–76; migrants as, 124–26, 138, 141, 143, 165; voice as, 26, 110, 149–52, 160, 162, 166–69; voice power for, 168–70

Sum, Ngai-Ling, 64
surveillance, 3, 174; biopolitical power as micro-, 14; as digital, 7, 22; inner border and, 185; intermediaries and, 63, 99; job centers for, 63, 68; modes of, 11–12; network commons and, 84, 98; NGO "guerrilla" activism on, 93; normalization of, 64–65; photographic theory for, 130–31; on smartphones, 16; social categorizations and, 7; social media for, 63, 65, 87; technology for, 185
symbolic border, 3, 171–72; biopolitical power relations as, 5; border exclusions using, 7; double articulation as, 6–7; economy of voice as, 124–27; grassroots agencies on, 161; media and stereotypes as, 7, 190; as media narratives, 105, 124; media on, 17–18; migrant voices and, 152–53; mobile technologies and, 15–18; news photography as, 129–30; platformed narratives of, 6, 106; remediation and, 128; 2015 migrant crisis and, 127; on "us" and "them," 6; visibility economy and, 143–47; voice and social media in, 148
Syria, 66, 137, 200n1 (chapt. 5)

Tacchi, Jo, 150
Tarnongo, Dickson, 166
Tazzioli, Martina, 63, 68
Techfugees.com, 74–75
technology: border exclusion and, 7, 21; borders and constructs of, 3, 171–72; camp identification bracelets as, 33; at Chios Island, 36; Code Your Future for, 89–90, 176; double articulation as communication, 6–7; racialized machine code for, 9; for surveillance, 185
techno-symbolic assemblages, 8, 18–20, 58
techno-symbolic infrastructures, 6, 36

territorial border, 23–24, 32–35, 58–59, 100–101, 183–85; camp identification and, 33; at Chios Island, 36; cities as, 58–59, 63–64; citizenship and, 59; civic participation and, 64, 74, 76–77; crisis and, 183; datafication of, 32–35; elasticity of, 148; employment prospects in, 196n5; entrepreneurial securitization in, 24; of Europe, 78; job center profiling and, 10, 12, 68, 98; networked commons and, 85–86, 97, 185; outer border as, 13; resistance and, 19, 24, 56–57; surveillance and, 63, 68, 185. *See also* outer border

terrorism: crisis and, 180–82; CVE policies on, 86; databases and, 34; as European foreign fighters, 181; migrants in, 108, 173; migration links with, 181–82; Paris attacks and, 42, 117, 181, 198n6, 199n8; protection against, 42; racism and images of, 144–45; RRN on, 163–64; UK *Prevent* Strategy on, 86–87. *See also* Paris attacks

threat: agency and malice in, 108; economy of visibility and, 130; victimhood or, 108–9, 113, 130, 132, 135, 144, 172; visuals of, 138–39, 144; young men as, 139, 144, 175

throwntogetherness, 82, 85, 89, 92, 97

transmediations, 20, 23–24, 82; of Chios Island, 32, 36; definition of, 172; digital connectivity and, 92; face-to-face cross-examinations in, 42; infrastructure for, 85; as meals and dry clothes, 51; migrant characteristics and security in, 42–43; of securitized care, 48–49

transnational governance, 58

Treré, Emiliano, 93–94, 98

Trilling, Daniel, 5

Trimikliniotis, Nicos, 82, 84–85

Tsianos, Vassilis, 36, 67, 84

Twitter: for Egypt protests, 84; migrants and, 5; NGOs using, 47; social media graphics of, 141–44, 146

2015 migration crisis: awaremigrants.org during, 152; Chios Island and, 23–24, 31, 195n1 (chapt. 2); emotions on, 115, 115–16, *119*; in Europe, 2–3, 10–11; humanitarian vs. defensive actions in, *123*; media reporting on, 111–12, 198nn5–6, 199n9; online news on, 105; perception and, 26–27, 177–78; politicians on, 113, 117–18, 124–25; RRN and, 163; symbolic border and, 127; victimhood and threat in, 109–10

2016–2020: EU border closures after, 66, 196n3; as post-crisis, 23, 67, 81

UGC. *See* user-generated-content project

UK. *See* United Kingdom

UNHCR. *See* United Nations High Commissioner for Refugees

United Kingdom (UK), 66

United Nations High Commissioner for Refugees (UNHCR), 31, 33, 44

Unmentionables (activist group), 94–95, 98, 100

urban networks: as coexistence and solidarity, 81; justice and, 84–85; migrants needing, 81; smartphones for, 24; throwntogetherness and, 82, 85, 89, 92, 97

Urban Studies, 59, 63, 83

user-generated-content (UGC) project, 154

Vaughan-Williams, Nick, 14

victimhood: economy of visibility and, 130; of migrants, 9, 22, 107, 134, 139, 173; threat or, 108–9, 113, 130, 132, 135, 144, 172

victim/threat binary, 5, 11, 144; activists and, 140; humanitarian care in, 17; media on, 16–17, 107, 134; on 2015 migration crisis, 109–10

violence: at borders, 33–34, 189; communal tensions for, 87; human rights or border, 189–90 visibility: symbolic border and economy of, 143–47; visuality and, 135. *See also* economy of visibility

visuality: of celebrity benevolence, 141–43; of hospitality, 140–41, 144; of migrants, 129; patterns in, 135–36; race and, 139; of responsibility, 135–43; scholars on, 135–36; of threat, 138–39, 144; visibility and, 135

Visual Security Studies, 131

voice: of anti-migrant rhetoric, 5; as articulated, 170; borders and citizenship, 22–23; context of, 120–24, *121*, *122*, *123*; dehumanization and lack of, 150; denial and rights of, 2–3; hierarchical structures of migrant, 37, 49, 55, 116, 174; journalistic economy of, 109; migrant naming and context as, 112; of migrants, 106–7, 152–53; migrants without, 109–10, 151; migrant trend on, 168–70; *Migrant Voice*, 161–62, 165–68, 200n2 (chapt. 6); migration news and, 107, 198n4; as narrative, 111–13; by NGOs and grassroots, 148; online media as migrant, 151–52; in online news storytelling, 25, 124; outer border for, 35; politics of, 110, 124–25; as resistance, 149; silencing, collectivization, decontextualization on, 112; silencing and hierarchy of, 116, 124; silencing of, 116; status of, 117–19, *118*, *119*; struggles on, 7; as subaltern, 26, 110, 149–52, 160, 162, 166–69; subaltern power and, 168–70; subjects of, 113–16, 199n11, *115*, *116*; symbolic border and migrant, 152–53; as ventriloquized, 169; West protection or migrant, 106–7. *See also* Refugee Radio Network

voluntary return and reintegration program, 156–57

volunteers, 49–53

WAHA, 44

Walters, William, 13

West: capitalism of, 16–17; citizenship norms of, 12, 22; hierarchical structures of, 19; land domination by, 3; media protecting, 134; on migrants and citizens, 119, 178; migrants entangled by, 141; protection or migrant voice, 106–7; racialized sorting by, 9

WhatsApp, 21, 47, 50–51, 56, 81

Wi-Fi, 91, 93

Willoughby-Herard, Tiffany, 139

Wodak, Ruth, 24–25, 189

Wood, Tim, 17

working-against-from-within, 99

Wyss, Anna, 61

Zaman, Tahir, 96

Zehfuss, Maja, 180, 182

zero-sum game, 139–40

ABOUT THE AUTHORS

Lilie Chouliaraki is Professor in the Department of Media and Communications at London School of Economics and Political Science. Her research focuses on human vulnerability as a problem of communication across media technologies, platforms, and genres. She is the author of, among others, *The Spectatorship of Suffering* (Sage, 2006) and *The Ironic Spectator: Solidarity in the Age of Post-humanitarianism* (Polity, 2013) and the co-editor of *The Routledge Handbook of Humanitarian Communication* (2021).

Myria Georgiou is Professor in the Department of Media and Communications at LSE, where she also serves as Research Director. Professor Georgiou researches and teaches on migration and urbanization in the context of intensified mediation. She is the author and co-editor of five books, including *Diaspora, Identity and the Media* (Hampton, 2006) and *Media and the City* (Polity, 2013), and the co-editor of *The Sage Handbook of Media and Migration* (2020).

www.ingramcontent.com/pod-product-compliance
Lightning Source LLC
Chambersburg PA
CBHW020250030426
42336CB00010B/700